FROM EAST AND WEST

FROM EAST AND WEST

RETHINKING CHRISTIAN MISSION

D. PREMAN NILES

CHALICE
PRESS

ST. LOUIS, MISSOURI

Cover art: "Te Ripeka" by Kura Rewiri Thorsen. Provided by
    Asian Christian Art Association
Cover design: Michael Domínguez
Interior design: Hui-chu Wang
Art direction: Elizabeth Wright

This book is printed on acid-free, recycled paper.

Visit Chalice Press on the World Wide Web at
www.chalicepress.com

10 9 8 7 6 5 4 3 2 1   04 05 06 07 08

Library of Congress Cataloging–in–Publication Data

Niles, D. Preman.
  From East and West : rethinking Christian mission / D. Preman Niles.
    p. cm.
  ISBN 0-8272-1033-7 (pbk.)
  1. Missions. I. Title.
  BV2061.3.N55 2004
  266—dc22

Printed in the United States of America

To the memory of my parents,
D. Thambyrajah (D. T.) Niles and Dulcie A. Niles,
from whom I received the faith

Contents

Introduction

"Of making many books there is no end" (Eccl. 12:12) comes to mind as one sits down to write a book on Christian mission or on missiology as the study of mission. Why another book on mission? With so many about with much repetition, one may reasonably say with *Qoheleth* (the Teacher), "There is nothing new under the sun!" (Eccl. 1:9).

For quite some time I put off writing this book, partly because of pressure of work and largely because I felt I had nothing significantly new to say on the subject. Friends both in the Council for World Mission, in which I served as general secretary, and in the various ecumenical organizations in which I worked disagreed. They persuaded, then insisted, that I bring together in book form the several papers I had written on the concerns for world mission today and the ways in which they challenge and elicit a missionary response from churches. They felt that it would be worth having a comprehensive articulation of the many ideas I had worked through with them.

In acquiescing to this pressure, I felt that there may be value in following in the footsteps of Norman Goodall, Michael Nazir Ali, Lesslie Newbigin, Bernard Thorogood, Max Warren, and several others who led mission organizations or mission departments and set down in writing their understanding and practice of mission. These writings make a different sort of contribution. Whereas a book on missiology as an academic discipline may propound several ideas or perspectives on mission and then leave it to the practitioners to put these into effect as best they may, a book from a practitioner has a somewhat different responsibility. At a planning meeting for a joint consultation between three mission organizations, I stated it in these words: "Good ideas in mission must not only be relevant, taking into account the signs of the time, but should also be translatable into action." This is the responsibility that I have taken upon myself in writing this book. So although there may not be anything significantly new in the way of ideas, it is in the way of putting these ideas into practice and my reflection on that practice that I may have something worthwhile to say. Let the reader be the judge!

I have chosen *From East and West* as the title for this book for several reasons. It reflects a position many Christians accept, that the mission of the church is not just from the West to the rest of the world but from everywhere to everywhere. More importantly, I have chosen this title because it comes in a passage of scripture (Mt. 8:11; cf. Lk. 13:29) that speaks of the mystery of nations from east and west coming to sit at the Messianic banquet. It comes in a context that not only extols the faith of one outside Israel but also presses for a paradigm for mission that would go beyond the paradigm of the modern Protestant missionary movement, which started with the formation of the Baptist Missionary Society in 1792 and the London Missionary Society in 1795. That missionary paradigm presents the Christian faith, and therefore the church, as over against the faiths of the nations. The intention to move beyond that paradigm is indicated in the subtitle of the book, *Rethinking Christian Mission for Today.*

I constantly repeat the words "for our time" or "for today" in speaking of the mission of the church for two reasons. First, I am not persuaded that the task for Christian mission is a continuous indulgence in seeking converts. As I will argue later, an important part of the mission history of the church is to finish an unfinished agenda. There is another stage in the missionary journey that has to be undertaken. Second, the missionary task requires us to read the "signs of the time." These signs change as the time changes and present new challenges as we seek to express the mission of the sending God who sent God's Son, who in turn sent the disciples in the power of the Holy Spirit. A static understanding of the missionary task contravenes "movement," which is another way of saying "mission."

A colleague of mine at the World Council of Churches (WCC) and later a bishop of the Church of South India, Samuel Amirtham, provided a clue on how I may bring together the ideas I deal with in this book. He said, "The Council for World Mission has provided you with an opportunity to harness your insights as an Asian theologian, your training as a biblical scholar, and your experiences as an ecumenical worker."

Being an Asian theologian is a matter of approach. Christian mission when seen from the perspective of one who has lived among people of many faiths is naturally going to be different from that of those who tend to see people of other faiths, so to speak, from a distance. Hence, two options for viewing the relationship between the church and the nations open to European and American Christian theologians may not really be open to Asian Christian theologians who take their location within people of many faiths seriously.

One option is to dismiss other faiths as purely human creations that are futile attempts to understand God, who, however, has been revealed in a defining way in Jesus Christ. This in large measure is the approach of neo-orthodox theologians. Because I will have occasion to engage this position in debate in the book itself, I will only point to the difficulties this approach poses for Asian Christian theologians. To do this, I will use two examples of actual encounters between Asian and European theologians.

The first is a conversation that my father, D. T. Niles, had with Karl Barth, arguably the greatest theologian of the twentieth century, which even the bishop of Rome, Pope Pius XII, is said to have conceded. During the conversation, there was a discussion about religions, including Hinduism, in which Karl Barth expressed his position. My father then asked him, "Professor Barth, how many Hindus have you actually known?" To which the professor responded, "None. But that is besides the point."

The second is a conversation that my compatriot Wesley Ariarajah had with the great ecumenical leader of our time, Willem Visser 't Hooft. As Ariarajah reports it,

> When pressed to respond to the Hindu witness to the experience of grace within their tradition, he answered, "I do not know whether there is salvation in Hinduism. All I know is that in Christ God wills to save all of humankind, and to this I am a witness."

Ariarajah goes on to say that though in some ways this answer was adequate, it was not satisfying.

> "Dr. Visser 't Hooft," I said, after a few moments of respectful hesitation, "your generation had to move from theological hostility to theological neutrality about the faith of our neighbours. Our generation needs to move beyond neutrality."[1]

The second option is to see all religions in varying degrees as partial revelations of the truth about God, each expressing this revelation in a way that is consonant with the climate of thought endemic to a particular geographical region. This is essentially the position of John Hick and others who follow him. Hick is right in criticizing the assumed preeminence of the Christian religion over other religions and in calling for a Copernican revolution in understanding the relationship between religions where all religions revolve not around Christianity but around God as center. He then speaks of the ways in which religious-minded people may learn from one another in truth-seeking dialogue.[2] Although accepting this basic thesis, the difficulties for an Asian Christian arise in the way he locates the various world religions as a consequence of a period of enlightenment, which started around 800 B.C.E. and swept across the world:

It suggests to us that the same divine reality has always been self-revealingly active towards mankind, and that the differences of human responses are related to different human circumstances. These circumstances—ethnic, geographical, climatic, economic, sociological, historical—have produced the existing differentiation of human culture, and within each main cultural region the response to the divine has taken its own characteristic forms...Thus Islam embodies the main response of the arabic [sic] peoples to the divine reality; Hinduism, the main (though not the only) response of the peoples of India; Buddhism, the main response of the peoples of South-East Asia and parts of Northern Asia; Christianity the main response of the european [sic] peoples, both within Europe itself and in their emigrations to the Americas and Australasia...We can see how these revelations took different forms related to the different mentalities of the peoples to whom they came, and developed within these different cultures into the vast and many-sided historical phenomena of the world religions.[3]

From a different perspective, the Jesuit Aloysius Pieris from Sri Lanka, a scholar of Buddhism, also makes the point that the main religions have not really succeeded against one another in winning converts, and therefore a different understanding of the Christian missionary task must be explored.[4]

But the fact remains that there were converts. How are these to understand their faith? Was it an aberration that my ancestors converted to the Christian faith, when some form of Hinduism would have been their proper religion? Also, how do we understand the movement of people of Hindu, Buddhist, and Islamic faiths to large parts of Europe, even converting European people to their faith positions? Speaking as an Asian Christian, my dilemma is that I can neither jettison my faith in Jesus Christ, which also calls for a missionary response, nor deny my identity as one who is culturally and ethnically related to my Hindu sisters and brothers.

Reflecting from an Indian context, Thomas Thangaraj proposes a way of dealing missiologically with the issue Hick raises. He takes as a starting point a picture that the World Development Forum offers:

If you lived in a representative global village of 1,000 persons, there would be:

- 300 Christians (183 Catholics, 84 Protestants, and 33 Orthodox)
- 175 Muslims
- 128 Hindus
- 55 Buddhists

- 47 Animists
- 210 without any religion or confessed atheists
- 85 from other smaller religious groups[5]

Thangaraj uses this picture to argue that—especially in a postmodern situation, which is suspicious of meta-narratives—no approach to any form of mission that is premised on what is uniquely Christian is likely to work. He therefore discards all Christian starting points, such as the Christian understanding of the word *mission* itself, *Missio Dei*, the Bible, and the church. Asking the question, "What is the most helpful starting point for constructing a theology of mission that takes the conversation with people of varying religious and ideological traditions as an important part of theological construction?" he proposes that we begin with *Missio Humanitas*. As the basis for a common human mission, he suggests three themes: "responsibility, solidarity, and mutuality." From this perspective, he addresses themes in Christian mission to explore at depth what it would mean to speak of "cruciform responsibility, liberative solidarity, and eschatological mutuality."[6]

Although agreeing with much of what Thangaraj has to say, my concern is to address a problem that he himself surfaces but does not treat adequately. In presenting his ideas on an approach to mission to students in India, the response was that "[the students] were very skeptical of sustaining the conversation with the other religions and secular partners once we introduce the concept of God in Christ." The students were conscious "that as Christian theologians their task is to talk of mission in the light of God, Christ and the church," though these could become blocks to continuing the conversation. He then goes on to say,

> Interestingly, however, a Hindu philosopher present at the seminar maintained that as long as one operates within the framework of responsibility, solidarity and mutuality, it still would be possible for a Hindu to continue in the conversation, even though a Hindu may bring his or her own particular understandings with regard to the elaboration of these basic concepts.[7]

The Hindu philosopher had in fact put his finger on the problem for understanding Christian mission today. What happens when the Hindu component is introduced into the conversation and then the Christian component? To avoid conflict and the erection of barriers, one suggestion would be to continue the reduction of positions within a framework of *Missio Humanitas* in the hope that it will produce a synthetic religious vision that is acceptable to all. However, such approaches in the past have failed.

The way forward is first to concede the position that Thangaraj has taken and maintain with him that an approach to Christian mission that ignores the reality of people of other faiths and ideological positions is not tenable in the pluralistic world in which we live. Such an approach would invariably involve a conversation about the challenge for mission, not just Christian mission, which a recognized historical human condition poses. In other words, it is within a commonly accepted project that this conversation needs to take place. In the introduction to his book *Man and the Universe of Faiths,* which he wrote as both a rejoinder and a companion to Hick's *God and the Universe of Faiths*, M. M. Thomas of India says,

> My conviction [is] that the common humanity and the self-transcendence within it, more especially the common response to the problems of humanisation of existence in the modern world, rather than any common religiosity, or common sense of the Divine, is the most fruitful point of entry for a meeting of faiths at spiritual depth in our time.[8]

The second step is to take into account the fact that in "a meeting of faiths at spiritual depth," we also encounter a problem that all religions pose. In his article "Togetherness and Uniqueness: Living Faiths in Inter-relation," Bishop Lakshman Wickremesinghe of Sri Lanka identified this problem. Wickremesinghe rejects Hick's position that the focal images, such as "Jesus is God Incarnate, Gautama is the All-Enlightened One, Ram-Krishna is the Absolute in Self-manifestation, and Mohammed is the Incomparable Prophet," which "express conflicting claims to normative truth for all," are only evocative and not cognitive and therefore in the end are not really conflictual but complementary. Wickremesinghe says,

> Those who claim that their religious visions are uniquely central and normative for all, and who accept conflicting truth-claims as part of the genuine context of inter-religious dialogue, would consider that Dr. Hick explains away, rather than explains, the distinctive role played by their respective focal images. These images are to them not merely mythic…or solely evocative. They are symbolic in that they are primarily illuminative and only consequently evocative. They illuminate because the basic analogies or "ways of describing" implicit in them convey insight into things as they are especially the nature of Transcendent Reality and the distinctive relation of such Reality to spatio-temporal reality…In terms of the Indian tradition, such a focal image is symbolic because it both elicits a way of seeing (*darsana*) and

also evokes a way of living (*pratipada*) in alignment with what is seen. Seeing and living are mutuality supportive.[9]

Wickremesinghe goes on to state what is for him and for other religious persons a precondition for interreligious cooperation and its contribution:

> There are small groups of persons from different religious faiths who are adopting new attitudes in relating to each other. First, they accept their own religious vision, their respective founder and scriptures, as uniquely central and normative for all, but not necessarily as complete or totally exclusive. They adopt an inclusive perspective. They expect that deeper sharing of life, devotion and insight with other religionists will result in a more comprehensive expression of their own definitively normative vision.[10]

He then presents in a comprehensive and dialogical way what it means for him to work with "Jesus is God Incarnate" as a focal image.

My approach to Christian mission in large measure follows the approach of my mentor, Lakshman Wickremesinghe, and addresses the problem for Christian mission as Wesley Ariarajah identifies it. He says that at several official ecumenical assemblies, where Christians from all parts of the world meet, there has been a tension between two theological positions: a recognition of God's presence in the lives and religions of peoples of other faiths, and the position that we are called to witness to what God has done in Jesus Christ for the salvation of the world and all its peoples. He shows that the theological tension between these two positions has never successfully been resolved. The position the San Antonio World Mission Conference (1989) took on this matter remains:

> We are well aware that these convictions and the ministry of witness (to Jesus Christ) stand in tension with what we have affirmed about God being present in and at work in people of other faiths; *we appreciate this tension, and do not attempt to resolve it.*[11]

As Asian Christian theologians, we must accept the tension between these two statements and turn that tension into a creative approach to Christian mission as do, each in their own way, Lakshman Wickremesinghe, M. M. Thomas, Aloysius Pieris, Wesley Ariarajah, Thomas Thangaraj, and many other Asian theologians outside the Indian subcontinent.

The contribution of this approach to an understanding of the task of Christian mission outside Asia resides in the fact that, as Thangaraj points out, American and European countries are also religiously plural. It is no longer possible to view people of other faiths from a distance. There is also the fact that many in these two continents do not subscribe to any religious persuasion.

It is this location that made me propose as a section heading for a mission roundtable, jointly sponsored by the Christian Conference of Asia and the Council for World Mission, the formulation "God's people in the midst of all God's peoples," which later was used for the title of the book that brought together the papers and discussions from that meeting.[12] This paradigm for understanding Christian mission today is a theological recognition of a global demographic reality. In speaking of the people of God or all God's peoples, I use three Greek words, namely, *laos, ochlos,* and *ethne,* to indicate understandings of people as church (*laos*); the multitudes (*ochlos*), among whom Jesus worked and in whose midst he received and expressed his identity as the Suffering Servant of God; and the nations of the world (*ethne*). I see the interplay among these concepts of people as crucial for rethinking the task for Christian mission in our time.

As I have already indicated, my approach in working with the paradigm "the people of God in the midst of all God's peoples," for understanding the task of Christian mission today, would be as a Christian who recognizes and works with the tension generated in the dual position of witnessing to Jesus Christ and accepting the fact that God is present and at work in people of other faiths.

A recognition of this tension shapes Christian witness in two ways that are worked out in the arguments in this book. The first is a rejection of all forms of witness that espouse a crusading form of mission. It is now a theological commonplace that Jesus proclaimed the reign/realm (kingdom) of God as good news, whereas the church proclaimed the risen Jesus Christ as good news. The two are interrelated in that the one who proclaimed God's reign and realm as good news to the people (*ochlos*) was the Messiah who understood his ministry in terms of the figure of the Suffering Servant of God. This is the ministry and mission to which we are called. It is a self-denying, self-emptying ministry that quite often contradicts and calls into question forms of worldly power that deny life for the people. In the end, such mission does become political in its manifestation.

The second is to recognize the fact that though we use Christian language and symbols to articulate the task of Christian mission in our time, because we have no other option open to us, we should concede that such language is provisional. As the passage of scripture from which the title of this book is taken indicates, the vision of the banquet to which people come from east and west is neither a purely Jewish nor for that matter a purely Christian feast. It is a Christian way of pointing to a mystery that cannot and should not be reduced to a Christian colonial argument that the nations can find their way into the Messianic banquet only through the history of Israel and the church. It must be remembered that the projection of that vision comes in the context of recognizing the faith of an outsider and before the Risen One sent his disciples in mission to the nations. Another such eschatological vision is that of the New Jerusalem that appears as God's gift when the old heaven and old earth have passed away (Rev. 21). Again, this is Christian language that refers to a mystery, which cannot and should not be reduced to a purely Christian position that the New Jerusalem is in fact "the Church." In fact, there is no "the Church" with a capital C. If anything, the New Jerusalem is an alternative to the church, for there is no temple there. In terms of the present historical situation, there are only churches, which, although geographically and denominationally specific, attempt to manifest their global interlinkage theologically and ecumenically. In this sense, one may use the term *the church* as a collective noun that refers to all churches. Although accepting the ecumenical argument that the unity of the church is not the result of human seeking but is ultimately a divine gift, I would hesitate to use that argument to speak of a universal "the Church" as a present historical reality. A Christian imperial and colonial intention, evident in the former use of the term *Christendom*, could lurk, and in fact often does, in such usage.

In 1 Corinthians 15, Paul hints at the provisional nature of a Christian way of looking at God's mission:

> Then comes the end, when he hands over the kingdom to God the Father, after he has destroyed every ruler and every authority and power. For he must reign until he has put all his enemies under his feet...When all things are subjected to him, then the Son himself will also be subjected to the one who put all things in subjection under God, so that God may be all in all. (vv. 24–25, 28)

Besides this critical note on the provisional nature of Christian language, which is in fact a specific application of the hermeneutics of suspicion, there is a positive reason for accepting the provisional nature of Christian language and symbols. In the exchange with people of other faiths, as Lakshman Wickremesinghe points out, Christian vocabulary is enriched with "a more comprehensive expression of [our] own definitively normative vision." This position can be illustrated with an example that Wickremesinghe himself provides in his article "Christianity Moving Eastwards." With the larger picture of what happens and should happen as Christianity in its Western garb meets and interacts with Indian Hindu and Buddhist religiosity, he pays special attention to the depiction of God as Mother. After acknowledging the effort of Western feminist theologians who have drawn our attention to the feminine attributes of God as found in Christian scripture, he argues that this effort needs a firmer theological base that certain Hindu myths could provide. He refers to two Hindu myths that portray the Creator God as mother and creation as taking place within the womb of God. In his words, these myths point to the fact that "in creation there is an emerging from within leading to a giving out or sacrifice from the hidden resources of the Supreme or Ultimate Reality," which "also means risk-taking and vulnerability."

There are two specific contributions of the maternal images from Hinduism for widening Christian scriptural symbolism. First, "the image of *ab divino* evokes naturally a personal and intimate relationship between God and human beings." It is more suitable than "the *ex nihilo* image to convey the dominant symbolism of a loving Creator. Second, "the image of the 'source-womb' evokes a sense of the all–encompassing, interiorized and pervasive presence of God within whom we live and move and have our being."

In the book of Revelation we have the Semitic imagery of the Lamb that is slain but regnant and the Hellenic imagery of the Alpha and the Omega on the same throne. "The time has come," Wickremesinghe says, "for the Indian imagery of the tender Divine Mother to be on the same throne. It will make explicit what is implicit in the Scriptures."[13]

This much will do to present my approach as an Asian theologian. The succeeding chapters will spell out this approach.

My training as a biblical scholar, especially of the Hebrew Scriptures, which Christians call the Old Testament, has made quite an impact on me in three particular but interrelated ways. First, there is an earthiness about the Hebrew Scriptures. They carry the address of God to a people, whom God accompanies, and the response of the people both in praise and in lament. Together both the word of God and the word of the people constitute scripture, which is given to us as the word of God. Unless we subscribe to the verbal inerrancy of scripture as the only way for understanding the Reformed doctrine of *Sola Scriptura*, we must recognize scripture as human words. In other words, it is literature with a mixture of history and legend, story and myth. It is in the reading of it and the preaching from it that the word of God meets us and confronts us.

This leads to the second impact of the Hebrew Scriptures. For, as a part and an important part of Christian scripture, the Hebrew Scriptures urge us to receive the whole of scripture as gospel, not law, as opening up avenues for liberation and imagination, not just as a set of stipulations to be obeyed. The Old Testament scholar and biblical theologian Bernhard W. Anderson, who was my professor at Princeton Theological Seminary, once said in class, "If you don't appreciate poetry, don't read the Bible."[14] To which I would add, "If you read the Bible and have no poetic imagination, you will not only kill yourself, you will kill everybody around you!" As the word of God, "the sword of the Spirit," the Hebrew Scriptures in particular enjoin imagination, which is the proper mode for appropriating the gospel. It is explicit in the prophecy of Joel, who presents the gift of imagination as an important gift of God's Spirit when old people will dream of new possibilities and young people will see visions that will break through the limitations of present realities (Joel 2:28). Because Christian mission is set in the context of God's mission of love, it cannot be conceived apart from the accompanying presence of the Holy Spirit (Acts 1:8; 2:1–47). Imagination defies and corrects every attempt we make to turn gospel into law, so that we may manage God's salvation.

The third impact has been the role of historical criticism in biblical interpretation. Historical critical readings of the Bible arose as a way of allowing scripture to speak for itself without imposing Christian doctrinal positions on it or using it simply as a source book for deriving Christian dogma. However, in an attempt to discover the authorial intention of biblical texts, source criticism has attempted to peel away assumed secondary material from primary material and has distributed the results into various presumed literary sources. At the end, one is not quite clear which text one is reading—whether the received text of the Bible or the reconstructed text of a scholar. Form criticism, in seeking literary forms and identifying their location and meaning in presumed original life situations, has many a time encouraged us to seek a text behind the text. There are two issues here. First, whether we like it or not, whether we agree with it or not, we have to deal with the Bible as scripture, warts and all. The major contribution of historical criticism in this regard is that it reminds us that the text has a history and cannot be read, so to speak, as a seamless whole. It throbs with historical memory. Redaction criticism, which attempts to identify the literary continuity of the text as we have it, has gone a long way in helping us read the Bible as scripture and prompts us to read portions of scripture in the context of the canon of scripture. Rhetorical criticism has encouraged us to look for literary structures and rhetorical prompts in the text itself that help us to read and interpret the text. Second, there is a question as to whether, despite our best efforts, we can find an authorial intention in an ancient text. In fact, if historical critical methods have taught us anything, it is that meaning resides not in the text itself but in our reading of the text. The social location from which we approach the text and the interpretative communities to which we belong shape the way in which we read the text.[15] I acknowledge this fact in using a reader-response approach in my biblical reflections as an exercise in imagination.

Clearly my interpretations of biblical passages are not definitive positions. When one's location changes and experiences multiply, the constant operation of the hermeneutical cycle of context addressing text and text illuminating and challenging context continues to generate a continually changing body of meaning.[16] There is also another reason why these are not definitive positions. What I have to say as a biblical theologian invites dialogue both for correction and for amplification from other communities of interpretation.

To illustrate the role of context in a reader-response approach, let us look at what Jesus had to say about the neighbor. In the account that Luke gives (10:25–37), the lawyer brings together Deuteronomy 6:5 and a part of Leviticus 19:18 to present the heart of the Torah, or God's commandment. Jesus says, in effect, "Well done! You have got it right." The lawyer then presses Jesus to identify the neighbor. Leviticus 19:18 is clear on this matter. The neighbor is from one's own people: "You shall not take vengeance or bear a grudge against any of your people, but you shall love your neighbor as yourself." The matter of what is to be the proper response in caring for the poor and the alien is already given in verses 9f. Yet given the social location of Jesus, working among the crowds or multitudes (*ochlos*), whom he characterized as "sheep without a shepherd," Jesus brings in the poor and the alien to give a different response to the question "Who is my neighbor?" The parable that answers this question not only points to the one who has been beaten and broken, robbed and ignored (the poor), as one's neighbor, but also holds up the untouchable outsider, the Samaritan (the alien), as the one who exhibits the qualities of neighborliness and teaches us how to identify and care for our neighbor. The exegesis of Jesus so mesmerizes the lawyer that he agrees. I am certain that if the conversation had continued, at some point the lawyer would have said to Jesus, "But that is not in the text!"

In the body of the book, I refer to the Hebrew Scriptures as the Old Testament to indicate their appropriation as a part of Christian scripture, together with the New Testament. Both need to be taken together to rethink the task for Christian mission in our time.

My varied experiences as an ecumenical worker contributed to my understanding and practice of mission. In describing the impact these experiences have had on my thinking, I slip also into the genre of memoir, which that will appear again and again in this book. But more needs to be said than in an introductory way of how these experiences shaped my thinking. This recounting of experiences and the shaping of ideas I present in the first chapter.

Although strictly speaking this book is not about the work of the Council for World Mission, it does figure quite prominently in it, especially in the first few chapters. There are two main reasons. First of all, it was in the Council for World Mission that my skills and theological insights, gained over many years, were brought together and brought to bear on leading it as its general secretary. It was also the place where I in turn was challenged to rethink. My ideas gained from this practical interplay.

The second and equally important reason is that it became my home and the context of my ministry. Rather sadly I had to say goodbye to Ceylon, as I still prefer to call the country of my birth. In March 2002 I visited my homeland of Jaffna and saw for myself the devastation a twenty-year-long war has wrought. Among other things, St. Peter's Church, the local church where my ancestor worked and several generations of the Niles family served, does not even exist anymore. There are not even ruins to see.

The dislocation from one context has meant that I have had to serve in many contexts. In my ministry in the Council for World Mission, I have had to be at home in several local contexts with a bewildering cultural variety stretching from the Caribbean to the Pacific. I have also had to respect and interact with the different ways in which the Triune God is worshiped and served. This culturally colorful situation and the symbiotic relationship that I have had with it have shaped my thinking in innumerable ways. Indeed, it is the lens, sometimes sharp, sometimes refracted, through which I express my thoughts on the task for Christian mission today.

I begin in chapter 1 with my personal story, which depicts my ecumenical formation. Chapter 2 presents a biblical reflection on the metaphor of "being on a journey" as an exercise in biblical imagination to chart the missionary journey on which communities of churches in mission, such as the Council for World Mission, have embarked. Chapter 3 presses for rethinking Christian mission in terms of the shaping of the *laos* for a new missionary situation. In this chapter we enter into a conversation with the theological insights that emerged in the Council for World Mission because of an axial change that took place when it changed from a Western mission society to a partnership of churches in mission. Chapters 4 and 5 look at ways of sharing personnel and money to express this axial change in concrete ways. Chapters 6, 7, and 8 are more argued chapters in which I bring together my ideas on rethinking the task for Christian mission today under the paradigm of the people of God in the midst of all God's peoples. Chapter 6 reexamines some of the thinking that lies behind concepts of mission that hinder a breakthrough into new ways of conceiving the task for Christian mission. Chapter 7 argues for the alternative paradigm for mission; chapter 8 tests this paradigm in the context of religio-ethnic strife that characterizes today's world.

In writing chapters 7 and 8, I have reworked and used parts of two articles I wrote for journals of the World Council of Churches. One is

"How Ecumenical Must the Ecumenical Movement Be?" which appeared in the *Ecumenical Review* (October 1991), and the second is "Toward the Fullness of Life: Intercontextual Relationships in Mission," which appeared in the *International Review of Mission* (October 2002). As I was writing this book, I had to deliver two lectures at the Union Theological Seminary for which I drew from some of the material in the book. These two lectures, "Costly Grace: Race and Reconciliation—An Asian Perspective" and "Called to be Channels of God's Peace: Remembering Dietrich Bonhoeffer" later appeared in volume 56 (2002–2003) of the *Union Seminary Quarterly Review (USQR)*. I am grateful to both institutions for giving me permission to reuse material.

A book of this nature could not have been written without the contribution of many colleagues who are also friends. Although some of these are mentioned in the book, there are many more. I am particularly indebted to my wife, Sherina, who has accompanied me in my ecumenical ministry and often patiently and sometimes not so patiently listened to my theological ramblings. I must also acknowledge the support of my children, who in various tangible ways helped me in this task.

While working in the Council for World Mission, I could not find the time or the needed space to write this book. Just the business of keeping the business going took all of my time and energy. The United Board for Christian Higher Education in Asia, under the leadership of President Richard Wood, provided the resources for Union Theological Seminary in New York to invite me as the Elisabeth Luce Moore Visiting Professor of Ecumenical Theology. It was extremely helpful to belong to a scholarly community of faculty and students to get the ideas flowing. My thanks are due especially to President Joseph Hough and Deans Rosemary Keller and James Hayes. It was good to have again the company of my friend James Cone, Charles A. Briggs Distinguished Professor of Systematic Theology, with whom I could test some of my ideas.

Following my teaching stint at Union Theological Seminary, I accepted an invitation from my friends Professor Archie Lee and General Secretary Luk Fai to teach at the Theology Faculty of the Chinese University of Hong Kong and conduct a number of seminars for the pastors and lay elders of the Hong Kong Council of the Church of Christ in China. While in Hong Kong I had time to finish the manuscript, largely because of the kindness of Dean Lo Lung Kwong, who asked me to teach just one course each semester for the year that I was there.

I am particularly grateful to my three readers: Rev. Jacques Mathey, who is the coordinator of the Commission on World Mission and Evangelism of the World Council of Churches; Rev. Tony Burnham, the former general secretary of the United Reformed Church in the United Kingdom and for a time also chair of corporations, which is a peculiarly British alternative for "honorary treasurer," of the Council for World Mission; and the Rev. Dr. Philip Wickeri, Flora Lamson Hewlett Professor of Evangelism and Mission at the San Francisco Theological Seminary and Graduate Theological Union in California.

In revising the manuscript for publication, I have taken into account as best as I could the comments and criticisms my readers made. There are two residual comments that I need to address. The first is that the approach in this book is not as "Catholic" as it could be. This is true, though from time to time I refer to Catholic theologians. I cannot with integrity jump out of my own location as an Asian Protestant theologian and address the task for Christian mission today in any other way than the way in which I have done. In this connection I remember what my father, D. T. Niles, said on this matter. He viewed the categories of Catholic, Orthodox, and Protestant not simply as specifying certain Christian churches but as theological positions that are to be found in all churches. Perhaps my contribution will be heard by the "Protestant" component in churches, who would then be able to interpret my position to others. The second comment from my readers is that sometimes my language is more turgid than it needs to be. I have heeded this criticism as best as I could. But there are times when in aiming for simplicity one could even end up being simplistic. Words carry not only meaning in a sentence but also a certain ambience, perhaps an emotional content and an excess of meaning, which another word and construction do not express as well. I do admit that at times the language and thought process are difficult. Although I would not and dare not aspire to the literary heights and intellectual talent of T. S. Eliot, I would still plead my cause with his words: "Since much thought has gone into the writing of it, I expect much thought to go into the reading of it!"

Two further comments need to be made. First, as far as possible, I have used inclusive language. I have not changed the language in quotations from authors who wrote at a time when inclusive language was not in practice. Similarly, when quoting from the New Revised Standard Version (NRSV) Bible and discussing biblical passages that refer to God as a male, I have made no changes. In using God's reign/realm to translate the Greek, usually rendered in English as the kingdom of God, I emphasize both its temporal and spatial aspects. Second, time and again I have quoted from remarks made in personal conversations with me or at meetings at which I was present. These have no footnotes. I have also referred to unpublished material, especially from the Council for World Mission, and given the reference in footnotes. These documents have now been stored with the School of Oriental and African Studies at the University of London, England, as the archives of the London Missionary Society and the Council for World Mission.

Recognizing my debt to the saints of God, those with us and those who have passed on, I am dedicating this book with love to the memory of my parents, from whom I received the faith: to my father Thambyrajah (better known as D. T.) and my mother Dulcie. From my father I inherited a passion for mission and my ecumenical vision. My mother helped me to appreciate "the ordinary as beloved of God," from which appreciation I was led to participate in the articulation of theologies of people (*Minjung/ochlos*) as the subjects of history. Because, time and again, I have occasion in the book to refer to the ways in which my father's thinking, both written and spoken, influenced me, I end this introduction with the words of my mother:

> But I wonder why he chose to follow and to guide me, an ordinary woman like me! Born in an ordinary home of ordinary parents! One who grew and lived an ordinary life! And yet has he not always chosen the ordinary things in life to glorify his name? He, too, was born in an ordinary home of an ordinary woman. His friends were all ordinary people, who lived ordinary lives. His teachings are built on illustrations from ordinary happenings. God must love the ordinary. He created so much of it!

> Whom the Lord chooses, however, are no more ordinary people after that. Nor is anything ordinary, when once the Lord uses it. That big fisherman of Galilee, that crossed piece of wood—they are ordinary no more. Why he chooses the ordinary, I do not know, except that he must love it. That is why he must have chosen me.[17]

1

My Ecumenical Formation

Alhough I had been involved earlier in ecumenical work locally in my hometown of Jaffna in Sri Lanka and regionally in Asia, my ecumenical formation as such began during my second stint as a teacher at the Theological College of Lanka starting in September 1974. Built on a hill in a village called Pilimatalawa in the outskirts of the city of Kandy, the Theological College of Lanka was intended to introduce the churches in Sri Lanka to ecumenical theological education on the soil of Sri Lanka. Until then, most from the Protestant and Anglican churches who offered themselves for the ministry went to India to the colleges of the University of Serampore, founded by Marshman, Ward, and Carey. The Anglican Bishop of Colombo started his own divinity school for those he wished to train as priests for his diocese, but the others continued to send most of their candidates for ministerial training to India.

With considerable difficulty it was argued with the Senate of the Serampore College, which granted the degrees, that Sri Lanka needed its own united theological college, which would prepare students in Sinhala and Tamil for degrees to be granted by the University of Serampore. After checking the qualifications of the teachers and the adequacy of the library, the Senate of the Serampore College permitted the founding of the Theological College of Lanka in 1960 to teach students in the two vernacular languages. Students had to sit for annual examinations set by Serampore. All the mainstream churches in Sri Lanka—two Anglican dioceses, the Methodist Conference, the Baptist Sangamaya, and the Presbyterian Church—decided to sponsor the college and send their ordinands for training there. The Jaffna Diocese of the Church of South India stayed out with the plea that those to be trained for the Tamil ministry should be trained in a Tamil college situated in a Tamil environment. The others were willing to risk an ecumenical venture.

17

The ecumenical challenge was twofold. First, many of us from an earlier generation had our high school and university training in English. English was our first language, so there was a natural linguistic bridge between Sinhala and Tamil people. Later on, English as a medium of instruction was dropped, and education was in the languages of the people. A commendable move, but it served to reinforce the ethnic division between the two language groups. Those who founded the theological college were of the opinion that students living together in a joint program of training, even though conducted in two different languages, would prepare themselves for a ministry that would hold together the two ethnic groups in the church. Friendships did develop across the language barrier. Second, though students trained for several denominational ministries, they began to appreciate one another's traditions and, with few exceptions, looked forward to a time when all the churches would unite to form the United Church of Sri Lanka. Ecumenical ministry for an ecumenical church was the vision.

Yet very little had been done to take the next major ecumenical step—namely, to relate the training to the various contexts of Sri Lanka. For ecumenism, in its fullest sense, involves the whole inhabited world and not just the Christian part of it. The challenge to take this next important step came from a problem posed by one of the church leaders to me.

When I returned to the college after receiving a Ph.D. in Biblical Studies from Princeton Theological Seminary, I was appointed director of studies (academic dean). Shortly after I returned, Lakshman Wickremesinghe, the Bishop of Kurunagala at that time, expressed his dissatisfaction with the ministerial training given at the theological college. He said, "You are producing candidates for the ministry with an academic training of sorts and little else. Most of these are quite inadequate as priests in my diocese, which is made up of many rural parishes. They also do not really know how to relate to the majority of people who are either Buddhist or Hindu." He was even wondering whether he should organize other supplementary forms of training for the ordinands from his diocese. I asked him to give me a year to try a different approach to ministerial training that might satisfy him.

My teaching colleagues and I had been dissatisfied for quite some time with the type of ministerial training we were giving the students, but we had done nothing about it. Change seemed difficult. One part of the difficulty was that, every year for four years, students were required to prepare for examinations of the Serampore College of the University of Serampore. With this requirement, there was not much more we could do. The challenge from the bishop was a spur to change the system to something more adequate for ecumenical ministerial training in Sri Lanka.

One of our senior staff colleagues, Cyril Premawardhana, was entrusted with the task of presenting our case to the Senate of Serampore. He argued at a meeting of its council that the Theological College of Lanka should be granted autonomy to have its own training program. The university could test the academic ability of the students through a number of comprehensive examinations toward the end of the fourth and last year of training. Permission was given, and we set about changing the program.

For the first year we provided introductory courses in Old Testament and New Testament. More important, to help Sinhala and Tamil students understand and appreciate their cultures and each other's culture, there was a course on the cultures of Sri Lanka. To understand their Christian heritage, we had a course on church history. It was a boon that my colleague, Donald Kanagaratnam, who taught the course on culture, not only knew both languages but also had an in-depth knowledge of both cultures. He was also our lecturer in church history. In this way, with my colleagues, I began to put into practice a conviction of mine, which I later stated methodologically as "the problem of the two stories."[1] As Asian Christians we inherit two stories, both as traditions and as narratives. One story, the Christian story, comes through the missionary movement, and the other story comes from our cultures. Their relationship to each other is not devoid of problems and tensions. Without suppressing either story or simply conflating the two, the task for Christian ministry and theology is to relate these two stories meaningfully and creatively.

The second year of training was devoted to intense theological studies. In the third year students went out two by two, one Sinhala and one Tamil, to work with churches, including the Roman Catholic Church and the Seventh Day Adventist Church. In this way they not only learned about other denominational traditions but also gained insights into what ministry in other churches entails. After a period of debriefing at the college, the same two went out to live and work among the Sinhala peasantry in the plains and the indentured Tamil workers, who had been brought from India by the colonial government to work the tea estates in the hill country. It was a time to test and put into practice what they had learned both at college and in working with churches.

During this time I started to evolve a theology of people, which I later developed more fully in collaboration with the Korean Minjung theologians.[2] Working with Korean and other Asian theologians, I began to realize that, as a corollary to the problem of relating the two stories, we also have to relate theologically an understanding of people as *laos* (the people of the church), people as *ethne* (the nations), and people as *ochlos* (the crowd or multitude).

In the fourth year the students brought together their experiences in ministry and mission together with their academic learning in a series of seminars working either with an individual lecturer or with teams of lecturers. A student of mine, who went on to do a doctorate in interfaith relations, said to me when I met him later, "I really learned nothing new since I left Pilimatalawa. Everything I learned subsequently simply helped develop the skills and knowledge I had acquired at the Theological College of Lanka."

The efficacy of such a model for ministerial formation became even more apparent when I was asked to reflect, many years later, on the method employed in the Institute for Theological and Leadership Development (ITLD) of the United Church in Jamaica and the Cayman Islands. Starting in 1990, ITLD has worked with a model of theological education and ministerial formation that is an advance on the experiment we tried at the Theological College of Lanka. In my preface to the book celebrating the tenth anniversary of the Institute, I summarize the intention of this form of ministerial training:

> Normally, for theological education and ministerial formation, persons are abstracted from the situations in which their ministry has to be exercised and validated, and gathered into theological laboratories. After the training, there is then the shock of re-entry with the concomitant need often to relearn and perhaps even reconfigure one's theological and ministerial task. To minimize this assault, most theological schools build in chunks of time for field training and internships with varying results. But the theological school remains the home for learning.
>
> What would it be like if the process were reversed and the actual place of ministry and mission became the home for learning and there were periods of retreat in learning centres with a community of peers for theological reflection and learning as well as spiritual refreshment? It is this reversal that ITLD understands as normal.[3]

I left the Theological College of Lanka and joined the Christian Conference of Asia (CCA) as secretary for theological concerns in January 1978. As a major part of my work, I organized several theological dialogues between theologians in a particular country and theologians from other Asian countries.[4] It was a way of encouraging new theological movements in Asia, to put into practice in Asia as a whole what M. M. Thomas had to say with regard to theology in India: "Indian theology must be judged in the light of the mission of the Church in India, and need not be brought to any other bar of judgment."[5]

Although the theme of moratorium on foreign missions and theology was not taken up in Asia with the same vehemence as it was in Africa, Asian theologians bemoaned the Teutonic and Latin captivity of theology. There was an increasing conviction that Asian Christians ought to free themselves from the requirements imposed by Western theological discourses, if mission and theology in Asia were to be relevant to the various Asian situations.

The problem lay in the way Asian Christians had received and internalized the message from neo-Orthodox theology. The message from neo-Orthodoxy, especially as Henrik Kraemer seemed to say at the World Mission Conference (1938) in Tambaram, India, was that one has to postulate a disjunction between religion as the human search for truth and God, which is riddled with error and therefore a failure, and God's once-for-all self-revelation and saving intention in Jesus Christ. Other religions may have some degree of truth in them, but in the end as systems of belief they are irrelevant or worthless.[6] This view informed our understanding of mission as essentially an effort to convince non-Christians of the error of their religion and the need to convert to faith in Jesus Christ. Although Kraemer was clear that Christianity as a religion also faced the same judgment as other religions, for Asian Christians Christianity was the only true religion particularly in the ways in which it was formulated in the West. On the one hand, this posture led to Christian triumphalism, and on the other it refused to have any serious engagement with Asian religions to articulate a theology that arose out of and spoke to Asian contexts.

Clearly, we could not ignore the Christian tradition, which had been brought to Asia by our missionary forebears. To do so would have been to suppress one of the stories. But there had to be a time for Asian Christians to reevaluate the theologies they had received and to set in motion new directions.

This was not an easy task because at that time liberation theology from Latin America was also beginning to have an impact on Asia. Several Asian theologians were persuaded by the "universalist" claim of some of the Latin American theologians who were of the opinion that they spoke for all oppressed people. This influence was particularly heavy in the Ecumenical Association of Third World Theologians, which was intended to be a forum for articulating theologies from the non-Western world. Utilizing Marxian social analysis, there was a tendency, later corrected, in Latin American liberation theology to ignore or downplay the role of religion and culture both in shaping the context and in theologically responding to the context. This trend also had to be combated.

In the first issue of the bulletin of the Commission on Theological Concerns of the Christian Conference of Asia, I reflected on this trend:

Asian theologians have usually been co-opted into theological agenda and theological positions which originate elsewhere. This is a constant danger, and is in many ways the reason why clear Asian theological positions are either slow to emerge or do not emerge at all. The danger of co-option is particularly evident when an organization seeks to speak for the whole of the Third World while taking its basic theological impetus from one section of the Third World, namely, Latin America.[7]

Aloysius Pieris from Sri Lanka was sharper in his criticism of the "narrow concept of religion" that Latin American theologians tend to espouse:

> But the two forms in which this tendency influenced liberationist interpretation of religion appeared only within the last hundred years. For the philosophical rejection of (the Christian) religion characteristic of certain intellectual movements in Europe (Enlightenment, scientific revolution, rationalism) found an ideological as well as theological formulation in the two Karls of "dialectical" fame. Marx's dialectical materialism set religion against *revolution*; Barth's dialectical theology opposed it to *revelation*. In their systems, religion was a major obstacle to liberation and salvation, respectively.[8]

Instead of simply belaboring the point that we needed space for Asian theology to develop, we actually got on with the job. The period from 1978 to 1985 was a particularly fruitful period for the doing of Asian theology recognizing "the problem of the two stories." This development has continued since then. To name but a few, Minjung theology (Korea), homeland theology and *chhu-thaau-thi'n* (Taiwan),[9] bicultural theology (Aoteoroa–New Zealand), and theology of struggle (Philippines) were Asian theological experiments that later spilled over to inform several movements of Christian mission in those countries. These theological expressions took into their analyses not only religious and cultural factors but also social, economic, and political factors. Through these theological dialogues we began to identify and bring together Asian perspectives on christology, ecclesiology, political theology, and social ethics.

While pleading for space, there was also a recognition of the fact that theology needed partners, which is implied in "dialogue" as a theological method. In my assessment of theological developments in Asia from 1979 to 1980 to the Commission on Theological Concerns of the Christian Conference of Asia, I reflected on this need:

> The question that is emerging now is, should we not also dialogue with others outside the Asian region who are

themselves involved in such a search? This has always been a vexed question because we have regularly argued that we break free from the Teutonic and Latin captivity of our theology. A certain isolation is necessary if we are "to do our own thing in our own way." But, is continued isolation or ghettoism desirable when we are coming through with our articulation of "living theology"? I am not arguing that we revisit the past from which we broke, but rather dialogue with others who are working out of their own contexts. Continued ghettoism may be a sign of both immaturity and insecurity.[10]

The experiences I had and the insights gained in theology and mission while working in the Christian Conference of Asia helped me appreciate the vision of the Council for World Mission, which stated that in making a different arrangement for mission the expectation was that "we may all learn from each other, for in that fellowship we believe that the Holy Spirit speaks to all through each."[11]

While serving in the Christian Conference of Asia, I was promoted (or demoted—depending on one's perspective!) from secretary for theological concerns to associate general secretary for finance and administration and was also asked to continue my work as a theologian. As I say to friends, "For a while I was serving both God and Mammon, and Mammon was clearly winning!" Although I had to spend considerably more time dealing with financial questions and the shrinking income base of the Christian Conference of Asia, I was also called upon to give several lectures on Asian theology, especially in the European and North American countries to which I went to raise money. Much to the disgust of Asian friends, my theological efforts in Asia seemed to come to an end. But a different kind of theological training was taking place.

Normally theologians tend to leave money matters alone. But in the new job I was given, I was realizing through experience the implications of the counsel of my predecessor, Ron O'Grady: "In this job you will acquire an entirely new understanding of the doctrine of human sin!" At the time I thought he meant that I would detect the propensity for fiscal sinning in others. Little did I realize how managing money would skewer my own judgment of people and shape my theology.

Valuable lessons on realism were learned at this time. For one thing, I tend to read budgets rather than theological statements to get a better understanding of the mission priorities of churches and organizations. Budgets do not lie. For another, I began to realize that the way in which we manage money is a spiritual matter. As I will argue later, this involves more than saying with Dom Helda Camara,

"Bread for myself is a material matter but bread for my neighbour is a spiritual matter."

My stint at the World Council of Churches, from September 1986 to June 1991, turned out to be my farewell to ecumenical innocence. I was led to believe by my parents that this was the Mecca of the ecumenical movement. So quite cheerfully I took on what many colleagues even in the World Council of Churches thought would be an impossible job: to be the Director of the "Conciliar Process of Mutual Commitment (covenant) to Justice, Peace and the Integrity of Creation," called JPIC or the Conciliar Process. Coming from Sri Lanka, issues of justice, of human rights, and of peace were daily matters. I had also lost friends and colleagues, such as Fr. Michael Rodrigo, in the struggle for justice and human rights simply because they stood by and with the people. So I assumed that with my passion for justice and peace and with all my local and regional ecumenical experiences, I could take on a job at the global level.

The job given to me was to tackle a demand placed on the World Council of Churches at its Assembly at Vancouver (1983). The Programme Guidelines Committee recommended and the Assembly accepted that "to engage member churches in a conciliar process of mutual commitment (covenant) to justice, peace and the integrity of all creation shall be a priority for World Council programmes."[12]

More than a program, it was an ecumenical vision or, better, an ecumenical expectation. On the one hand, it was a desire to get the commitment of churches to the struggles for justice, peace, and the preservation of God's creation. On the other, it was an attempt to bring together the Life and Work Movement and the Faith and Order Movement, which had always tended to stay apart in the Ecumenical Movement, so that they could speak in concert to help churches make the needed commitment of faith translated into action to the perceived threats to life at the time. But there were problems.

One of the things that made the vision almost unworkable was the vagueness of the terminology. What does "a conciliar process of mutual commitment" mean? Is it simply another way of saying "a process of covenanting"? In which case, although churches and people from the Methodist and Reformed traditions warmed to "a process of covenanting," it left other churches cold. They too had their own terms, rich in theology, to speak of churches coming together to express their commitment.[13] "Conciliar process" created further difficulties. English, the usual working language of the ecumenical movement, blurred two different understandings of the term *council*. One understanding of *council* is that it is an official gathering of the church called by a designated authority. Vatican II would be such a council. But who is the designated authority that can call together such a council of all the churches?[14] The suspicion that the World Council of Churches would pretend to be such an authority raised all the concerns and fears that were addressed in the document "The Church, the Churches and the World Council of Churches" (Toronto 1950).[15] This document clearly states that the World Council of Churches is not and cannot pretend to be the supreme council of the church, but is a fellowship of churches on the way to such a council. So it was made clear that there was as yet no one recognized church authority that could call an official council of all the churches. The other understanding of *council* was similar to what Dietrich Bonhoeffer had in mind when he called for "a Council for Peace." In 1932 and 1934 Bonhoeffer asked the churches, especially in Europe and America, to respond to the growing menace of National Socialism in Germany. Bonhoeffer wanted the churches to come together to speak together in a united voice a word that the world cannot ignore. If this were to be the model, then it would be possible to think of *council* more in terms of the French *conseil* or the Russian *sobornost,* meaning the coming together of representatives of churches to take a particular position on matters relating to "justice, peace and the integrity of creation." To avoid the confusion endemic to the term *council,* it was decided to call the coming together of churches, which took place at Seoul, Korea (February 1990), a *convocation.*

Another area of confusion was the term *integrity of creation.* Does *creation* have a perceivable integrity, or is "the integrity of creation" a theological construct? The vagueness inherent in *integrity of creation* was shown up by the German and French versions of the Vancouver call, which preferred to speak of "preserving" or "safeguarding" the creation. "The integrity of creation" too raised hopes that something radically new could be said about human relationship to the rest of creation. As Heino Falke, a pastor and theologian from the former East Germany, put it, "Thank God the ecumenical movement has finally given us a concept without content so that we can put into it what we like!" But this expectation was short lived.

Another problem that made the vision of "coming together" almost unworkable were developments both within the Life and Work Movement and the Faith and Order Movement. In the Life and Work Movement there was a clash of approaches on matters relating to ecumenical social thought. Some insisted that the model of "responsible society," formulated at the Oxford meeting of the Life and Work Movement (1938) and later refined at the 1948 and 1956 assemblies of the WCC, was still the only relevant approach to matters of justice, peace, and the environment. Others wanted to operate with models for social action and ethics drawn from liberation movements and liberation theology.[16]

Gains in the Faith and Order Movement also began to militate against its coming together with the Life and Work Movement, because there was already a sense of coming together in the Faith and Order Movement, which had its own method of careful doctrinal enquiry with agreements and "negotiated differences." The Roman Catholic Church, with representatives from the Vatican, was playing a major role in this movement. It also included Orthodox churches with their emphasis on "the unity of the church." Already many things had been said together, and all these and more were brought together in the celebrated *Baptism, Eucharist and Ministry* volumes.[17]

The sense that unity on doctrinal matters is not only possible but also required spilled over into the JPIC Preparatory Group, which was preparing for the World Convocation. The group had representatives from the Vatican and Christian World Communions in addition to representatives from the member churches of the World Council of Churches. A conflict in the process of preparation arose from the fact that predominantly, though not exclusively, most of those who came from the Faith and Order Movement together with representatives from the Vatican expected that theological and doctrinal positions on JPIC would be agreed on first and then put through a process of reception culminating in the world convocation on JPIC. For others, the ecumenical process of commitment to struggles for justice, peace, and the integrity of creation was the primary thing, which would then yield an agreed-on theology to resist the threats to life in our time. This conflict stood on its head the old ecumenical adage supposedly coined by Archbishop Nathan Soederblom, the principal architect of the Life and Work Movement, that "doctrine divides while service unites." With the gains of Faith and Order, it soon became evident in JPIC that although doctrine unites, service tends to divide.

Finally, for the previous administration, with Philip Potter as the general secretary of the World Council of Churches and Konrad Raiser as his deputy, the conciliar process was a way of bringing the member churches of the World Council of Churches on board a comprehensive program thrust. Under the next administration, the process was broadened to include as far as possible all churches. Once this move had taken place, it would have made no sense to leave out the Roman Catholic Church, which is the biggest Christian church in the world. This effort created its own strains both for the World Council of Churches and the Vatican. The process leading to the convocation was slowed down until the Vatican could respond to the invitation of the World Council of Churches to co-sponsor the convocation. After some nine months of internal deliberations, the Vatican declined the invitation. It also said that it would not send official representatives but would send observers.[18]

I speak of this period as my farewell to ecumenical innocence because many of the presuppositions and assumptions with which I came were blasted during my tenure at the World Council of Churches. This was my first experience of dealing with churches in their confessional or denominational particularity, with some proving to be more difficult than others. More to alleviate my frustration than anything else, in my mind I started classifying churches into those with "high-density ecclesiologies" and those with "low-density ecclesiologies"! In Asia, in the midst of people of many faiths, Christian ecumenism is a way of life. Denominational differences, even if they are not subsumed in movements for church union, are not usually major points of division. The whole approach of Faith and Order, with its emphasis on "negotiated differences," was new to me. At the same time I came up against churches and their leaders who insisted on "getting the theology right" as a precondition for responding to the "signs of the time" in the conciliar process. Yes! But whose theology are we talking about?

Another troubling experience had to do with communication. The local and national churches, which were the ones addressed primarily in the Vancouver call, either were slow to respond or simply ignored a major ecumenical vision and concern. What was happening seemed to be a symptom of postmodernism, namely, a suspicion of the meta-narratives and meta-visions of the ecumenical movement. That this was not the case became apparent when, in many countries, local movements for justice, for peace, and for the preservation of the environment took on the concerns of JPIC. These "peoples' movements" not only contributed to making the JPIC process a matter of ecumenical importance but also began to relate their specific struggles to the global JPIC process as it developed; in addition, they adapted as needed the global emphases and language of JPIC to address local situations.[19] A good case in point was the way in which Christians in the former German Democratic Republic (East Germany) took up the theme of peace as their response to the global JPIC process. When the government protested that matters of peace were political issues and therefore rightly the concerns of government, East German Christians said that they were only responding to a global ecumenical invitation and by implication not of much local political relevance. Steadily that movement grew to bring down the Berlin wall and a despotic government.

Struggling with the churches, I began to realize a truth D. T. Niles, the first general secretary of the East Asian Christian Conference, later the Christian Conference of Asia, said many years earlier (1968) to justify the need for an ecumenical organization in Asia that would also include Christian movements:

The churches as institutions are geared more to conserving the gains of the past than attempting the tasks of the future. The necessity, therefore, is for the churches to have those frontiers-people who are willing, as it were, to venture into unchartered [*sic*] territory, whether of thought or action or organisation, and to risk the mistakes that that kind of adventure demands. To give to these frontiers-people a sense of solidarity, encouragement and sharpened insight is a prime concern for such an organisation as the EACC.[20]

Another experience, peripheral to the actual work at the WCC but seminal to gaining a measure of ecumenical realism, was a meeting in Geneva with M. M. Thomas, who had been a moderator of the Central Committee of the World Council of Churches. He was passing through Geneva on his way to Princeton Theological Seminary, where he was a visiting professor. I knew him personally. But almost all my previous conversations with him had to do with Asian theology or Asian ecumenical matters. This was the first time I was meeting him with other colleagues to tease out of him his wisdom on global ecumenical matters. The meeting was, as my Hindu friends would describe it, a *satsang* with a *guru*. In the course of conversation he said, "The ecumenical movement was originally a movement of friends. Then it became a movement of movements. Later it became a movement of the churches. And the last has turned around and is killing off the first two."

Thomas's entry into the ecumenical movement was through the World Student Christian Federation, which was a gathering of several national student Christian movements. He then went on to the Life and Work Movement and chaired the important meeting of Church and Society in Geneva in 1966 that had a major impact on the Life and Work program of the WCC, evident especially at its 1968 Assembly in Uppsala. The Programme to Combat Racism (PCR) and the Commission of the Churches' Participation in Development (CCPD), two of the most radical programs the WCC ever had, came out of that assembly. He valued friendship. It was through his several debates and altercations with friends that his ecumenical ideas and commitment were shaped.[21] As a moderator of the Central Committee, he had to deal with churches, which as members of the World Council of Churches saw themselves as the subjects or bearers of the ecumenical movement. These were at loggerheads with the movement itself. His reproach of churches was understandable and helped me to comprehend the struggle I was having with churches in JPIC. But I could not stop there.

The statement of a colleague at the World Council of Churches got me thinking: "When you come down to it, the ecumenical movement is a movement of about three thousand people!" With the breakdown of communication or the difficulty of communicating with local churches and eliciting a response from them, the tendency, perhaps even the fallacy, of ecumenical work is to stay with like-minded people, "friends," who understand the issues and the concerns and are willing to work together. We do this largely because the churches tend to be cautious, even conservative. But to ignore the churches is to let the concerns of the ecumenical movement stay at a level that makes the churches suspicious and perhaps even antagonistic to the movement.

An incident at a meeting of the General Committee of the Christian Conference of Asia, at which I was present as a staff person, illustrates this situation. A bishop from Malaysia criticized the writings coming from the Theological Commission of the Christian Conference of Asia as difficult to understand and perhaps irrelevant for the churches. To which I retorted, "If those on the frontiers with workers and peasants in Urban Rural Mission can understand and appreciate what we are saying, what is the problem with churches?" Bishop Lakshman Wickremesinghe responded, "The reason why Preman Niles and George Ninan [then secretary for Urban Rural Mission] can understand each other is because both of them are on the frontier. But who is talking to us?"

When I came to the Council for World Mission, I began to realize that nothing is gained by, so to speak, writing off the churches and letting the staff run programs, however good such programs might be. The churches had to be brought into the movement. Speaking specifically of the Council for World Mission, a major effort had to be made to help churches become missionary churches in the sense in which David Bosch speaks in evaluating the mission concerns of Paul. Bosch says that there are few specific references in Paul's letters to the direct missionary involvement of churches. He then goes on to say,

> But this is not just to be seen as a deficiency. Rather, Paul's whole argument is that the attractive lifestyle of the small Christian communities gives credibility to the missionary outreach in which he and his fellow-workers are involved. The primary responsibility of "ordinary" Christians is not to go out and preach, but to support the mission project through their appealing conduct and by making "outsiders" feel welcome in their midst.[22]

In a word, churches are called to be bearers and sustainers of the missionary movement. This cannot and will not happen unless the vision is earthed. Speaking specifically in terms of the Council for World Mission, it was important for me as general secretary to ensure with staff colleagues that a creative tension was maintained between the Council for World Mission as Council, which has overall responsibility for expressing the character of the Council for World Mission as a missionary movement, and the churches that constitute it, which despite their institutional worries and priorities had to be the instruments for discharging the missionary responsibility of the Council for World Mission.[23]

I end this recounting of learning from ecumenical experience with a word on relating to people of other faiths. Although there had been for quite some time a subunit on dialogue with people of other faiths and ideologies in the WCC, this issue remained a thorn in the work of JPIC. There was first and foremost an ecumenical problem. If ecumenism is concerned with the whole inhabited world, then Christian ecumenism is only a small part of it. It cannot pretend to be the whole of the ecumenical arena. Second, there was a problem with JPIC itself. Justice, peace, and the preservation of the environment are not purely Christian concerns. Partnership with people of other faiths and beliefs on these matters is imperative, not just important. This is an area that cannot be ignored in discussing the task of Christian mission.

In searching for a broader framework than just interdenominational and interchurch relations for understanding the concerns of ecumenism, I found the opening of Psalm 24 to be most helpful:

> The earth [land] is the LORD's and all that is in it,
> the world, and those who live in it;
> for he has founded it on the seas,
> and established it on the rivers. (Ps. 24:1–2)

The motif of creation presents this larger picture for ecumenical commitment with some important emphases. Everything that fills the land, which we may call the totality of God's creation, with an emphasis on the flora and fauna, belongs to God. The "world," which the Septuagint translates as *oikoumene*, with all its inhabitants belongs to God, because God created both the earth and the world. In a word, it is a biblical witness to the integrity of God's creation. The integrity resides in the fact that in creation God has established order over disorder, cosmos over chaos. For the Hebrew reader, the words "seas" and "rivers" would immediately recall the ancient chaos monsters, which inhabited the seas and rivers.[24] In attenuated form, the theme of mythic conflict in which creation arises out of the subjugation and shaping of chaos is there. There is the possibility that the earth and the world can revert to chaos because of human sin and disobedience. Bemoaning the calamity let loose by Israel's revolt against God, the prophet Jeremiah sees the whole of creation reverting to chaos (Jer. 4:23–26).[25] That this could indeed become a reality is foreseen in the next four verses of Psalm 24, which depict the kind of person who could approach and remain in God's presence: "Those who have clean hands and pure hearts, who do not lift up their souls to what is false" (Ps 24:4). In a positive vein, the Psalmist assigns to humanity, made in God's image and placed in the midst of creation as God's representative, the responsibility for maintaining creation. This is the ecumenical vision that is set before us and the task to which we are called.

Work in the ecumenical movement—locally at the Theological College of Lanka, regionally with the Christian Conference of Asia, and globally with the World Council of Churches—both by accident and by design helped me acquire a more comprehensive ecumenical vision and shaped my thinking on mission as I moved to join the Council for World Mission as its general secretary in July 1991. I joined the Council at an exciting time, when it was attempting to express for our time the founding vision of the London Missionary Society, articulated two centuries ago:

> It is declared to be a fundamental principle of the Missionary Society [later the London Missionary Society] that our design is not to send Presbyterianism, Independency, Episcopacy, or any other form of Church Order and Government (about which there may be differences of opinion among serious Persons), but the Glorious Gospel of the Blessed God to the Heathen: and that it shall be left (as it ever ought to be left) to the minds of the Persons whom God may call into the fellowship of His Son from among them to assume for themselves such form of Church Government, as to them shall appear most agreeable to the Word of God.[26]

The Council for World Mission became a conduit through which I could express my ideas. It was also a conduit for a reverse flow of ideas from others—staff colleagues, members of Council, and church leaders, as well as many ecumenical leaders. All these helped to shape the mission thinking and practice of the Council for World Mission into an exciting arrangement and movement for mission. In the next four chapters we will reflect on what it means to be the people of God as *laos* with a missionary vocation, grounding this rethinking within the ebb and flow of ideas and experiments in the Council for World Mission.

In the next chapter, with the help of the metaphor of "being on a journey," we will engage in some imagining to see what it would be for a missionary community, such as the Council for World Mission, to be a movement of churches in mission.

2

Exploring a Metaphor for Mission

Metaphors can play an important role in articulating the self-understanding of a missionary community. At their best, they could also perform a reverse function, namely, to provide the imagination to shape the community's missionary ethos and project a vision to which the community could aspire. After recalling a few other metaphors for mission that performed a function in shaping the identity of the Council for World Mission, we will indulge in some imagination for mission using the metaphor of "being on a journey," which emerged to challenge the Council for World Mission to become a movement of churches in mission.

Recalling a Few Metaphors for Mission

A small boat with a cross for a mast on a storm-tossed sea has been a logo and an image of the ecumenical movement for quite some time. It symbolizes the church, if not the whole ecumenical movement, on turbulent waters with the cross as a mast, signifying that only the cross is its protection and guide. For the early period of the modern missionary movement, the symbol was a ship. It stood for the voyage of the missionaries taking the gospel from Europe to distant places of the world. In Britain the halfpenny coin with an image of a ship on its flip side, called "the ship ha'penny," was for a long time the unit of collection for the work of the London Missionary Society.

In 1972 the Congregational Council for World Mission, which continued the work of the London Missionary Society and the Commonwealth Missionary Society, changed its name to the Council for World Mission when the English Presbyterian Committee for Mission and the Missionary Committee of the Christian Church Disciples of Christ joined it. This newly formed British missionary society did not have a metaphor describing its missionary ethos. But one soon emerged, given to it by those who were not full members of the council. The image was that of a dining table in Britain.

As Christopher Duraisingh from India, the second general secretary of the Council for World Mission, described it:

> In a traditional dinner at a rectangular table, as I have often experienced it during the past several years, the host and hostess sit at the head of the table [i.e., at either end] with their bountiful resources laid clearly before them, demonstrating clearly that the resources are theirs and that they are in control. Most importantly, when I as a guest would like to have some more, it is the accepted norm that I keep quiet until the host/hostess decides to offer a second helping. Everything that happens at the table is a clear demonstration that I am a passive recipient, entirely dependent upon the decision and good will of my hostess.[1]

At an important consultation in 1975 at Singapore, a new metaphor emerged to capture the imagination of the churches that were to form the *new* Council for World Mission in 1977. Representatives from the constituent churches of the British missionary society from Britain, Australia, and New Zealand and participants from associated or related churches, which were founded by the missionary activities of the constituent churches, were meeting together outside Britain. Several participants from the associated churches voiced their unhappiness at being excluded from the actual decisions of the Council. Although they were included in a consultation on world mission, the actual decisions about the deployment of missionaries and resources for mission would be made at a board meeting of the missionary society in London. Why should they also not participate in the making of crucial decisions on the use of resources for mission? It would be wrong to assume that they were, so to speak, simply "mission churches" that were the objects of mission planned in London and not themselves "missionary churches" that were responsible for the task of mission in their own lands and abroad.

Out of this argument arose the conviction that what was needed at this time was mutuality or partnership in mission. We will reserve for treatment in the next chapter the actual theological and missiological arguments that led to and arose from this change and speak only of the metaphor of the round table that was used to describe this new arrangement.

The metaphor was employed to signify two related ideas. The first had to do with authority and importance. When people are seated at a round table, no one is at the head of the table, as would be the case when people are seated in a boardroom. All are equal. Second, all bring their food (their resources) to the table and share. Each contributes as each is able, and each receives as each requires. It was a way of recapturing for modern times the fellowship of the early church in which "no one claimed private ownership of any possessions, but everything they owned was held in common...and it was distributed to each as any had need" (Acts 4:32–35).

The metaphor of a round table itself was probably prompted by mealtimes in Singapore. The Chinese prefer round tables and not the rectangular tables used in British homes. Usually the food, either served in restaurants or brought in by several people when meals are held in church halls, is placed at the center of the table, and the diners help themselves to what they need.

The hymn writer Fred Kaan, who was also for some time a moderator of the Council for World Mission, was inspired to turn this metaphor into an image for the church. I quote the first two verses of the hymn:

The church is like a table,
a table that is round.
It has no sides or corners,
no first or last, no honours.
Here people are in oneness
and love together bound.

The church is like a table
set in an open house;
no protocol for seating,
a symbol of inviting,
of sharing, drinking, eating;
an end to "them" and "us."[2]

Although the metaphor of the round table serves both to illustrate and to shape the concern for mutuality, it leaves out of the reckoning two important facts that also interplay in any arrangement for mission. First, partners are not always equal. In fact, most partnerships are between people who are equal and unequal in different ways. The metaphor of the round table does not address this problem, which can easily be skirted in setting up a partnership. For instance, the adage attributed to Swami Vivekananda of the Ramakrishna Movement that "although the West is materially rich the East is spiritually rich" has often been used to describe a basis for partnership. Whatever merit this description may have, it certainly does not address the issue of economic justice. Although we may agree with the biblical injunction that "one does not live by bread alone" (Deut. 8:3), it is clear that without food no human being can live. The statement of the Swami needs to be counterbalanced with a statement of the Mahatma, Mohandas Gandhi, who said, "To a poor man God appears as food." Or, as Masao Takenaka of Japan, echoing the words of the Korean poet Kim Chi-ha, puts it, "God is rice."[3] A partnership that ignores this issue—and does not address the problem of power relations, which underlies this issue—is not a partnership at all. Second, the metaphor of the round table, although illustrative of the aphorism "each contributes according to ability and each receives according to need," does not address the spiritual discipline required for proper sharing in partnership. Remember Ananias and Sapphira (Acts 5:1–11). There are often many unasked and unanswered questions. When does need transgress into greed? What role do fiscal prudence and proper management of money play in any sharing of power? When does partnership deteriorate into benevolence that masks paternalism? Or worse, when is it tinged with skepticism or suspicion? In the account in Acts, the resources were laid at the feet of the apostles, who made sure that justice was done.

A metaphor such as "being on a journey," which is intended to build community and trust, cannot fully address all these questions. But it certainly can open up issues implied in mutuality or partnership, which we will explore in later chapters.

"Being on a Journey"

We will use this metaphor of being on a journey to explore some of the issues and imbalances in partnership—the matter of food, the matter of power or leadership, and the demands on all to be part of a common venture.

"Being on a journey" has its source in the Puritan understanding of the church as a pilgrim people[4] and is used as a metaphor for engagement in mission. With its connotation of movement, it places the accent rather more firmly on mission. The round table is a good image for describing mutuality. But mutuality by itself can easily become a grand exercise in communal selfishness, unless it activates and sustains partnership *for* mission. As my colleague on the staff of the Council for World Mission, Andrew Morton, asked, "When do we move from a community of self-interest to a community of common-interest that is engaged in mission?"

Mission before it is translated into action is a posture. It is to turn in love toward a suffering world, which God loves and for which the Son of God gave his life. Bernard Thorogood, the first general secretary of the Council for World Mission, got this point across with a verbal picture derived from the metaphor of the round table. "When people are asked to stand in a circle, they usually stand facing each other.

What would the Council for World Mission be like if we stood in a circle facing the world?" The metaphor of being on a journey picks up on this concern.

The Council for World Mission, which I use as an example, is a diverse group of churches at various stages of a common journey. Today it is made up of thirty-one churches, which are called constituent bodies because together they constitute the Council for World Mission. There are two churches in the Caribbean, five churches in Europe, five churches in Africa, five churches in South Asia, five churches in East Asia, and nine churches in the Pacific.[5] Almost all of them in one way or another trace their ancestry as churches to the work of the London Missionary Society and the other missionary societies that joined it. This ancestry has often proved to be too fragile a basis for a common journey in mission. They also vary in size. The Church of Jesus Christ in Madagascar (FJKM) and the United Church of Zambia, to take just two examples, have millions of members. The Congregational Union of New Zealand has a total membership of around 299 people, which is about the same size as the congregation in which my wife and I worship in Orpington in England! The Ekalesia Kelisiano Tuvalu is the only church in Tuvalu, or claims to be the only church, and gets very upset when other denominations or sects try to gain a foothold in that small country of eight islands. In other countries, Council for World Mission churches are not only one church among many, but often are part of a minority religion, as in India and Bangladesh. In Europe the churches are losing members, whereas in East Asia and Africa churches are growing.

Like the people of Israel who were on a journey from Egypt to Palestine, the Council for World Mission too, like similar mission organizations, is a motley group on a journey. We will use one part of the journey as given in the book of Numbers, without ignoring the larger context of the wandering in the wilderness, to interweave with it the journey of a missionary organization and the challenges it faces. I quote this passage in full because the story carries the argument.

> Now when the people complained in the hearing of the LORD about their misfortunes, the LORD heard it and the his anger was kindled. Then the fire of the LORD burned against them, and consumed some outlying parts of the camp. But the people cried out to Moses; and Moses prayed to the LORD, and the fire abated...
>
> The rabble among them had a strong craving; and the Israelites also wept again, and said, "If only we had meat to eat! We remember the fish we used to eat in Egypt for nothing, the cucumbers, the melons, the leeks, the onions, and the

garlic; but now our strength is dried up, and there is nothing at all but this manna to look at."

Now the manna was like coriander seed, and its color was like the color of gum resin. The people went around and gathered it, ground it in mills or beat it in mortars, then boiled it in pots and made cakes of it; and the taste of it was like the taste of cakes baked with oil. When the dew fell on the camp in the night, the manna would fall with it.

Moses heard the people weeping throughout their families, all at the entrances of their tents. Then the LORD became very angry, and Moses was displeased. So Moses said to the LORD, "Why have you treated your servant so badly? Why have I not found favor in your sight, that you lay the burden of all this people on me? Did I conceive all this people? Did I give birth to them, that you should say to me, 'Carry them in your bosom, as a nurse carries a sucking child,' to the land that you promised on oath to their ancestors? Where am I to get meat to give to all this people? For they come weeping to me and say, 'Give us meat to eat!' I am not able to carry all this people alone, for they are too heavy for me. If this is the way you are going to treat me, put me to death at once—if I have found favor in your sight—and do not let me see my misery."

So the LORD said to Moses, "Gather for me seventy of the elders of Israel, whom you know to be the elders of the people and officers over them; bring them to the tent of meeting, and have them take their place there with you. I will come down and talk with you there; and I will take some of the spirit that is on you and put it on them; and they shall bear the burden of the people along with you so that you will not bear it all by yourself..."

So Moses went out and told the people the words of the LORD; and he gathered seventy elders of the people, and placed them all around the tent. Then the LORD came down in the cloud and spoke to him, and took some of the spirit that was on him and put it on the seventy elders; and when the spirit rested upon them, they prophesied. But they did not do so again.

Two men remained in the camp, one named Eldad, and the other named Medad, and the spirit rested on them; they were among those registered, but they had not gone out to the tent, and so they prophesied in the camp. And a young man ran and told Moses, "Eldad and Medad are prophesying in the camp." And Joshua son of Nun, the assistant of Moses, one of his chosen men, said, "My lord Moses, stop them!" But Moses said to him, "Are you jealous for my sake? Would that all the LORD's people were prophets, and that the LORD would put his spirit on them!" And Moses and the elders of Israel returned to the camp. (Num. 11:1–17, 24–30)

There are three phases in the journey in which God accompanies the people, and at each phase there is a different challenge.

Phase 1 brings to the fore the fact that Israel was more a collection of tribes, each with its own tradition and perhaps even its own god, than a community. This heterogeneous group had to be welded into a community. This was the first challenge.

Initially a common experience brought them together. They had escaped from crushing social, political, and economic conditions both in Egypt and in other city-states. They were brought together under the understanding that it was the god Yahweh who had saved them.[6] The crossing of the Jordan was like a baptism, heralding a new beginning. It was an experience that was intended to bring them all together.

Like us, Israel too had a mission. These tribes had to become the people of God. They had to separate themselves from the oppressive sociopolitical and religious world of their time, so that eventually they might turn back to the world of nations as a blessing (cf. Gen. 12:3; Isa. 19:24). As the book of the prophet Isaiah was to put it later, God says to them, "I have given you as a covenant to the people, a light to the nations" (Isa. 42:6b).

There was a forty-year period of wandering in the wilderness to face up to this challenge. Forty years! Why forty years? It was to be a time of testing. A time to learn the truth that one does not live by bread alone but by every word that proceeds from the mouth of God (Deut. 8:3; cf. Mt. 4:4). Why does it take forty years to learn this seemingly simple lesson? Because everyone, not just the leaders, had to learn and experience this truth. And it is this lesson that is fundamental to a motley group becoming a cohesive community of people with a mission. This takes time.

Kosuke Koyama says that we are so used to jetting about, apparently doing God's work, that we forget that the God we serve is a walking God. God is a three-miles-an-hour-God! God walks with people at three miles an hour.[7] God walks with every one of them. This takes time. As every missionary knows, it takes time to build a missionary community. It takes forty years for all to learn to live in complete and daily dependence on God's all-providing grace.

Being sent in mission is not a picnic. It involves rejection and hardship. It requires endurance. People cannot live by food alone. They need the empowering and supporting presence of God.

This truth is hammered home to Israel. What began as a perilous but joyous journey turned into a nightmare. Israel had to fight battle after battle. There were casualties. There were endless impediments.

So the people started complaining. And they complained about everything. They complained that Moses had taken a foreign wife (Num. 12). They complained that there was not enough water (Num. 20:1–13). And so on and so on, with a refrain that ran, "'Would that we had died in the land of Egypt! Or would that we had died in this wilderness'" (Num. 14:2). From the perspective of Egypt, Palestine looks like a land flowing with milk and honey. From the perspective of Palestine, Egypt looks a lot better! As the people might put it, "Milk and honey is the vision that is held out. But what we keep on getting is this wretched manna stuff!"

Manna, or bdellium, as the dictionary describes it, is "a resin with an acrid taste and a more or less agreeable smell." Imagine forty years of this! The late Professor George Caird of Oxford said in one of his lectures to us, "Say, manna. Think, semolina!" One can bake it or roast it or boil it. One can do whatever one likes with it. But it endures!

No wonder the people of Israel complained. We can feel for them. Oh, for the good old days! Oh, that we had meat to eat! Think of the fish, the cucumbers, the melons, the leeks, the onions, and the garlic—all for nothing. In a dry and parched land with manna for food, this menu does make one's mouth water. It may not be the favorite food of many, but for Asians and the like this is great stuff!

Under this stress, the old fissures of tribe and group seem to reemerge. "The rabble," as they are called, are the troublemakers. These are the ones who when on an arduous journey look back, and thus attempt to halt the movement forward, because moving forward entails hardship and risks. These are the people who keep talking of the good old days of the London Missionary Society, the Paris Missionary Society, the missionaries of the English Presbyterian Church, or the missionaries of any other parent missionary society who looked after them and provided them with the needed material resources.

Like Joseph, the missionaries had good intentions. They protected "their people." But we are in different political and social times. We live under Pharaohs who don't know Joseph. However good their intentions in taking care of "their people," the missionaries created, as we were to say later, "a mission compound mentality," or "hothouse Christians." These find it hard to survive in a changed situation and in a different world. These are the ones who keep moaning, "We had all for nothing."

When thinking of the good old days, memory is always selective. Therefore, Israel had to be reminded that, on the one hand, one couldn't have the luxuries without the bondage of the past; on the other, God's grace may be boring, but it is sufficient.

Yet the cry for meat is not forgotten. Before "the rabble" took over and turned the cry for meat into a basis for rebellion, the cry had to be answered. In itself it was a legitimate request for protein. Strength was needed. The story continues. A strong wind brings in a plentiful supply of quails, so the meat for strength was provided. But in the tension between the cry for meat and the answer, various aspects of the lesson that one does not live by bread alone had to be learned. The story is not about denial of rightfully felt needs for the journey, but rather about proportion. Like the manna, the quails too are brought by a wind from Yahweh (Num. 11:31–35). The quails too are a symbol of God's accompanying presence. Though food is important and needs have to be met, these needs must not override the required discipline. The emphasis is on sufficiency, not hoarding, because even the wretched manna could not be hoarded. In brief, the challenge was to depend on the sufficiency of God's grace as a basis for a community of sharing.

Phase 2 raises the issue of leadership. The challenge has to do with the type of leadership that can sustain a forward movement.

The challenge about leadership is raised before the cry of the people for meat is addressed. It appears at a point of crisis. Do we continue on this arduous journey trusting in God's grace, or do we return to the fleshpots of Egypt? Do we go forward, or do we turn back?

At this time of crisis even God does not play fair by Moses. Every time the people complain, God's displeasure blazes out as fire and consumes some outlying part of the camp. The people complain even more! Finally, Moses can stand it no longer, and he complains: "Look! I didn't ask for this job. This is not my people. I didn't bring them into this world. I was asked to adopt them and play nursemaid. And you penalize me for all their faults. This is too much!" This is the complaint of almost every leader at some time or another: I would have been happier minding my father-in-law's sheep than these goats!

One would expect God to give greater authority and power to Moses so that he may control this motley group much better and weld them into a community. Instead, power and leadership are devolved. The charisma of Moses is now shared and passes to the many. God says to Moses, "You don't have to bear the burden alone. However, the burden of guiding these people away from Egypt into Palestine, from bondage to freedom, has to go on." The journey has to continue. The mission must be accomplished. Only devolution of leadership seems to be the way forward.

The message is simple and yet so profound. When the going gets tough, the normal tendency is to look for more power and authority for those who exercise leadership. This is the worst of all possible solutions, because that would lead to another form of slavery. Look rather, says the narrative, for a more broad-based and informed leadership in which the vision and spirit bestowed on the pioneer are shared out. At a time of crisis, the paradoxical solution is to devolve, not to centralize authority. This is the essence of the second challenge.

In the process of leadership being devolved, certain important insights appear and lessons are learned.

First, sharing the burden and involving more people in the leadership may be both good and inevitable if the people are to own the vision and to learn that they do not live by food alone but by every word that proceeds from the mouth of God. But there is a problem. When leadership becomes broad-based, efficiency is sacrificed. There will be wastage. This is to be expected as a legitimate consequence of devolution. As the parable of the sower reminds us (Mt. 13:3–23), not all the seeds fall on good ground. Yet as that parable shows, the results more than compensate for the loss. Patience is needed. Remember forty years in the wilderness walking with a three-miles-an-hour God!

There is a lesson to be learned from our missionary forebears, who were known for their "stickability" because they knew there would be no quick results. They were prepared for wastage in many forms.

To give an illustration, missionaries from the United States of America had worked in Thailand for some nineteen years without any result. Just as they were planning to withdraw, there was one convert. It was the man who had helped them to translate the Bible into Thai. The culture of Thailand is Buddhist. It is a culture that values silence. It takes time. He with his family was the beginning of a Thai church. Today, there is a small but strong church in that country. Among other things, the church in Thailand is noted for the work it is doing to rescue girls from prostitution (sex tourism is rampant in Thailand) and to rehabilitate them. It is also at the forefront in combating the menace of HIV/AIDS. In brief, it is a small church that is a blessing to the nations.

Second, the leadership of the elders is not independent of the leadership of Moses. They share in the leadership of Moses. Moses is not set aside. His position as leader remains. A share of the Spirit is taken from Moses and put on the elders. The elders do not constitute either a rival or an alternative model of leadership. There is collegiality, yet with a clear leader, who will eventually step aside so that another can take his place (cf. Deut. 34). However, the collegial style of leadership continues.

Third, as Professor Bernhard Anderson reminded us in a lecture at Princeton Theological Seminary, institutionalized leadership is also charismatic leadership. There is an orderly passing of the charisma from Moses to the elders. At first the elders exhibited pentecostal tendencies—ecstasy in the Spirit—when they "prophesied." But later they prophesied no more. Charisma and leadership are institutionalized. Order is not necessarily against the Spirit.

Fourth, with order and institutionalized leadership, there is always the temptation to settle down at a convenient spot. The temptation to settle for the fleshpots of Egypt can happen anywhere and at any time. These are the points at which we feel comfortable and settled and so refuse to move.

Phase 3 on the journey deals with the prophesy of disruption as a manifestation of the Spirit when we succumb to the temptation to settle down at a convenient spot. For continued movement not only involves risks, it also demands constant change. "Have we arrived?" is the question that is often asked. The answer "Not yet" is most debilitating. To settle down at a convenient spot is a temptation that institutionalized leadership often faces. Complacency is the enemy of mission.

When we succumb to the temptation to settle down and ignore the demand for movement that is of the very essence of mission, allowance is made for the prophecy of disruption.

Two persons who were chosen remained in the camp. So, unlike the other leaders, so to speak, they were not ordained properly. They started prophesying. The institution of the church derives its credibility from the Spirit. But the institution of the church cannot domesticate the Spirit.

Just when we have settled down and are comfortable, here comes the disturbing and disrupting Spirit of God through two outsiders who are also part of the journey and part of the leadership. They too were chosen, but were not ordained or given a share of the leadership from Moses. They come from the camp where the people are. They represent the spirit of the people. They come, so to speak, from the cutting edge where the church meets the world and thus bring the challenge of the world to the church, calling for greater missionary faithfulness. It is a challenge against complacency and a challenge that calls the church to move on.

The leaders do not always welcome such a challenge. Joshua, a general (perhaps even a general secretary!), is a man of order. As is often the case, bureaucrats are mesmerized by order. Then they lose the capacity to imagine. Consequently, vision perishes. Joshua says to Moses, "Stop them. The situation is getting out of hand."

To which Moses responds, "Are you worried about me and my leadership?" Moses understands what God has done in bringing more people into the leadership. Moses presses on further: "Would to God that all God's people were prophets!" It is his vision and his hope that all people, not just he or for that matter Joshua or even just the elders, would come to share in the Spirit of God. The call to be a light and a blessing to the nations needs to be the vocation of all God's people. The vision needs to be earthed. An informed total democratization of the leadership must take place if the journey is to continue.

Would to God that all God's people were prophets! We would reach the land of promise when all learn that we do not live by food alone but by every word that proceeds from the mouth of God. The prophet Jeremiah speaks of this stage as a new covenant (Jer. 31:31–34). It is not just a covenant relationship of grace and mercy with a leader, but with all. "And I will write [my law] on their hearts [i.e., minds]... No longer shall they...say to each other, 'Know the LORD,' for they shall all know me, from the least of them to the greatest."

Would to God that all God's people were prophets! Each person who has been baptized and has crossed through the Jordan from the old to the new has received a gift of the Spirit. All these gifts need to be received for the enrichment and work of the missionary community. To receive and deploy these gifts is the task of the elders.

Would to God that all God's people were prophets! For each person to be a prophet is important because prophecy is not about prediction but about discernment. It is the power given to us through the Holy Spirit to be on the Lord's side and thus to know what is right and what is wrong, what is acceptable and what is not acceptable, at a particular moment in time.

It is the Spirit who gives us the assurance of God's grace and the discernment to witness to God's work of salvation in and for the world. It is to speak and do the truth, even when the truth may not be popular.

At Pentecost, the Spirit of God was poured out on all so that old people could dream of new liberating possibilities and young people could envision a new future in hope (Acts 2:17).

Who said it was easy? "But you will receive power when the Holy Spirit has come upon you; and you will be my witnesses in Jerusalem, in all Judea and Samaria, and to the ends of the earth" (Acts 1:8). Thus, the prayer of Moses was fulfilled and continues to be fulfilled.

But what about Moses himself?

The words of my father, D. T. Niles, come to mind in response to this question. Toward the end of his ministry, and as it turned out, toward the end of his life, he said,

> We never begin anything; we never end anything.
> We begin where someone else left off;
> and we end where someone else begins.
> And across all of our lives are written the words, "Move on!"

In his inimitable way he was reflecting on the mystery of leadership in the Bible as a truth about Christian leadership in general. I have often wondered why elected or appointed leaders, such as Jeremiah and Paul, were protected and strengthened during their ministry and then required to step out or allowed to be martyred. The answer seems to be that, in the end, leadership belongs to the people. The role of the appointed leader is to enable the people to move on. A leader exhorts, cajoles, and even rebukes the people so that the movement toward the vision is sustained. Then as one steps out, another takes on the role of leader. Moses is a good example. He was responsible only for a part, albeit an important part, of the journey.

As his responsibility ends, Moses goes up to a high mountain, and God shows him the promised land. God says to him, "I have let you see it with your eyes, but you shall not cross over there," although, as the text says, "His sight was unimpaired and his vigor had not abated" (Deut. 34:4–7).

During his leadership, Moses had to contend not only with vision outstripping reality but also with reality contradicting vision. At the end, as he steps out, he sees the pure vision. It comes to him as an expression of comfort and a word of hope. It is an assurance that the future is in God's hands and that the goal is secure.

How are these experiences encountered in a missionary community on the move? How are these insights to be appropriated? In the next chapter, we will face these questions as they emerged in the Council for World Mission.

3

A New Arrangement for Mission

One of the factors that divides the missionary community, the *laos*, into segments is the separation between sending church and receiving church, between missionary society and mission church or "younger church." It is a separation made along the line of power between those who have the financial resources and therefore the personnel resources for mission and those who are powerless and therefore can only receive. Some think of themselves as active participants in mission, as called to go out into the whole world to proclaim and to share. Others see themselves as passive recipients, whose duty is to receive and receive graciously. This division has an impact on the self-understanding of the two segments. The one feels that it not only has the resources and skills for mission but also the right understanding of the faith, which the other segment needs to heed and receive. To the other segment, receiving becomes a habit that is hard to break. Enormous effort is needed from both segments to break free from such stereotypical behavior. But before that can happen, there has to be a structural change in power arrangements.

To abolish this separation structurally is to treat all equally, irrespective of the varying contributions each brings to the common enterprise, as illustrated in the metaphor of the round table. All are expected and challenged to be missionary churches. This expectation and challenge is addressed not just to former receiving churches but also to former sending churches. Those who previously only received have to learn to contribute to the missionary task, and those who previously contributed have to learn to receive. The metaphor of being on a journey captures the difficulties inherent in this challenge and the ways in which attitudes from both sides reappear. Lee Ching Chee, the first Education in Mission Secretary of the Council for World Mission, said when she began her work, "All need to be educated for mission to fulfill their calling to be missionary churches." As we saw in the previous chapter, the way forward resides in a greater sharing of authority and power, which is consonant with a theology of people as *laos*, and not through any form of centralized authority.

In this chapter we will tease out the ingredients of a theology of people as *laos*, taking the rethinking in the Council for World Mission as a test case. The thinking on a new arrangement for mission began at a consultation in 1975 and was put into effect at the Council meeting in 1977. In large measure, critical Asian thinking on mission prompted the transformation of the Council for World Mission into a new arrangement for mission. The various accounts of what happened at the consultation in Singapore make one common admission: The change was neither planned nor expected. It just happened. It happened partly because the representatives at the consultation were open to one another and to the leading of the Holy Spirit, so that something new could emerge. It also happened partly because they were together in a part of the world where churches were debating the task for mission in Asia and the issue of partnership in mission. Peter Leung, the chaplain at the Singapore consultation, drew heavily on Asian ecumenical thinking on mission in his addresses to the consultation. The General Secretary of the Christian Conference of Asia, Yap Kim Hao, also addressed the consultation on the concerns of partnership in mission and Asian theological understandings of mission. These opened up fresh avenues for thinking on mission to which participants particularly from the so-called associated churches warmed because these ideas were not strange to them.[1] Another trigger for change was the presence of two churches in the Council for World Mission—namely, the Church of Jesus Christ in Madagascar (FJKM) and the United Church of Zambia—which were also members of Cevaa. This was the old Paris Missionary Society transformed into a new arrangement for mission. In fact, the member from the church in Madagascar said when asked that he preferred to be a member of Cevaa because all were treated equally.

I will first present briefly the Asian theological milieu in which protest was seen as a legitimate starting point for Asian thinking on mission and theology. Second, I will present the new directions in mission thinking and practice that emerged in the new Council for World Mission to earth the expectations raised in Asian discussions on mission and the ways in which a theology of people as *laos* found expression. Third, I will discuss how these new directions in mission thinking, which led to a theological understanding of people as *laos*, were used to articulate the task for mission in our time. Fourth, as a consequence of these changed understandings, I will examine how the issue of authority and power was addressed in the Council for World Mission.

The Asian Theological Milieu

As far back as 1910 at the world conference on mission at Edinburgh, Asian participants in particular had already raised the concerns expressed by representatives from "the associated churches" or "Third World churches" at the Singapore consultation of the Council for World Mission.

In a total of about twelve hundred participants at the conference, there were only seventeen Asians, and these represented the whole of the non-Western world. The Asian participants were invited to the conference by the Western missionary societies that had founded their native churches. Their own churches did not send them. Yet at the conference they chose instead to represent the distress and concerns of "the younger churches" from which they came. Their protests formed a foundation for later non-Western theological articulations on mission. Despite their number, they made a tremendous impact on the conference.[2] This fact was acknowledged by the conference itself in spite of the irritations many missionaries felt at the interventions of the Asians. In its message to the churches in non-Christians lands, the conference said, "None have been more helpful in our deliberations than members from your own Churches."[3]

In his later celebrated, but at that time deemed notorious, evening presentation on mission, "The Problem of Co-operation between Foreign and Native Workers,"[4] V. S. Azariah of India, who was later to become the first Indian bishop of the Indian church, startled and angered the representatives of missionary societies gathered at the conference. Despite his courteous and sometimes even obsequious presentation, he raised a number of issues that were important for subsequent discussions on Christian mission.

The first was his insistence that the present structure of relationships between Western missionaries and native workers must go. It was a structure that not only encouraged missionary control of power, with statements such as "our money" and "our control," but also openly encouraged what later came to be called racism. His opening statement itself sees this as the heart of the issue: "The problem of race relationships is one of the most serious problems confronting the Church to-day."[5] He gives many examples to support his criticism of "missionary racism," but perhaps the most telling is the disgust a missionary expressed when an Indian deigned to shake hands with him just because the Indian had a university degree. Azariah blamed not so much individual attitudes as the institutional power missionaries exercised in which they were the paymasters and the Indians the servants. He called for a change:

> I plead, therefore, that an advance step may be taken by transferring from foreigners to Indians responsibilities and

privileges that are now too exclusively in the hands of the foreign missionary. Native Church Councils should be formed, where Indians could be trained in the administration of their own Churches.[6]

The second subsidiary but important point he made was that the selfhood of the Indian church would not emerge if it were treated as a child. Although Indian Christians were happy to be treated as children by those who first shared the Christian faith with them, younger missionaries who came later also wanted to maintain this paternalistic attitude. This attitude was not only resented by Indians Christians, but they also felt that it prevented them from growing in maturity: "There can never be real progress unless the aspirations of the native Christians to self-government and independence are accepted, encouraged, and acted upon." He then went on to say:

I am fully aware of the fact that all advance in responsibility should be transferred *gradually* and not by the sudden withdrawal of foreign funds and control. But gradually, but none the less [*sic*] steadily, it *should be done.* For, without growing responsibility, character will not be made. We shall learn to walk only by walking—perchance only by falling and learning from our mistakes, but never by being kept in leading strings until we arrive at maturity.[7]

The third point he made was that for true cooperation to be possible, there needs to be a recognition of India's spiritual heritage: "No personal relationship will be true and permanent that is not built on a spiritual basis. India is a land that has a 'religious atmosphere'…In such a land, therefore, the easiest point of contact with the heart is on the spiritual side."

His speech rejects any form of what later came to be called moratorium. Instead, he held up, as we were to say later, "mutuality in mission." This required two things. First, it required that missionaries practice love as Jesus practiced it when he called his disciples friends, not servants (cf. Jn. 15:12–17). Second, mutuality in mission is needed not only for the Indian Christians but also for Christians in the West:

It is in this co-operation of joint study at the feet of Christ that we shall realize the oneness of the Body of Christ. The exceeding riches of the glory of Christ can be fully realized not by the Englishman, the American, and the Continental alone, nor by the Japanese, the Chinese, and the Indians by themselves—but by all working together, worshipping together, and learning together the Perfect Image of our Lord and Christ. It is only "with all Saints" that we can "comprehend the love of Christ which passeth knowledge, that we might be filled with all the fullness of God." This will be possible only from spiritual friendships between the two races. We ought to be willing to learn from one another and to help one another.[8]

Then, ringing the changes on 1 Corinthians 13, he ended his speech with these now famous words:

Through all the ages to come the Indian Church will rise up in gratitude to attest the heroism and self-denying labours of the missionary body. You have given your goods to feed the poor. You have given your bodies to be burned. We also ask for *love*. Give us FRIENDS![9]

Many of the missionaries present at the conference found this speech so upsetting—almost tantamount to sedition from one whom they had invited—that a special informal meeting of missionaries was called to make a public protest. Finally, Azariah was quietly reprimanded in a closed session.[10] How difficult is the sharing of power!

I have quoted extensively from Azariah's speech because it opens up issues in the formation of partnerships in mission, which we will explore both in the present chapter and in subsequent chapters.

Azariah's speech seems to have opened the floodgates at Edinburgh. The other Asian delegates also began to voice their protests, even though they too, as Azariah, represented not their own churches but were guests of foreign missionary societies. C. H. Yun of Korea was even more explicit than Azariah in his condemnation of missionary paternalism. Although recognizing the principle that money raised in the West for missions in Asia needs to be accounted for by the missionary, he appealed to a higher "principle of Christ." This requires that the money be so used as to avoid the suspicion of Koreans:

Missionaries have and must see to it that native leaders are taken into frank consultation in the distribution of the money, because that money is not for a selfish purpose, but for the advance of the Kingdom of God in that particular land, and that cannot be done unless you have the hearty and sympathetic co-operation of the native leaders.[11]

K. Ibuka of Japan, who also gave an evening address, made two important points. The first was a division of missionary history in non-Christian lands into the following three periods: the period of the pioneer missionaries, the period when foreign missionaries and native

Christians were coworkers, and finally the emergence of the indigenous church "when it is sufficiently equipped with the institutions necessary to its vigorous maintenance and advance, and when foreign missions have given place to home missions in strength." This way of setting the periods of church history in the so-called non-Christian lands was also assumed in other Asian interventions. All these, although critical of the middle period, were attempting to usher in the third period. The second point Ibuka made may be seen as a forerunner of the emergence of Asian contextual theological expressions. He raised questions about the cumbersome Western creeds, with their underlying complicated theologies, that were being foisted on Japanese Christians. He admitted that these creeds had their place in the Western church history in which they were shaped in Western theological debates. But they have little meaning for Japan. Instead, he spoke of a simple Japanese creed, which may be crude by Western standards but is adequate to express the Christian faith in Japan.[12]

Like C. H. Yun of Korea, C. Y. Cheng of China also spoke of the need to consult native workers: "For after all it is not your particular denomination, nor even is it your particular Mission that you are working for, but the establishment of the Church of Christ in China that you have in view."[13] He spoke about his vision for the Church of Christ in China, to the building of which he hoped the missionaries would also contribute:

> Speaking plainly we hope to see, in the near future, a united Christian Church without any denominational distinctions. This may seem somewhat peculiar to some of you, but, friends, do not forget to view us from *our* standpoint, and if you fail to do that the Chinese will remain always a mysterious people to you![14]

Whereas Ibuka spoke of the need for an indigenous contextual confession of the faith, inchoate but necessary, which would set aside Western theological impositions, Cheng, representing the London Missionary Society, called for a church that would indeed put into practice what the founders of that missionary society had articulated as a principle. The intention of that society was not to foist any form of church government on indigenous churches but to allow indigenous churches to choose for themselves a form of church government that they found to be most agreeable to the word of God.[15]

It is said that the boldness of the Asian participants was in no small measure due to the encouragement they received from John R. Mott, chairman of the conference and one of the pioneers of the ecumenical movement, who had already seen the partnership that was emerging between East and West in the Christian associations of young people.[16]

This thinking, which was in the air in Asia, triggered new thinking at the Singapore consultation. By the 1970s, the plea Azariah made that the religious heritage of India be taken seriously in the task of mission had also begun to unfold in a new way, no longer simply as a pre-understanding for Christian mission but as a recognition of God's presence in the religions and histories of people of other faiths.

Reserving for a later chapter a fuller treatment of this contribution, its basic position may be stated in the words of two Asian theologians, one from Korea and the other from India. Addressing the task for theology in Korea and the use of historical and religious themes from the religious culture of the Minjung, Hyun Younghak stated his position in these words: "I do not believe in an invalid God who was carried piggy-back to Korea by some missionary. God was already active in our history long before the missionaries came." At a meeting on mission sponsored by the Council for World Mission, some theologians, who had accepted as normative the whole approach of "church planting" as the goal of Christian mission, began to speak of "reaching the unreached." At this point Bishop Victor Premsagar, who was then the moderator of the Church of South India, said, "This language of reaching the unreached sounds like God is fast asleep and we are running around like busy-bodies. God reached India centuries ago, while Jesus Christ is a new comer. How do we relate these two realities? That is the problem for mission in India."

Hans-Ruedi Weber, who was himself a missionary in Indonesia, notes a significant lesson missionaries, and by implication Western Christians, had to learn:

> Witnessing, they enter into that risky dialogue where one faith meets the other, where they may lose their own faith (or at least many familiar securities and feelings of superiority they inherited in the West), and then discover that Christ is not some*thing* they transmit to the other, but some*one* who has preceded them and now teaches both, the missionary and the convert. Serving, they learn the lesson of self-sacrifice, discerning in the suffering world the already present suffering Servant.[17]

In essence, the contribution of non-Western Christians to the missionary task may be stated thus: We, too, have a story to tell, which is not simply a parroting of your Western European story. Our story too must be heard if the task of Christian mission worldwide is to unfold in a new way.

A New Arrangement for Mission

Through their own experience of the missionary enterprise from the West, theologians from other Third World countries had also begun to echo the concerns raised by the Asians at the Edinburgh world mission conference and later. In fact, a common language was emerging by 1975. The record of the Singapore consultation says that the regional group discussions and the small group discussions made it clear that it was necessary "to achieve greater mutuality in mission." The report then goes on to say,

> It became evident that although the present Consultation may be seen as an advance on previous methods, there is still too far a distinction between the Constituent Bodies [the "sending" churches] and the Associated Churches [the "receiving" churches], as though only the former are active participants in world mission. It therefore appears to be necessary that a new structure be created which would enable all the churches related to CWM to participate fully and equally in all the responsibilities of CWM.[18]

This criticism is more evident in the section on the historical setting of the consultation found in *Sharing in One World Mission:*

> The consultation came to the unanimous view that as now constituted the Council represents only a restricted understanding of the missionary task (from the West to the developing nations of Africa, Asia, the Pacific, and the Caribbean); that it perpetuates the relationship of donor and recipient; and that it gives inadequate place to the talents of every church in the one co-operative enterprise. So the major recommendation from the consultation was that CWM should make a thorough and urgent attempt to reform its structure so that the associated churches might share fully and responsibly in the one missionary task.[19]

To put it differently, given the present structure of relationships, the consultation may take place in Singapore, but the actual decisions will be made at the "center" in London. Such an attitude represents the interests of financial and theological power. It advocates a donor-recipient relationship. It assumes that where there is a concentration of power in the form of money, there, too, are the real resources of ideas and personnel for mission. It precludes the truth that each church, wherever it may be placed, has its own God-given gifts for mission. The challenge for the participants at Singapore was not simply to reform a structure but to change it, so that this false assumption could be exploded and the resources of all churches in all its forms (not just money) could be acknowledged. Then there could be a genuine sharing of power.

Such power sharing could not be an end in itself. On the one hand, power sharing should be designed to remove the negative, inhibiting pressure that stifles self-expression. It was this negative experience of Western missions that prompted some African churches to call for a moratorium on mission. They were, in effect, saying to Western mission boards, "We need the space to be obedient to God's calling in our own context in our own way." On the other hand, power sharing should enable a genuine sharing of resources and a method for sharing them that would enable each church to pursue in its own place the mission that Christ has entrusted to the church in every place. It was the recognition of this dual function of power sharing that led the consultation to choose mutuality, rather than moratorium, to signify the new relationship of partnership and accountability.[20] This in turn led to a fresh statement of the basis for mission:

> We believe that we become participants in mission not because we hold all the answers and all the truth, but because we are part of the body of Christ. All of us are still searchers... Therefore we seek a form of missionary organisation in which we may all learn from each other, for in that fellowship we believe that the Holy Spirit speaks to all through each.[21]

This confession acknowledges three important truths: (1) Mission is not just a function of the church or of a few individuals who may claim to have all the answers and all the truth, but is of the very essence of being the church in the world. Mission is implicit in being part of the body of Christ. (2) Not all members of the body are equal in strength, but all are important members of the body and have a function to perform. Each has to support the others. The metaphor of the body carries the tacit understanding that partnership is not among equals (cf. Eph. 4). We are all equal and unequal in different ways. (3) It is not just the churches in the Council for World Mission that are part of the body of Christ. Implicit in the acknowledgment of being part of the body of Christ is the recognition that the partnership goes beyond the Council for World Mission.

If the openness to one another and the Holy Spirit precipitated the change in relationships, openness to the ecumenical movement and the willingness to be involved in it helped to change and shape the theological thinking of the Council for World Mission. As *Sharing in One World Mission* admits, "As one small section of the world church we are indebted to the ecumenical movement for helping us to understand aspects of mission as they become particularly significant at moments in history."[22]

Besides the concern for power sharing, other impulses coming from the ecumenical movement also helped to shape the theological thinking of the Council for World Mission.

The first was the emphasis on world mission as the task of the whole people of God (the *laos*). The structure of the Council for World Mission as a council of churches in mission was intended to reflect this emphasis.

The second was the recognition of the multifaceted character of mission identified in the following key terms:

conversion—forgiveness—new life—eternal hope
reconciliation—peace—community
liberation—justice—humanization
sacrificial caring—healing—wholeness
preaching and teaching—baptism—church growth

The document then goes on to say:

It is our belief that all these aspects of Christian mission are true to the New Testament and that none of them can be isolated from the others and made the one controlling emphasis for all missionary work. As we recognize the variety of God's gifts to his servants and the multitude of human situations, so we seek to share in *many-sided mission*.[23]

It was assumed that the ways in which these relate to one another and augment one another would become evident as the journey of the Council for World Mission continued.

A third impulse coming from the ecumenical movement was the conviction that the world, not just the church, is the object of God's love and that the church is called to participate in God's mission. This impulse was appropriated in the form of a confession:

But there is a central belief which is our guide and our hope. It is that Jesus Christ lives for all humankind. He lives for humankind, for human development, for our peace, unity and joy. He lives for all humankind and not primarily for the church or for any section of humanity. He lives and is neither myth nor dead hero; he is with us, walking our road and sharing bread and wine. It is Jesus Christ, the man of Nazareth, who lives, who came from the Father, who healed and taught and was crucified. We believe that as we commit ourselves to him, so the Holy Spirit enables us to share in the demonstration of his love, a healing love which is unsentimental enough, wide enough, patient enough, to change the world.[24]

In its original setting, this confession was clearly intended to impel what was a racially, ecclesiologically, and missiologically limited mission organization into becoming an international ecumenical instrument for world mission and to affirm a more complete understanding of the *laos*—the whole people of God from all parts of the world—in the task of mission.

Intrinsic to the founding vision of the Council for World Mission was a sense of proportion. (1) No triumphalistic claims were made. There was an honest recognition of the fact that as a partnership of churches in mission, the Council for World Mission was only a small part of the world church, to which it was indebted for broadening its vision. Although it envisaged drastic changes of structure to put into practice ideas on partnership in mission that had emerged in the ecumenical missionary movement, it did not claim to be the forerunner or even the trendsetter of a new ecumenical thrust. (2) No utopian claims were made for the new Council for World Mission. Nowhere do we find assertions that it would change the world. In fact, the admission was that it is the Holy Spirit who "enables us to share in the demonstration of his [Christ's] love," which alone can change the world. (3) Neither were assertions made that the new arrangement of relationships between churches would immediately replace old relationships of inequality and injustice created by the colonial system as a whole, which had an impact on the Western missionary enterprise. It would take time for changes to become effective.

However, the vision of the new model did carry the expectation that with God's grace old relationships based on the donor-recipient model would change to new relationships based on justice and openness. There was the conviction that diversity can be held together so that we may learn from one another. The new model of relationships was intended to enable each church to become an equal participant in God's mission. For these changes to take place and for the movement to continue, two changes were necessary. The first was a broadening of the theological basis of the missionary task. The second was an acceptable arrangement of power and authority, so that the division of the *laos*, into those who have the power and the resources to give or send and those who are powerless and therefore can only receive, could be overcome.

Toward a Holistic Understanding of Mission

Using the affirmation on many-sided mission given earlier, the Council for World Mission attempted to work out an understanding of Christian mission that was patterned on the ministry of Jesus. "Many-sided mission" was later translated to "a holistic understanding of mission,"[25] which attempted to draw together all aspects of the ministry of Jesus into a comprehensive understanding of Christian mission. Drawing from a document of the World Council of Churches, "Mission and Evangelism: An Ecumenical Affirmation,"[26] the 1983 meeting of the Council for World Mission accepted the following spelling out of its theology:

> Christ's commission to all Christians is "You shall be my witnesses both in Jerusalem and in all Judea and in Samaria and to the end of the earth" (Acts 1:8). The risen Christ says, "As the Father sent me, so send I you," and he empowers his disciples by the Holy Spirit (John 20:21–22). That commission is given further expression in Paul's words "God was in Christ reconciling the world to himself...and he has given us the ministry of reconciliation" (2 Cor. 5:18–19). So Christians are called to share in the purpose of the God who is revealed throughout the Bible as the Creator and Redeemer of the world. In this purpose God uses the Church—the body of people for whom Jesus prayed, "Father I pray that they may all be one. May they be one, so that the world may believe that you sent me" (John 17:21).[27]

Reflecting on this statement, the general secretary at that time, Christopher Duraisingh, remarked that to begin with Acts 1:8 rather than Matthew 28:18–20. to understand the task of Christian mission is to open up a perspective rather different from the traditional one. The absence of any reference to Matthew 28:18–20 seems to imply that there could be a different and more comprehensive basis for understanding the mission of the church in our time. To make Acts 1:8 the starting point for understanding the mission of the church today is a tacit acceptance of the fact that "mission is first and foremost of the Spirit" in which the church is called to participate.[28]

Besides the important point noted by Duraisingh, Acts 1:8 also brings out other emphases. As in all the other New Testament commissions to mission, the call to mission is not so much a command as a promise. "You will receive power when the Holy Spirit has come upon you; and you will be my witnesses." Furthermore, Acts 1:8 envisages a progressive movement from home (Jerusalem) to the end of the earth. It does not provide a mandate for seeing mission as simply "out there."

The statement is also striking in that along with dropping any reference to Matthew 28:18–20, it also does not use the term *evangelism*. In this way, it parts company with many of the theological statements on mission of that time and even later. The term *evangelism* may have been dropped either because its usage and meaning were both confused and misleading or because evangelism as the proclamation or manifestation (incarnation) of the good news should inform all forms of mission and therefore need not be singled out or coupled with mission as is usual in the phrase "mission and evangelism." We will return to a fuller treatment of this position in chapter 6.

The commission in John 20:21–22 is as specific as Acts 1:8 in drawing attention to the work of the Holy Spirit in mission and accentuates mission in Christ's way. Just as the Father sent the Son, the Son sends out his disciples after breathing on them the empowering Spirit of God. The commission in John, with the words, "Peace be with you," is amplified in Paul's words, "God, who reconciled us to himself through Christ...has given us the ministry of reconciliation... entrusting the message of reconciliation to us" (2 Cor. 5:18, 19). This text places the mission of the church in the context of God's reconciling work in the world. God's mission is far more comprehensive than what often passes for the church's mission.

To empower the church to participate in God's mission, Jesus prays for the church: "I ask...that they may all be one. As you, Father, are in me and I am in you, may they also be in us, so that the world may believe that you have sent me" (Jn. 17:20–21). This text emphasizes the nexus between unity and mission. As Duraisingh pointed out, "It indicates that CWM believes that mission and unity inseparably belong together. They are tandem realities. One without the other has no credibility."

A Partnership of Churches in Mission

Without the transformation of the Council for World Mission into a partnership of churches in mission, all the rethinking on mission described earlier would have, so to speak, no carrier. So the issues of partnership are as important a part of rethinking Christian mission today as the theology that arises from and supports the required change.

The terms *partnership* and *partners* are bandied about so much in mission circles today that it is never quite clear what they mean. Quite often the use of these terms is adjudged to be cosmetic—to mask old missionary relationships, which continue the donor-recipient model.

In an article titled "Structural Changes in Mission: New Shoes or Stocking Feet?" Jan van Butselaar, a Dutch missiologist, maintains that this is the case also with the Council for World Mission.[29] He alleges that it continues with a "British scent" and does not reflect the cultural plurality that should be evident in a new arrangement of relationships. He goes on to say that the Council for World Mission is not really grounded on common concerns in mission but on old historical relationships. Such relationships, he argues, though not bad in themselves, can severely limit the ecumenical relationships of a partner church and, in the final analysis, may turn out to be more inhibiting than liberating. Although the indicators he uses for judging the Council for World Mission may not be the most adequate, and his examination itself is rather cursory, he does point to real dangers.

Has the Council for World Mission made a real effort to transform old historical ties based on the donor-recipient model to more liberating relationships that could enable churches to be real partners in mission?

From the very beginning the Council for World Mission wrestled with this problem and gave it a theological answer implicit in the following admission from *Sharing in One World Mission*:

> No particular church has a private supply of truth, or wisdom or missionary skills. So within the circle of churches which we serve, we seek to encourage mutuality. This is a recognition that to share in international mission every church is both a receiver of help and a giver of its talents. At the present time we are seeing a shift in the world church's centre of gravity from Western Europe to Africa, Latin America and parts of Asia and the Pacific. We therefore long to take this present opportunity for change as a moment when we who are British may welcome more fully the influence of our partner churches in the Third World. But we are aware that this willingness to learn does not come easily.[30]

By using mutuality to define partnership, the Council for World Mission did three things. First, it brought into the equation other forms of power besides the power of money. It rightly pointed to the shift in the world church's center of gravity from Western Europe to the so-called Third World. The power of money could not have been the indicator for perceiving this shift.

Second, it abandoned the understanding of power as control and instead viewed power, in its various forms, as gifts and resources for enabling (empowering) all churches to engage in mission. This was the argument advanced in a letter from the United Church of Jamaica and Grand Cayman to the Council for World Mission:

> Chronically dependent churches cannot function effectively as partners if they are not able to move with integrity towards the optimum value of interdependent relationships. We envision therefore a policy of resource sharing which enables Churches, which demonstrate the maturity and the readiness, to be empowered for genuine partnerships.[31]

The letter went on to say that such a policy of resource sharing could provide "all Member Churches with the opportunity to participate systematically in a plan which liberates and empowers other Member Churches for Mission at home and abroad."

Third, if power is to be effective, it must be shared. As the statement given above from *Sharing in One World Mission* confesses, this is not an easy lesson to learn.

In his article "Council for World Mission's Partnership in Mission Model,"[32] Maitland Evans, who has been intimately associated with the Council for World Mission as a founding member, a member of staff, and then a moderator, addressed the problem of power sharing and how it may be accomplished. He brought in the perspective of one who was the descendent of African people whose rights were stolen and taken as slaves to work the sugar plantations in the Caribbean.

As the first principle, he argues that the initiative for mutuality, if it is to be real and effective, must come from the poor or victimized. Using what he calls "the Onesimus perspective on partnership in mission relationships," he contends that it is the refusal of Onesimus to be part of the old relationship, however inadequately that refusal is expressed, that precipitates a crisis that demands a new relationship between him and Philemon. The initiative of Onesimus, the victim, identifies the first principle of partnership. The initiating action for liberation and liberating relationships can only come from the powerless and not from the powerful. When the initiative for partnership comes from the rich and powerful, it is at best a sharing of wealth in acts of benevolence. Power is retained. Such acts simply continue old relationships of patronage and dependency and do not lead to a real sharing of power.

The second principle of partnership, Evans points out, is the insistence of Paul that only when Philemon is also liberated from the old relation of master to slave can both Onesimus and Philemon really be free and be affirmed as true children of God. This can be accomplished only by the return of Onesimus carrying the challenge of Paul to Philemon. Paul's challenge embodies the kingdom demand of the gospel for just relationships. Philemon is required to accept Onesimus as an equal, as a brother in Christ. It is only when Philemon embraces Onesimus, in an act of solidarity expressing his repentance, that the structure of relationships between them could change. That embrace will free and unite both, leading to a real sharing of power.

As we have noticed, the impetus for forming the new arrangement came from the representatives of the "associated churches" at the Singapore consultation. They were clear that the donor-recipient model was not conducive to mature and horizontal relationships. Their challenge not only questioned relationships based on the power of money but also brought into the equation other resources of churches from the so-called Third World. At a time when Christianity in the West is shrinking, churches in Africa, Asia, the Caribbean, and the Pacific are growing. Their voices had to be heard.

Consequently, the following changes took place:

1. It was agreed that all should be valued as equal contributors. To this end they set up a decision-making structure that equalized the power relations between the churches. The Council, its executive committee, and its executive staff are constituted to reflect as far as possible the multi-church and multicultural reality of the Council for World Mission. Furthermore, all churches, big and small, have a minimum of two delegates at each Council meeting, ensuring that debates and decision making are as democratic as possible. Clearly, those with experience and a better command of the English language have an advantage. But efforts are made to reduce this advantage by having interpreters and using small group discussions to enable greater participation in discussions and in the making of decisions.

2. The resources of wealth that belonged to the old London Missionary Society in Britain were placed in a common financial pool. The European churches continued to make further monetary contributions for the work. The European churches have never insisted that their representatives should have a control over decisions regarding the disposal of the money. Those decisions were left to the Council as a whole. The European churches were also willing to ask for resources from the common pool of finance and personnel for their mission work. These responses may be seen as concrete and significant signs of change (repentance) and a willingness to be in genuine partnership with the former associated churches.

The former associated churches also have demonstrated their willingness to be part of this new relationship, not just in receiving but also in giving. They have given in two ways.

First, they have shared their personnel resources. Although the number of missionaries from European churches is decreasing, other churches are sending more missionaries, especially in south-to-south sharing. Furthermore, the number of missionaries going from these churches to European countries is increasing. Some of these churches also participate in the ecumenical sharing of personnel. More than 50 percent of the missionaries going through the Council for World Mission are from non-European churches.

Second, churches from the Third World are also sharing their financial resources. Until the influx of new financial resources from the sale of a piece of land in Hong Kong, the annual giving of member churches to the work of CWM increased by around 5 percent. Using the gross national product (GNP) of the country of a church and the size of that church, an analysis was made of the contributions received in 1992. The analysis revealed that in real terms, though not in the actual amounts they gave, poorer churches gave as much as, and in a few cases more than, the richer churches. It was revealing to see that on the basis of this analysis, which took into account the economic situation and the size of each church, the Church of Bangladesh, which is the smallest church in a predominantly Muslim country that is one of the poorest countries in the world, should head the table.[33] The economically poorer churches have also given unstintingly to emergency appeals to help the work of a partner church during times of national/natural calamity and disaster.

Along with these positive indicators of the growth of partnership, regressive tendencies also continue. Some churches still view the practice of partnership in the Council for World Mission merely as a pie-sharing exercise. The situation is compounded by the fact that quite a few of them have other mission relationships that do not follow the principles of partnership as practiced in the Council for World Mission. Instead of the partnership within the Council for World Mission transforming other relationships, donor-recipient relationships practiced outside begin to color relationships within the Council for World Mission.[34] For some other churches, membership in the Council for World Mission is peripheral. Their main resources of personnel and money are used in mission enterprises that do not reflect the mission principles or partnership discipline of the Council for World Mission. In both instances, the Council for World Mission as a corporate entity has "interfered" in the life and work of these churches and challenged them. Churches are constantly being called to account for their membership in a community of churches in mission. This challenge is slowly but surely producing changes. Denominationalism is still rife, often preventing the practice of unity in mission and the forming of broad-based ecumenical partnerships. Another area of concern is the absence of partnership within churches. The Community of Women and Men in Mission, Youth in Mission, and Mission with Children are attempts to address the issue of partnership and power sharing within churches. Clearly, there is a long way to go.

Yet in attempting to put into practice the principles of partnership in mission, the Council for World Mission, together with other such missionary organizations, is earthing the issues raised at the World Mission Conference in Edinburgh 1910 and later. These attempts provide an understanding of the mission of the *laos*, the church, that may be stated in summary thus:

Partnership in mission is essential for all churches. In that fellowship we learn from one another as we support one another. As Azariah said so eloquently at the Edinburgh conference, "The exceeding riches of the glory of Christ can be fully realized not by the Englishman, the American, and the Continental alone, nor by the

Japanese, the Chinese, and the Indians by themselves—but by all working together, worshipping together, and learning together the Perfect Image of our Lord and Christ."

Furthermore, it is in that fellowship that we also learn the challenges for Christian mission today, especially as they arise from churches in the non-European world who have usually been receivers rather than contributors to the task of Christian world mission. As an important part of the exercise of power sharing, the challenges and the voices from the so-called poorer churches, unless these happen to be simply pale reflections of colonial Western missionary positions, need to be listened to. So, too, the challenges from women and children, who too are often treated as peripheral to partnership in mission.

In this fellowship we learn that churches participate in God's mission because they are part of the body of Christ. There is no place for triumphalism or triumphalistic claims to special knowledge and skills for mission, or even claims to change the world.

A clear sign of the church's participation in God's mission is the manifestation of the unity of the church. Unity and mission are inseparable and should be seen as inseparable in the life and witness of the church.

There needs to be a holistic understanding of mission, which draws from the various ways in which Jesus expressed his ministry of love in which the church is called to participate. No one aspect of that ministry should be held up as the fundamental or exclusive aspect of mission.

The primary, though not exclusive, focus of the mission of any church is its specific location. When people go out from a particular church as missionaries, that church shares its resources of people and ideas in a missionary task that arises out of its membership in the body of Christ, which is universal.

In the final analysis, the abiding test of the practice of partnership will be twofold. First, will a missionary organization continue to value and use all resources and contributions in the practice of power sharing for the sake of the mission of the church? Second, will it continue to encourage liberating initiatives for real partnership? Without submitting to this twofold test, the movement of a missionary organization as a partnership of churches in mission could cease.

In the next two chapters we will seek the answers, looking at and reflecting on the practical ways in which the Council for World Mission faced these questions through the sharing of people in mission and the sharing of money in mission.

4

Sharing People in Mission

At the world conference on mission and evangelism with the theme "Salvation Today" (Bangkok 1973), Emilio Castro, who was to become the director of the Commission on World Mission and Evangelism of the World Council of Churches, caught the mood of the time and the changing global context for Christian mission with the words, "We are at the end of a missionary era; we are at the very beginning of world mission." The old era of mission was thought to be passing away and a new era dawning. The old missionary societies had carried the responsibility, as the London Missionary Society put it, "to send the glorious Gospel of the Blessed God to the Heathen." One of the surest signs of the end of that era was the dwindling number of missionaries going from the West to the East and the South.

With a sense of joy at the end of the old and the birth of the new, Choan Seng Song spoke in 1975 of a celebration: "This celebration will in fact be a manifesto of liberation from missions largely shaped, conditioned and carried out by the churches in the West." The end of Western foreign missions would signal the birth of the new when the church in the Third World

> makes demands for entirely new relationships with the church in the West. She lets it be known that man does not live by bread alone, that she is awakened to the truth that the freedom of spirit is far more essential than the abundance of financial aid. She refuses to be judged and evaluated by ethical, cultural, and religious standards and values prevailing in the West. Moreover, she is confronted with the need to probe into the depth of the mystery of God's salvation in her own social, cultural and political contexts.[1]

Those were indeed heady days! The decade of the 1970s was a time of great expectations in mission thinking and a changing context for world mission. This was the time when the Council for World Mission as a new missionary arrangement was born to deliver on the expectation that it would and could be a new model for Christian mission today. The debates and experiments in the Council for World Mission provide a good backdrop for evaluating the role of missionary service in expressing the task for Christian mission today.

To do this, we will first make a sober assessment of what really transpired after the world mission conference at Bangkok in 1973 and the challenge that situation posed. Using the mission thinking and action in the Council for World Mission as a test, we will see how the challenge was met. Second, against the background of this assessment, we will briefly revisit the era of Western mission that has ended or is ending. The intention will be to get behind interpretations of a missionary era that have to do with later manifestations of that era and identify the vision and initial emphases that impelled the modern missionary movement, which, as we will see, still have a bearing on the practice of missionary service today. Third, we will look at the ministry of Jesus with the people understood as *ochlos*—that is, the crowd or multitude—to give greater theological depth to the impulses that led to the modern missionary movement. Fourth, in terms of what we have discovered in our explorations, we will identify some of the major ingredients, as well as demands for missionary service today.

The Postmissionary Reality

The euphoria about the birth of a new era for mission did not last very long. Just as political independence soon gave way to the reactionary forces of neocolonialism, the new era of world mission had to submit itself to the reassertion of the old in what may be called the neomissionary period, not so much because the former "missionary" churches demanded it but because the "missioned" churches wanted it. In this sense, neomissionary is rather different from neocolonial, but there are similarities.

Just as the nations created and shaped by the colonial era inherited the political structures bequeathed to them by their former colonial masters and then had to struggle with them to express indigenous political aspirations and arrangements, the churches in the so-called Third World or Two-Thirds World inherited ecclesial institutions and structures shaped and bequeathed to them by their "mother" churches. Little or no attempt was made to create institutions and structures that would suit new, emerging situations in which the mission of the church would have to be expressed. Old church structures remained, raising not only questions of relevance but also doubts about their financial viability. Consequently, by and large, financial considerations became paramount in most interchurch relationships between the former missionary churches and those spawned through that mission.

There has been a strengthening of links preserving old denominational alliances in order to receive financial help. Even several united churches, which were supposed to be harbingers of a new period in mission relationships, reverted to encouraging the old denominational links of the churches that came into the union. They did this knowing that they could draw on the financial help of many so-called partners. Sadly, partnership in mission, instead of being a sharing in Christian world mission, did often become a partnership for the sending and receiving of money. In the neomissionary era, the sending and receiving of money has replaced to a large extent the sending and receiving of missionaries.

Often, even when there is the sending and receiving of missionaries, financial considerations are paramount. Unless there is a tangible financial gain in having persons from abroad, few missioned churches are really interested in receiving missionaries. On the other side, many former missionary churches still use missionaries as both conduits and controllers of funds to the missioned churches.

By becoming central in interchurch relationships, financial considerations have brought a distortion into the practice of partnership in mission. In her report on the Caribbean North American Council on Mission to the meeting of the Council for World Mission in Jamaica (1993), Jet den Hollander pointed to this distortion:

> Today, two decades later [after the concept of partnership in mission was promoted at the World Mission Conference in Bangkok in 1973], genuine partnership still seems to be an elusive commodity. For, while resource-sharing between North and South has in effect become more multi-directional, there seems to be a new one-sidedness about it all. Mutuality in mission is running the risk of becoming a kind of barter, whereby churches in the North share their material resources with the South, while churches in the South are expected to share their spirituality with the "emptying" churches in the North.

The justification for the barter approach to interchurch exchange, to which Jet den Hollander refers, is based on the questionable adage coined by Swami Vivekananda to which we referred in chapter 2. Partnership relationships created on the basis that "whereas the West is materially rich, the East is spiritually rich" are perilous.

For one thing, a crisis is looming in the West, where churches are shrinking in membership (the "emptying" to which Jet den Hollander refers) and, consequently, financial resources are dwindling. Churches in certain European countries that relied on "church tax" to boost their financial resources are now facing the fact that this tax is soon to be abolished or has been abolished. An important source of church revenue is drying up. A missionary relationship in which missioned churches say to former missionary churches, "Give us the money and we will do the mission" or "Send us missionaries with the money" is likely to come to an end sooner rather than later.

For another thing, there are really no spiritual resources from the missioned churches to share. There is a rising tide of theological conservatism and biblical fundamentalism that refuses to listen to, let alone accept, indigenous faith expressions that could be the basis of a real spirituality. The theologies that emerged at the frontiers of the mission of the church in the 1970s by and large stayed at the periphery. With one or two notable exceptions, both in their life and in their worship, the churches as institutions continue as before. To give just two examples: (a) Although there are many small Minjung churches, it is extremely difficult to find the influence of Minjung theology in the thinking of many of the mainstream Protestant churches in Korea. By and large, many church leaders in Korea think that Minjung theology is a vaguely Christianized form of North Korean Marxist ideology. (b) In India, theological work in relation to people of other faiths, which has gone on for decades if not centuries, has had little or no influence on the churches. To illustrate: At a worship service during one of the synods of the Church of South India, a presbyter of the church, who is also a theological teacher, got into serious trouble for using a prayer incorporating indigenous elements from local religious piety. It was of little consequence that the prayer had been used in the East Asia Christian Conference (now the Christian Conference of Asia) during the time of and with the blessing of D. T. Niles, considered by many to be one of the greatest church leaders Asia has produced.

Along with theological conservatism has emerged missiological conservatism. The richer churches, especially in Asia and the Pacific, feel that it is now their turn to send out missionaries using the old missionary model. As justification they point to the many churches in poorer countries that keep begging them to send missionaries who are also expected to take along with them much-needed money, thus reintroducing old missionary relationships riddled with paternalism and dependency. Sometimes missionaries are sent to found rival missions without any consultation with local churches. Many a time, evangelical zeal overrides both common sense and common courtesy.

Typical of this form of mission is the language of crusades and "reaching the unreached." Whether we like it or not, every time we speak this language, we touch a raw nerve. This is especially so because such mission ventures have at their disposal large financial resources, which have replaced military and colonial power. People who are the targets of such mission see it in its old guise as an attempt to conquer others. Shutters come down, and mission comes to a dead end. We might try to brush aside this criticism saying that we only want to win souls for Christ, but this will not do. Mission, which is an alliance between financial strength and evangelical zeal, can easily pervert the very gospel to which it attempts to bear witness. Furthermore, such mission is also not sensitive to those churches, which have worked out a legitimate and relevant form of mission in their own countries. If mission is to be meaningful today, we must not only change our language and attitude to those to whom we go in mission but we must also control the use of financial power in mission.

Also, because Western colonial expansion and Western Christian mission took place at the same time, many countries still view the church as a foreigner in their midst. The Chinese saying that "one more Christian means one less Chinese" is symptomatic of the opinion of many people. This opinion is an outcome of a missionary policy that urged on converts a discontinuity between the religion, culture, and politics of the land and the Christian faith. This was done especially during the later stages of modern Western Christian mission, because in return for supporting and protecting mission work, imperial powers depended on Christians in the colonies to support them against national hostilities. In a way, this policy put into political and social practice the neo-orthodox postulate of a disjunction between the gospel and all religions and by implication between the gospel and all forms of non-Western and non-Christian political and social life. This isolationist policy has created in many Asian Christians and churches a mission-compound or ghetto mentality.

The expectation of many, which Choan Seng Song so eloquently expressed, that an old era was ending and a new exciting period of mission relationships was emerging, simply evaporated. This is the situation—may we even say reactionary situation—in which the purpose and practice of missionary service must be conceived.

Tied into the problematic nature of missionary service in the post-missionary period is the uncertainty in many missionary organizations about the use of the term *missionary* itself. There is a tendency not to use this term anymore because Christian mission is often viewed, rightly or wrongly, as a handmaid of colonialism. So, for instance, when the old Paris Missionary Society transformed itself into a community of churches in mission and became Cevaa, the French initials for the Evangelical Community for Apostolic Action, it dropped the term *missionary* and began to use the term *envoy.* Many other mission societies and churches in Western Europe and North

America prefer to use terms such as *partners* or *fraternal workers* rather than *missionaries*.

Despite these questions and uncertainties, the Council for World mission decided to retain the term *missionary service*. Bernard Thorogood, its first general secretary, gave the following reason:

> Should we wind up one era and call it a day? At Singapore (1975) we said, "No." The former CWM board said, "No." We cannot plan to conclude missionary service, for it is too close to the centre of the gospel...But how are we to view the purpose of it?[2]

Even when missionary organizations use terms such as *envoys* or *partners,* there is a tacit understanding that missionary service is at the center of the gospel. The Council for World Mission kept the term *missionary* because it wanted to keep the motif of "sending" for understanding the task for Christian mission today.

So missionary service as being at the center of the gospel was not in dispute. What was in dispute, however, was the form missionary service should take today. It was clear that the old form of missionary service, in which missionaries went from European churches to other churches, was no longer adequate.

When I joined the Council for World Mission, there was the possibility, if not the danger, that with the return of missionaries from abroad to Britain, missionary service in all its forms would gradually cease. My colleagues, Andrew Prasad and later Andrew Williams, who were secretaries for personnel sharing, ensured that the old missionary service did not wind down without having something else to take its place. Once a movement of this nature stops, it is very difficult to start it up again. It was assumed, rather than explicitly reasoned, that the purpose for sending and receiving missionaries in a new situation had to be found perhaps in analyzing the old arrangement in new settings. So the sending and receiving of missionaries between the churches in the Council for World Mission continued. This was possible, as we shall see later, by not allowing the power of financial resources to dictate the direction and nature of missionary service. So in the first instance, the desire to continue missionary service was prompted more for reasons of strategy than theology.

To keep the momentum going while reevaluating the worth of missionary service, I began to urge my colleagues "to put more bodies on the road." The slogan was picked up, and churches were encouraged to receive and to send missionaries. To crank up missionary service, I even put the identity of the Council for World Mission as a missionary organization on the line. I made it clear that to talk of a missionary organization without missionaries is a contradiction in terms.

The program on personnel sharing, as the name itself implies, rightly began to focus on the resources of people in all the churches in the Council for World Mission and began programs such as long-term missionary service, short-term missionary service, voluntary service, various forms of short-term exchanges of personnel, experience enlargement programs, and leadership development, including a scholarship program. It helped to maintain a *people-centered approach* to mission, while CWM began to face the question Bernard Thorogood left dangling: "But how are we to view the purpose of it?"

To find some insights to answer this question, which has not as yet been properly done, we will examine the beginnings of the modern missionary movement and identify the impulses that led to it.

The Impulses That Led to the Modern Missionary Movement

Our view of the missionary period, which began the era of modern missions as a movement from European churches to the rest of the world, is colored by an opinion, perhaps often justified, that these were heavily identified with Western colonial aspirations and are therefore tainted. It is this opinion that is at the root of much of the political resistance to missionary work today. It is also this judgment that prompts many Christians to be shy of our missionary history and even to argue that the words *missionary* and *mission* should be dropped from Christian vocabulary. But a more careful reading shows that, at the beginning, Western Protestant missions, particularly those from Britain, wanted to tread a path very different from Western mercantile and colonial interests.

This is the judgment of T. V. Philip, the Indian Church Historian, in a series of lectures he gave on Western Christian Missions at Serampore College in India. He argues, "The background, attitudes, methods and commitment of those who came after 1830 were distinctly different in many ways from those of the early Protestant missionaries."[3]

He identifies several impulses that went into the beginnings of Western Protestant missions. Principal of these was the pietistic movement and the evangelical awakening, which pressed upon these missionaries the belief that the whole world had to be won for Christ. Underlying pietistic faith was the conviction that each person was worthy to be saved and Christ had died to save everyone who turned to God in true repentance. So underlying the missionary impulse that emanated from this conviction was gratitude.

In 1794 one of the founding fathers of the Missionary Society (later the London Missionary Society), Mr. Bogue of Gosport, in calling for the formation of a missionary society to send the gospel overseas, said,

> *Gratitude* calls loudly to us to be active instruments in the hands of Christ, in proclaiming to the most distant parts of the earth that grace of which we hope we have ourselves been made partakers. *Justice* too unites her strong and imperious voice and cries, "Ye were once Pagans, living in cruel and abominable idolatry. The servants of Jesus came from other lands and preached His Gospel among you. Hence your knowledge of salvation. And ought ye not, as an equitable compensation for their kindness, to send messengers to the nations which are in like condition with yourselves of old, to entreat them that they turn from their dumb idols to serve the living God, and to wait for His Son from heaven? Verily their debtors ye are."[4]

Despite its dissonance with views that we would hold today on the subject of "pagans," the important point is that the word *pagan* is not used here in a racist way. Those in distant lands are compared with the British who are deemed to have been pagans before missionaries from other places arrived on Britain's shores. In other words, a pre-Christian person is called a pagan. The radical nature of this understanding of pagan is often lost because it is not compared with other viewpoints of church leaders in Britain, especially from the state churches in England and Scotland, which were downright racist in refusing to engage in mission overseas. For instance, a speaker at the General Assembly of the Church of Scotland in 1796 argued, "I cannot otherwise consider the enthusiasm on this subject than as the effect of sanguine and illusive views, the more dangerous because the object is plausible." Listening to his views, the Assembly passed a motion that "to spread abroad the knowledge of the Gospel among barbarous and heathen nations seems highly preposterous, so far as it anticipates, it even reverses, the order of nature."[5] This was a time when the questionable use of *race* as a term to distinguish between people on the basis of skin color and physical features was in its heyday. Having settled, not without some disagreement, the fact that Adam and Eve were the parents of all humankind, attempts were made to answer the question, Why then all these differences? Theories drawn from the Old Testament were advanced to say that with the cursing of Noah's son, Ham (Gen. 9:22–25), the negroes as a lower order of humanity emerged. Of course, there is no evidence in the Genesis accounts that Ham was black or was made black. Environmental factors and later a kind of social Darwinism were used to argue that there was "a Great

Chain of Being," with the Africans at the bottom. It was even alleged that the Negroes had no souls. The other races were arranged in an ascending order, with the white Europeans at the top.[6] It was this massive prejudice that the early Western missionaries cut through when they said, as did Mr. Bogue of Gosport, that "gratitude" for their salvation leads to the demand of "justice" that they work for the salvation of the so-called pagans, which, as we shall see later, was more than a project simply to garner souls for heaven.

A second impulse for mission overseas came from the travels of Captain James Cook in the Pacific, which, T. V. Philip contends, was the secular contribution to the making of a vision for mission overseas. Cook's travels together with the invention of steam as a source of energy, rather than the control over many lands through the expansion of European mercantile and commercial interests, made it possible to traverse large expanses of land and sea to proclaim the gospel.[7]

The text in Matthew that came to be known as the great commission (Mt. 28:18–20) was foundational for the mission thinking and action of that time. The process of interpretation itself was quite complicated. The "nations" intended in this passage, as in the gospel according to Matthew as a whole, are not the Gentiles thousands of miles away, but the "Gentiles down the road" with whom Jewish Christians refused to associate. Equally important for Matthew was the Jewish nation, which as a whole had not received Jesus as the Messiah. Matthew is concerned not so much with, so to speak, "mission overseas" as with "mission near at home."[8] Matthew's commission simply says, "Therefore go." It does not say, "Go into all the world." The commission to mission that does talk of those in distant lands is that of Luke (Acts 1:8), who has a programmatic account of the spread of the gospel in his Acts of the Apostles. In the process of interpreting the so-called great commission, the mission understanding in a part of Acts 1:8 was conflated with the commission in Matthew. It is also clear, at least in William Carey's tract "An Enquiry into the Obligations of Christians, To Use Means for the Conversion of the Heathen" (1792), which heavily influenced the missionary movement of the time, that Mark 16:15 was also drawn in and given a particular slant. Carey speaks of going "into all the world to preach the gospel to every creature" (i.e., to every human being), rather than "to the whole creation" as intended by the Greek. In this way, biblical texts were removed from their contexts, conflated, and skewed in a particular direction to justify a particular understanding of the missionary task.

On the one hand, this interpretation served to argue against those who were against mission overseas. It is said that when William Carey wanted to embark on his mission journey, elders in his church tried to prevent him. The chairman is supposed to have said, "Young man, sit down. When God pleases to covert the heathen, he will do it without your aid and mine. If it was in God's plan to save the heathen, He would find his own way."[9]

On the other hand, and more important for us, it inspired a counter outward movement to the aggressive mercantile and military movement, which was intent on conquering lands and plundering nations to build an empire. A missionary movement arose with the desire not to exploit nations but to take to them a divine treasure.

This vision, which impelled the modern missionary movement, was in many ways a vision for resistance. On the one hand, it led to the formation, in the late eighteenth and early nineteenth centuries, of several missionary societies independent of ecclesiastical and church control. On the other, this vision also functioned to resist what were deemed to be the evils of colonial and mercantile interests. This latter aspect of resistance is worth following up in greater detail.

As T. V. Philip observes, almost all of those who went out as missionaries in the earlier period—and this was true also of those who went from the London Missionary Society—were "a distinctive social class in British society...of craftsmen, small traders, shoe makers, printers, ship builders, school teachers."[10] William Carey, for instance, plied the trade of a cobbler to supplement his meager earnings as a village schoolteacher and Baptist pastor. He taught himself the classical and European languages and several subjects such as botany and zoology, that he might be a greater witness for the Lord. But it was his social background and his identification with people of his class in the countries to which he went that influenced his attitudes and shaped his theology.

First and foremost, Carey saw world mission, understood as foreign mission, as an obligation or duty that called on him and others to carry the gospel to all parts of the world. As T. V. Philip comments, "It was Carey more than anyone else who gave to the modern missionary movement its geographical perspective."[11]

The second great contribution that Carey made was to give a strong social perspective to Christian mission. He was not alone in this matter. Instead of denying their social background, the early missionaries used their class orientation to sharpen their theological perspectives. At a time when Church of England prelates were berating the French Revolution for its subversive teaching, the spirit of democracy, and its blasphemous character, Carey welcomed the new spirit of liberty, equality, and fraternity. According to Carey's biographer, Pearce Carey, Carey greeted the French Revolution as "God's answer to the recent concerted praying of his people." He viewed it as opening doors that will continue to open wide "for the

Gospel by the spread of civil and religious liberty and by the diminution of Papal power."[12] He and many of his fellow missionaries viewed the French Revolution as leading people to a more complete humanity. But he was convinced that these ideas and visions had to be grounded in Christ if they were to bear fruit.

These convictions led to a form of missionary action that was radical. Carey and his fellow missionaries were fierce in their criticism of the slave trade, which had reached disgraceful proportions in their time. Carey abandoned the use of sugar as a sort of personal economic boycott of the slave trade. For him, sugar seemed to represent the blood of the poor slaves. Others in England, especially those in the Church Missionary Society, saw Africa as a place for their special concern. They spoke of "the miseries which had entailed on them by the slave trade" and "the duty of making some recompense for the injuries and wrongs, which by our participation in that nefarious traffic, we had inflicted on Africa." This position not only challenged the view of other clerics in Britain for whom the pagans were, so to speak, "a lower order of creation," but also led evangelicals to argue that Britain's role in Africa should be that of guardian and protector of the people.[13]

To illustrate, I give two examples of this position in action in the history of the London Missionary Society (LMS), one from the former British Guyana and the other from South Africa.

John Smith went to British Guyana in 1817 as an LMS missionary. He was to share the work with the senior missionary, John Wray, who was already there. His reception by the colonial authorities was anything but cordial. When the governor quizzed him on how he intended to work with the Negroes, Smith answered, "By teaching them to read; by teaching them Dr Watts' catechisms; and by preaching the Gospel in a plain manner." To which the governor replied, "If ever you teach a negro to read, and I hear about it, I will banish you from the colony immediately." Although the authorities frowned on his activities, those whom he came to serve welcomed him gladly. His work in the Demerara region flourished, and there quickly grew a black church with some 800 persons in a few years. However, the condition of the slaves remained awful. In a letter he wrote to England in 1822, John Smith sketches the appalling conditions of the slaves—their utter dependency on the slave owner, the cruel conditions of labor with even Sundays, which should have been days of rest, taken away from them through vexing tasks laid upon them. The representations through letters sent to England finally began to bear fruit, and acts of Parliament for the better treatment of slaves were enacted in Britain. The British government addressed circular letters to the colonial governors recommending reforms, including the limiting of a day's labor to nine hours and absolutely forbidding the flogging of female slaves. The governor deliberately held back announcing the orders, resulting in speculation on what the orders contained. One rumor was that the king had ordered the slaves to be freed but the governor was not willing to do it.

Despite John Smith's advice to the slaves to be patient because something good was going to happen, with interminable delays, patience ran out. In 1823 arms were seized and revolts broke out, spreading from estate to estate. In the ensuing conflict no white soldier lost his life, but there was a terrible slaughter of the slaves. Disregarding the ameliorating role that John Smith had played, a hostile colonial government arrested him and tried him for instigating the slave uprising, if not actually participating in it. He was condemned to death, but as a British subject he could not be executed without the order being confirmed by the British government. His fellow and senior missionary, John Wray, left for England to plead his cause.

In the meantime John Smith was shut up in a prison cell with wooden floorboards over stagnant water. Physically he was not a robust person. In prison his health began to deteriorate rather rapidly. His friends in England managed to get him a reprieve, but it was too late. He died in prison.[14]

John Smith was a nonconformist. He did not have the protection of the state church. He worked among the poor—a white man on the side of black slaves. So the rich and powerful disliked him. He was vulnerable. He died a martyr. When the slaves were emancipated, they built the John Smith memorial church. They deliberately chose to build the church in a North-South direction rather than the usual East-West direction to commemorate a missionary who was martyred because he stood with them.

The history of the London Missionary Society in South Africa, beginning especially with the arrival of the Dutch LMS missionary Dr. Van der Kemp, was anything but calm. Dr. Philip, who followed Van der Kemp, was equally determined as Van der Kemp to resist the wrongs done to the native African tribes. Commenting on this aspect of missionary work, which continued with the work of later missionaries, the historian Richard Lovett wrote in 1899:

> No aphorism is more common...than that missionaries as such have nothing to do with politics. Sound as this maxim may be, it is from the Christian standpoint inevitable that if the Government of a country allies itself with cruelty, social wrongs, and oppression, the Christian missionary, working within the sphere of such Government, *must* find himself in active opposition to those things.[15]

Sharing People in Mission   77

After detailing the problems that Dr. Philip ran into in resisting the anti-African policies and practices of the colonizers, especially his conviction of the charge of libel in the Supreme Court of the colony for publishing his famous tract *Researches in South Africa*, Lovett writes,

> Any man of any common sense, who studies the facts will see that the great vice of all missionary institutions, in the eyes of the colonists, was that they enabled the Hottentot to learn that, as a human being, he had rights; they taught him to claim these rights, they often enabled him to secure them, and they confronted Dutchman and Englishman alike with a power that said, "You shall not enslave and oppress and harry to death, just as you will, men whose great offence is that they are the aboriginal inhabitants of the land you covet."[16]

Against overwhelming odds missionaries not only fought for the people of the land in South Africa but also argued in Parliament in Westminster and did manage from time to time to get laws passed to protect the indigenous African populations. It is perhaps no exaggeration to say that these missionaries, beginning with Van der Kemp and Philip, provided the foundation for the freedom movement in South Africa that finally brought down the apartheid government.

Understood as an intrinsic part of evangelical and pietistic commitment, this social and critical dimension, which affirmed the worth and dignity of every person, gave the early missionary movement its distinctive character. At a time when state churches either overtly or covertly colluded with national political and military powers, the dissenters trod a different path both at home and abroad. Nonconformism was at one and the same time a political position and a theological conviction. These missionaries were not mere evangelists. They were also social reformers who challenged what they deemed to be wrong in society, theirs as well as those to which they went. William Carey, for instance, braved personal danger to express his resistance to the Hindu practice of *sati* (the immolation of widows at the funeral pyres of their husbands) at the very places in which these were being carried out.

Within such an understanding of the beginnings of the modern missionary movement, it is possible to detect the revolutionary impulse of the founding vision of the London Missionary Society: "To send the Glorious Gospel of the Blessed God to the Heathen." Although we might deplore the use of the term "heathen," with all of its connotations, we must remember that at a time when colonialism was interested in exploiting the heathen and accumulating treasures in Britain and other European countries, these missionaries were more interested in taking to the heathen a heavenly treasure that they felt had been entrusted to them. This was an act of love that should and could overcome any danger.

The task for today is to find a similar revolutionary meaning and practice for Christian world mission, so that we may express God's compassion and love for people through the kind of solidarity that these early missionaries expressed in taking the side of the oppressed. To grasp at greater depth the revolutionary character of mission as the expression of solidarity through compassion, we will look at the way in which Jesus expressed God's compassion, which provided the model for these early missionaries.

Jesus' Mission with the Multitudes (*Ochlos*)

Solidarity is the crossing of frontiers to embrace another, defying and overcoming existing boundaries or walls of separation. Compassion is solidarity in action. The early missionaries of the modern missionary period crossed the boundary between European and pagan, affirming that the so-called pagan was also a child of God, and expressed their solidarity in their compassion, much to the chagrin of colonial political authorities. To unpack their practice of compassion, we need to go beyond the understanding of the word *compassion* that prevails in the English language. The English word *compassion* has come to mean feeling sorry for another who is in misery and indulging in acts of compassion or charity in an attempt to alleviate the pain of the other.

The compassion of the early missionaries was more in line with the way Jesus showed compassion. They crossed the barrier of race at a time when the pagan was classified not only as unenlightened but also of a lower order of creation. It was their solidarity, redolent of the solidarity that Jesus exhibited in identifying himself with prostitutes, tax collectors, and all those who were labeled sinners, that often led them into trouble with colonial governments and to their being charged with sedition.

Mark, who is followed by Matthew and Luke, uses the collective word *ochlos* ("crowd," "multitude," or "mob") to designate the motley group on the margins of society with whom Jesus identified.[17] They also provide us with an important clue for understanding the character of Jesus' compassion, which the early missionaries of the modern era of mission expressed and which we are called to emulate in our missionary service.

The gospel writers use the Greek verb *splanchnizomai* to describe the character of Jesus' compassion. Although the noun form *splanchnon* occurs elsewhere in the New Testament (Rom. 9:15; Col. 3:12; Heb. 10:34) to refer to God's love or the practice of God's love, the verb occurs only in the synoptic gospels and is reserved for use with Jesus.

It is used either to describe the attitude of Jesus to people defined as the *ochlos* and the actions that ensue from that attitude (Mk. 1:41; 6:34; Lk. 7:13), or when Jesus speaks in parables to explain the nature of God's reign/realm and the nature of divine compassion (Mt. 18:27; Lk. 15:20). In all these instances, it is preferred over another verb, *oikteiro*, which also means to have compassion, and over verbs such as *eleeo*, "to have mercy" (Mt. 20:30), which is used in the liturgical *Kyrie eleison* ("Lord have mercy"), and *sumpatheo*, from which we get the English "sympathy."

The verb *splanchnizomai* denotes a strong emotional, physical response. Its literal meaning is "to be moved in one's bowels." Or to put it in our language, it is to say that it is a gut-wrenching response. It is not just a mental attitude—to have pity or to feel sorry for people. It is a physical response to human conditions that leads to action. It is the response of Jesus when he sees the crowds or multitudes, the sinners and prostitutes, the nobodies of society whom Jesus described as "sheep without a shepherd."

A good example of the compassion of Jesus is found in Mark 6:30–44. Jesus tried to get away from the crowds to a lonely place to rest awhile. He got into a boat with the Twelve and moved away to another part of the shore of the Sea of Galilee. Seeing him leave, the crowds ran along the shore to the place where he was to land. "As he went ashore, he saw a great crowd; and he had compassion for them, because they were like sheep without a shepherd; and he began to teach them many things" (v. 34). He also fed them.

Jesus' compassion found expression in his teaching. Through the stories or parables that he told and through his preaching, Jesus presented to the crowds the reign/realm of God as a reality made known in him and through his ministry. They were invited to repent—to return and come home to God and to the place where God reigns—and be forgiven and restored. For them, the reign/realm of God was good news (Mt. 5:3–10).

Jesus' compassion found expression in his healing. As Jesus was leaving Jericho for Jerusalem, two blind men sitting by the roadside heard that Jesus was passing by and cried out, "Lord, have mercy on us, Son of David!" The crowd rebuked them. But Jesus called them to him and asked, "What do you want me to do for you?" They said, "Lord, let our eyes be opened." And Jesus *had compassion on them* and touched their eyes, and they received their sight (Mt. 20:29–34).

Compassion could also find expression in anger. Jesus told a parable comparing the kingdom of God to a king who wished to settle accounts with his servants. One of these owed him much money. The king ordered him to be sold with his family and possessions to recover what was owed. The servant fell on his knees and implored the king to have patience with him and promised that he would eventually pay back everything. The king *had compassion on him* and released him and forgave his debt. The same servant found another servant who owed him money, and demanded repayment. The other servant in turn asked him for patience and a time for repayment. But he refused and put the man in prison until the debt was repaid. His fellow servants in distress reported what had happened to the king. Then the king summoned the servant and scolded him: "You wicked slave! I forgave you all that debt because you pleaded with me. Should you not have had mercy on your fellow slave, as I had mercy on you?" And in great anger the king delivered the servant to the jailers until he paid all that he owed (Mt. 18:23–34).

The compassion of Jesus expressed as anger resisted the unjust demands that the religious authorities placed on the people. Listen to this: "But woe to you, scribes and Pharisees, hypocrites! For you lock people out of the kingdom of heaven. For you do not go in yourselves, and when others are going in, you stop them. Woe to you, scribes and Pharisees, hypocrites! For you cross sea and land to make a single convert, and you make the new convert twice as much a child of hell as yourselves" (Mt. 23:13–15). This is strong language, and there are many more instances in the gospel accounts of Jesus crying and weeping in anger and anguish.

In him and through him, the compassion of God was expressed in the strongest of terms. To the dismay of religious leaders of his time, Jesus broke a line of untouchability and had table fellowship with the *ochlos* (Lk. 15:1–2). In him and through him, it was also revealed that compassion is the quality of the Messiah. It was this close identification with the crowds—the victims of injustice, the prostitutes and sinners, and those on the periphery of society—expressed in his compassion for them that led to his death on the cross.

What he did was dangerous. It opened up dimensions of hope for those who were considered to be sinners or unclean and those on the periphery of society. Through Jesus the Messiah, the compassion of God expressed itself in affirming the human dignity of those whom society treated as outcasts. The compassion of Jesus, expressed in acts of love for the people and as resistance against those who shut the gates of the reign/realm of God in the face of the people, was seen as dangerous political activity. This was why he was executed. Jesus was not stoned to death as was Stephen, who was accused of blasphemy— a religious offense. Rather, Jesus was crucified for an alleged political offense. For sure, the religious authorities whom Jesus questioned and resisted participated in the arrest and trial of Jesus. They found him dangerous and were convinced that he could imperil the nation in the eyes of Rome (cf. Jn. 11:47–52). The charge against Jesus was a political interpretation of what he did for and with the people (*ochlos*). In proclaiming the kingdom of God, Jesus opened up avenues of hope for the people. But for Rome that was sedition. He was indicted for calling himself or permitting himself to be called the King of the Jews. The execution was ordered and carried out by the authorities of the Roman Empire. In other words, Jesus was crucified not because he was considered to be a bad theologian, but because he was perceived to be a political menace.

The Purpose of Missionary Service in World Mission Today

The mission of the early missionaries of the modern missionary era resonates with the ministry of Jesus with the people. It provides us with directions for the understanding and practice of missionary service today, and would in large measure answer the question Bernard Thorogood raised: "But how are we to view the purpose of it?"

First, it is the clearest expression of the international nature of the church and that we are all part of the one body of Christ. Maitland Evans, the general secretary of the United Church in Jamaica and the Cayman Islands, which both receives and sends missionaries, said to me, "At present we need missionaries because we are short of trained personnel. But even when we have made up this deficit, we will still receive and send missionaries as we now do to demonstrate in Jamaica and the Cayman Islands that we are part of the world church." It is a way of expressing the solidarity that should exist within the body of Christ—a solidarity that crosses barriers of race and nationality within the church.

Second, missionary exchange today can demonstrate in a tangible way what partnership in mission is all about if the power of money does not control the sharing of personnel. If the power of money is the determining factor, only those with money will feel that they can engage in mission and will indulge in a form of mission that brings back the worst characteristics of the previous missionary era.

To overcome this danger, in the Council for World Mission, the church that sends the missionary is not required to accept financial responsibility for the person it sends. In sending a person, it is already sharing its resources. It is the responsibility of the receiving church to provide the salary and other material needs, as well as pastoral care for the missionary. If the receiving church does not have the needed financial resources, then the common pool of money, to which all churches in the Council for World Mission contribute, is used. In this way the nexus between personnel and financial control is cut. To contribute to a common pool is itself an act in which a church says that it is willing to share the power of money. Furthermore, in this missionary exchange there is also an agreement between sending church and receiving church not only about the nature of the ministry in which the missionary is to be involved but also about the level of financial support that is needed. Most churches in the Council for World Mission, even the financially poorest, provide in this missionary exchange at least what it provides as the financial component of a church worker's emolument.

As already noted, with the separation of personnel resources from financial resources, more churches in the non-Western world are sending missionaries. Particularly, though not exclusively, through South to North exchanges, churches have begun to put into practice forms of mutual challenge that have begun to raise in new ways both justice and peace issues. Some of the important issues in which churches from the South and the North are collaborating are combating the debt burden, which is exacerbating the woeful condition of people in many countries of the so-called Third World; fighting the HIV/AIDS pandemic, which is devastating populations in Africa and Asia; and seeking economic justice for the poor in an era of economic globalization. Missionaries, even from churches that have refused to move on in mission thinking, seize their freedom as missionaries to be far more progressive and challenging in these matters. In a new way, missionaries today are attempting to bring back into mission thinking and practice the character of mission as expressed in the early period of modern Western Protestant mission and the ways in which they expressed solidarity through the practice of compassion.

Third, missionary exchange could manifest in exciting ways the concept of the missionary as a frontiersperson. This is best done by linking missionary service not so much to length of service as to place of service. Through the ages missionaries have crossed borders and boundaries to witness to the liberating and saving word of God. Today, too, we have to perceive frontiers and cross boundaries that are not only geographical but also ideological, political, economic, religious, racial, and so on.[18]

Fourth, missionary exchange has a role to play in an era of economic globalization. Konrad Raiser, the general secretary of the World Council of Churches, calls this a reemerging ecumenical emphasis on the mission of the laity (inclusive of clergy and lay), or "lay participation towards inclusive community." He explains:

> The goal of lay commitment is the rebuilding of viable, non-exclusive social forms that will produce a community with a human face in which human dignity is recognized, basic human needs are satisfied, and the diversity of cultural identities and human talents are duly recognized.[19]

The world as we know it today is subject to global economic and political forces that are largely faceless and thus nonaccountable to people and democratic institutions. These are forces that not only exploit people and indeed the whole of God's creation but also exacerbate divisions in human community. In this situation the church as the people of God (the *laos*) is called on to be involved with others in erecting civic institutions through which the causes of democracy and accountability can be expressed. The mission of the laity is to be involved in processes of setting up alternatives and resistance movements to these global forces, especially in their local manifestations. Missionary service in this vocation is an expression of solidarity across geographical and economic divisions. It would not only support the struggles to build community but would also provide a human face to partnership in mission.

All these reasons for continuing missionary service reconnect us with the character of missionary service as it ought to be: solidarity expressed through compassion. These also bring back a people-centered approach to mission. Freed from the control of money and open to negotiations between sending church and receiving church, missionary service could continue to be a sign and expression of the one body of Christ to which we belong, and which belonging sustains Christian mission. The releasing of missionaries to perceive frontiers and cross boundaries should enable a greater sharing of experiences of the gospel touching ground and taking root. The missionary takes the experience of the way the gospel has been incarnated in a particular context on a missionary journey. In returning, the missionary brings back the experience of the incarnation of the gospel in another context. In this way the missionary enables the process of learning from one another, thus opening the views of the sending and receiving church to new understandings of Christian mission.

In the next chapter also we will use the twofold test implied in this chapter in looking at the sharing of resources of money in mission. First, would a missionary organization continue to value and use all resources and contributions in the practice of power sharing for the sake of the mission of the church? Second, would it continue to encourage liberating initiatives for real partnership?

5

Sharing Resources of Money

Three experiences in particular shaped my thinking not only on the problematic nature of sharing resources of money in mission but also on the problematic nature of money itself. In fact, the two are interlinked. The first was my experience as an associate general secretary in the Christian Conference of Asia. I learned there that money is not only a bad master; it is not even a good servant. Money has an intrinsic allure, which is expressed in its power to seduce.

The second was my experience in the Council for World Mission, when as general secretary I was confronted with shrinking financial resources. With the sale of a piece of land belonging to the London Missionary Society in Hong Kong we replenished our financial resources. However, the arguments that had to be advanced to claim that land against competing claims and the magnitude of the sum that was finally received raised other issues involved in the acquiring and management of money. (Because much of what is to be said in this chapter concerns the Council for World Mission, I will often use just the initials CWM.)

The third experience was with a consultation of representatives from three mission organizations, the Evangelical Community for Apostolic Action (Cevaa, its French initials), the Council for World Mission (CWM), and the United Evangelical Mission (UEM). These three organizations had transformed themselves from European mission societies into global communities of churches in mission. For the consultation, which was an evaluation of how we had fared as partnerships of churches in mission, each organization provided its own evaluation in advance on three areas that were framed as questions: (1) How does the organizational structure enable power sharing and the participation of member churches in planning and discharging the mission of the church? (2) What are the principles for financial cooperation? (3) How have we helped one another to be missionary churches? At the meeting there was a joint evaluation with efforts to learn from one another. All three organizations had struggled to express in practical ways the sharing of power to create and sustain communities of churches in mission.

The sharing of money was an important aspect of that exercise. Reflecting on our experiences, a small group of six persons drawn from the three organizations made a statement on the responsible management of finances, saying that the management of money is a spiritual matter. I was in that small group. The composition of the group of six is worth noting, because it was not a European group, as one might suspect reading the statement. Besides one from Germany, all the others were from outside Europe: two from Sri Lanka, and one each from French Polynesia, Hong Kong, and Tanzania. Of these six only two, both from outside Europe, were professional accountants, though all of us had had previous experiences in managing money.

Using these three experiences, I reflected on the problematic nature of money in a biblical reflection on Luke 16:1–13, the parable of the dishonest manager, at a meeting of the Finance Advisory Group of the Council for World Mission in April 2000. The statement of the joint consultation states succinctly concerns involved in the management of money,[1] so I use it both to introduce and close the biblical reflection. After the biblical reflection, we will see how the insights presented in the biblical reflection were evident in the ways in which the Council for World Mission attempted to manage and survive a windfall.

The Management of Money as a Spiritual Matter

> The ways in which money is acquired, used, and managed are spiritual matters. Faith, theology, and financial matters should be seen as one whole. We feel the need for renewed reflection on these matters as recent developments in the world economy challenge our model of mission.[2]

I quote the following parable in full because it is replete with irony and is a good illustration of Jesus' sense of humor.

> Jesus said to the disciples, "There was a rich man who had a manager, and charges were brought to him that this man was squandering his property. So he summoned him and said to him, 'What is this that I hear about you? Give me an accounting of your management, because you cannot be my manager any longer.' Then the manger said to himself, 'What will I do, now that my master is taking the position away from me? I am not strong enough to dig, and I am ashamed to beg.

I have decided what to do so that, when I am dismissed as manager, people may welcome me into their homes.' So, summoning his master's debtors one by one, he asked the first, 'How much do you owe my master?' He answered, 'A hundred jugs of olive oil.' He said to him, 'Take your bill, sit down quickly, and make it fifty.' Then he asked another, 'And how much do you owe?' He replied, 'A hundred containers of wheat.' He said to him, 'Take your bill and make it eighty.' And his master commended the dishonest manager because he had acted shrewdly; for the children of this age are more shrewd in dealing with their own generation than are the children of light. And I tell you, make friends for yourselves by means of dishonest wealth so that when it is gone, they may welcome you into the eternal homes.

"Whoever is faithful in a very little is faithful also in much; and whoever is dishonest in a very little is dishonest also in much. If then you have not been faithful with the dishonest wealth, who will entrust to you the true riches? And if you have not been faithful with what belongs to another, who will give you what is your own? No slave can serve two masters; for a slave will either hate the one and love the other, or be devoted to the one and despise the other. You cannot serve God and wealth." (Lk. 16:1–13)

The parable is about a manager who is called an economist (*oikonomos*). The Greek word literally means one who is in charge of the law (*nomos*) of the home (*oikos*). In this case, the "economist" was managing not the law of his own home but the law of the home in which he had been put in charge. The money he was asked to manage was not his own. It had been entrusted to him as an economist. The manager, or economist, proved to be dishonest and irresponsible. He was squandering the property of his master.

In the parable of the talents, the fault of the man who had been given one talent lay in the fact that he simply buried the money in the ground and waited for his master to return so he could return it intact. He was frightened to do anything with it lest he made a mistake and lost it. But did he return it intact? The value of the money would have gone down between the reception and return of the money. That would have been the cause of the master's anger. Just leaving it in the bank to accumulate interest would have been better than doing nothing (Mt. 25:24–28). Fearing to take risks, to do nothing with the money entrusted to us, is disobedience. In the parable of the dishonest manager, the "sin" is in squandering the money entrusted to us. Not investing wisely and spending the money irresponsibly are two sides of the same coin. Both are spiritually culpable offences in that they are presented as tests of our Christian stewardship.

As in the parable of the talents, there was a day of reckoning. The external auditors were to come to examine the books. The master says to him, "Give me an accounting of your economics, because you cannot be my economist any longer." He realizes that his dishonesty would be found out and he would be sacked. With a touch of homespun humor, the dishonest manager says, "I am too old to dig and I am too proud to beg." So he fixes the books before getting thrown out. He fixes the books in an interesting way. Realizing that the sacking was inevitable, he squanders even more of his master's money to win friends. He forgives debts owed to his master! He works on the assumption that when he is thrown out, he will fall into the laps of his newly won friends.

But did they receive him? Were they as magnanimous as he expected them to be? Or did they also turn him out? At this point the parable assumes that his ruse worked.

The parable goes on:

> And his master commended the dishonest manager because he had acted shrewdly; for the children of this age are more shrewd in dealing with their own generation than are the children of light. (Lk. 16:8)

It is not the dishonesty but the shrewdness that is commended. The dishonest manager knew the character of money, its seductive power, and used it shrewdly even though it was for selfish ends. His shrewdness in knowing how to use money is used as a yardstick for measuring the "children of light," who are contrasted with the "children of this age."

Quite often we tend to posit a clear division between managing money and living our faith, because we think dealing with money is such a materialistic enterprise. For many of us the question is, What does money have to do with our faith or spirituality? This position leads to disengagement in one form or another. In the face of economic globalization and the exclusion of many from the system, one response is condemnation. We spend so much time demonizing and rejecting globalization that we fail to deal responsibly with its threat. Such action is doing theology from the sidelines of life. No one, neither the controllers nor the victims of globalization, will take us seriously, because no amount of theological ranting will deal with the problem. As a Dutch theologian, Bert Hoedemaker, said at a consultation on justice, peace, and the integrity of creation, "Exhortations and incantations don't work anymore, even if they ever did work." They don't work because we are not simply dealing with individuals but with "systems of injustice," as the World Council of Churches phrased it at its assembly in Vancouver (1983),[3] or with "structures of sin," as Pope John Paul II stated in his encyclical *Sollicitudo Rei Socialis*.[4]

Another response is to ignore it altogether and expect others to do what is needful. I give two instances of this response from within the Council for World Mission.

A small group of scholars, most of them from CWM churches, wrote a document called *World Mission Today*.[5] The document provides an analysis of economic globalization, among other issues, as a way of discerning the signs of the time and suggesting avenues for expressing the mission of the church. Great care was also taken to edit the document so the language was as clear as possible in dealing with some rather complicated issues. The document was sent to all the CWM churches and to several ecumenical organizations.

At a subsequent meeting, a leader from a CWM church from one of the poorest countries of the world, who constantly complained about the dire straits of his church and people, blasted the document for being difficult and filled with jargon and therefore irrelevant to the needs of the church. To this diatribe I responded: "My friend, there are no prizes for ignorance in the church. While you refuse to put in the required effort to understand what is happening, the forces of globalization are ripping off your people. You cannot simply sit on the sidelines and moan at what is happening."

I visited a church in the Pacific, which had debts running into a few million pounds sterling. The church had got into this big debt because it had borrowed a large sum of money from the bank to expand its business venture. Previously, there had been several small businesses scattered over the country, which catered to small clientele. These were all brought together under a large management under the mistaken notion that if small works well, then big should work better. The business collapsed when it could not compete with cheaper products from business corporations. The planning of the business project was also poor and so, too, the debt management. The consequences of economic globalization on the country, devaluing of currency, and political instability also played a part. The moderator of the church said to me that, when he went to see the bank manager to seek a rescheduling of debts, the bank manager said to him, "Oh you are from the church that does not keep its promises!" When he inquired what this was all about, the manager told him that his predecessor had said to the bank, "Do not worry about the debt. CWM will settle it." He asked me whether I could give him a letter saying that CWM would do nothing of the sort. Because no such promise had been made and would be made, I gave him the letter he asked for. He shared this letter with the manager of the bank to show him that the previous moderator had simply indulged in some wishful thinking.

The way out of this problem for the church was far more arduous and involved. With skills available from outside, the church shrewdly negotiated with the bank to reschedule its debts. The church used financial resources allocated for it in the common pool of the Council for World Mission to get the bank to relinquish its lien on valuable church property that had been used as collateral. Gradually but surely, the church is pulling out of its financial problems.

The economic world, the market, and all financial transactions and movements have their own rules, including the rule of the invisible hand first propounded by Adam Smith. All of these must be studied. We must know how to play the game. This is not simply a matter of accounts or accounting that can be left to experts. It is a theological task for which economic shrewdness is essential, for we have to deal with the allure of money.

Jesus goes on,

> And I tell you, make friends for yourselves by means of dishonest wealth so that when it is gone, they may welcome you into the eternal homes. (Lk. 16:9)

Wealth, called "mammon," is dishonest. It is deceitful. It can and will entice. I had an interesting experience of the seductive power of money when I was working in the Christian Conference of Asia. Its financial resources were going down. A considerable and difficult part of my job was to raise money. Having raised the money, I loved to see the bank balance grow. It seemed to assuage all my pain at having to plead, beg, and cajole donor organizations in Europe and America to contribute to the budget of the Christian Conference of Asia. Seeing money in the bank was so sweet! Consequently, I hid it from others. I blocked program plans that called for what I considered to be high expenditure. I realized what was happening to me when my fellow associate general secretary, Park Sang-jung, who was responsible for supervising all programs, screamed at me: "Why is it that finance boys are more interested in preserving money than in the mission of the church?" I came to understand what Ron O'Grady meant when he said, "You will have an entirely new understanding of the doctrine of human sin." Wealth is dishonest. It is deceitful. It can entice. It tends to twist our priorities. But it has to be used wisely, shrewdly, for the right purposes.

At this point the issue of the ethics of using "dishonest wealth" surfaces in the exposition of the parable. Scholars are not clear whether verses 8b to 13, from "children of this age are more shrewd than..." to

"...you cannot serve God and wealth," were originally part of the parable. These verses seem to be separate allegorizing commentaries on the parable, applying the parable to test one's faith and faithfulness.[6] That this may be the case is suggested by the fact that beginning with verse 9, matters of "faith" and "unfaith," as well as "honest" and "dishonest," are contrasted. The contrast culminates in the assertion that one cannot be faithful to God and mammon at the same time. However, because they come together in the text as we have it, we will read them together. To help us read this section, these commentaries on the parable have been arranged in couplets, which would befit Hebrew/Aramaic poetry, where the second line of the couplet amplifies the verse line.

> Whoever is faithful in a very little is faithful also in much;
> and whoever is dishonest in a very little is dishonest also in
>   much.
> If then you have not been faithful with the dishonest wealth,
> who will entrust to you the true riches?
> And if you have not been faithful with what belongs to another,
> who will give you what is your own?
> No slave can serve two masters;
> for a slave will either hate the one and love the other,
> or be devoted to the one and despise the other.
> You cannot serve God and wealth. (Lk. 16:10–13)

Using the first couplet to interpret the second couplet, not being faithful with "dishonest wealth" is the "little" that becomes a yardstick for not trusting the person with "true riches," which is the "much." The contrast is between "dishonest" (Greek: *adikos*) and "honest" or "what is really true" (Greek: *alethinos*). Whereas *adikos* as an adjective is followed by the noun "wealth," or "mammon," *alethinos* is not used as an adjective but as a substantive. It is a nonpersonalized neuter noun meaning "what is really good." The contrast then is not between "dishonest mammon" and "true riches." There is nothing called honest wealth or riches. Wealth remains dishonest. So a more felicitous translation would be, "If then you have not been faithful in the way you have managed dishonest wealth (mammon), who would entrust you with the things that indeed make for truth?" The suggestion seems to be that the way in which we manage money—that is, dishonest mammon—is a test of our spirituality that has to manage the things that make for truth.

The next couplet expands on what has been said. What is another's is the wealth that is entrusted for our management, as was the wealth entrusted to the "dishonest manager." In managing what belongs to another, there should be a distance, so to speak, "from one's soul," so that one need not be seduced by dishonest wealth. Clear accounting practices and responsible management would be required. We would also know that external auditors could and indeed would check our management. If, even with this clear knowledge, we are irresponsible, how could we be trusted with the management of the things that make for truth? For there is no objective way of checking one's spirituality. Here, each of us alone is responsible for maintaining faithfulness.

The contrast is now broadened in the next few lines. It is not possible to give one's allegiance both to God and mammon, for they contradict each other. The moment the acquiring, using, and managing of money becomes our all-absorbing vocation, and we invest that activity with absolute value, we have lost it! Then we worship mammon. Remember! Wealth is dishonest.

Mammon, which indicates more clearly than the term *wealth* its inherent character to lure us and capture our allegiance as if it were a deity, must be used for a purpose. It must be used against its own ethos, which is expressed as greed with its desire to accumulate capital. This is the prevailing goal of global economic systems. Instead, the wealth entrusted to us must be used against its own ethos to serve the poor, whom the system of mammon has disadvantaged and will continue to disadvantage. But such service cannot be simplistic, ignoring the very character of money. Discipline and shrewdness are required from both those who provide and those who receive, so that we are not deceived.

Concentrating on this problem only within the circle of churches that constitute the three mission organizations, the statement on the management of money went on to say:

> The three organizations should make an extra effort to follow the key principles of management—accountability, mutual trust and transparency. Transparency should be applied not only in the three organisations, but also between and within each of the member churches up to the congregational level. It is important also to find out what proportion of their resources the member churches are putting to mission work and what proportion they set aside for maintenance.

> Ethical considerations in raising and investing funds in the organisations should be clearly formulated and regularly evaluated.

> The budgets of the three organisations and of the churches should be regularly reviewed with a view to finding out whether they still reflect the mission priorities they seek to practice...

With regard to financially struggling churches, we recommend that the three organisations undertake a study of the exact situation of the churches, and provide short-term help. They should also work towards the long-term goal of financial self-reliance of these churches. We recommend that the three organisations supply consultancy teams made up of professionals—accountants and financial experts as well as theologians and pastors. These should be preferably from churches in the same region.[7]

It was an invitation to demonstrate our faithfulness over a little in a small circle so that it could become the test of how we would and could respond to a larger circle. This was the test the Council for World Mission had to face when it received and tried to survive a windfall.

Managing and Surviving a Windfall

Considerable shrewdness, financial and otherwise, was required to deal with proceeds from the sale of a piece of land in Hong Kong. In his booklet *In All Good Grace,*[8] Andrew Morton provides an account of the negotiations and legal wrangles with the Nethersole Hospital Committee, which took the position that the proceeds from the sale of land should actually be transferred to them for their continuing medical work in Hong Kong. He also describes the various concessions, such as the setting up of a trust for the benefit of the Chinese in Hong Kong and mainland China and a contribution to the Nethersole Hospital Committee for chaplaincy work in a new hospital, that had to be made to get the bulk of the money—something like 65 percent—for the work of CWM. Andrew Morton shows how CWM dealt legally with the question, Was it right to take this money from Hong Kong for the general work of CWM?

My concern here is not to rehash this process but to look at the theological issues that the claiming and reception of this resource raised in managing "dishonest wealth." The issues also had to do with my personal story.

When I was interviewed for the post of general secretary of the Council for World Mission, the first stage of the interviewing process was a conversation with Aubrey Curry, who was then the secretary for finance as well as the acting general secretary. Aubrey wanted me to say something about my intended vision for the Council for World Mission. With my previous experiences in two other ecumenical organizations in which I had to find the money required to do the work, I was more interested in finding out what resources there were to do the work. What use is vision without money! So within a few minutes of this interview, I asked for the budget. Looking at the figures, I knew that financial resources were inadequate for the work at hand. Where would more money come from? The CWM churches were already contributing quite a lot. From previous knowledge, I could compare the contributions of some of the Asian churches to the Council for World Mission, which were considerably more than what they gave other ecumenical organizations to which they belonged. Could the CWM churches give more? Not really. A rent review was soon due on rents received from Livingstone House and St. Andrew's House, which the Council for World Mission owned. At the time the property prices and rents in London were high. When the rent review actually took place, the property market had dropped. The rent review with the occupants of St. Andrew's House was a disaster. We could not agree and so went for arbitration. The arbitrator fixed an amount that was numerically 60,000 pounds sterling less per year than what they had paid for the previous thirty years! Add inflation, and the loss was tremendous. Quite a number of rooms in Livingstone House, which had previously been rented, were now empty. So when the matter of the land in Hong Kong came up, I was already miffed that the needed financial resources for mission were not available.

It was around February or March 1993 that I was told that the land on which the Nethersole–Alice Ho Miu Hospital stood would have to be transferred to a trust in Hong Kong nominated by the member church, the Hong Kong Council of the Church of Christ in China. I was aware at the time that resources of the London Missionary Society outside Britain were to be transferred to the member church in that country. However, I was not aware that an actual policy decision had been made in 1977 that said that "properties outside the UK be transferred into the ownership of the local organisation nominated by the constituent body in that country."[9] I doubt that even if I knew about this decision, I would have acted differently.

I persuaded the Finance Advisory Group of the Council for World Mission, in effect, to go against this policy decision. I began to inquire about the history of the land and why it was now being vacated. In brief, the London Missionary Society had provided the land for a hospital. It was an ecumenical venture. The hospital had done well. So the government provided better facilities of both land and building in the New Territories of Hong Kong. The site was no longer needed for the original purpose for which it was given. The land and property were now being vacated. The member church of the Council for World Mission in Hong Kong had at no time used it for its own mission, as it had used the schools founded by the London Missionary Society, which were later transferred to the church.

With this knowledge in mind, I felt that because no member church in Hong Kong had used this property, it should now come back to the Council for World Mission for the work of the whole community. At the meeting of the Finance Advisory Group, Aubrey Curry, the secretary for finance, followed the decision quoted earlier. He said that the land had to be transferred to a charitable trust in Hong Kong. However, he felt that the persons proposed for the trust in Hong Kong looked like an ad hoc group rather than a properly formed trust and that they should be requested to constitute themselves as a proper legal trust with objectives similar to those of CWM before the land could be transferred to them. My argument, or lack of it, had a dramatic opening. I banged the table and said, "That's my money! I want it." After the hilarity had died down, I was asked to explain in clear, sober language what on earth I was on about. I argued that the Nethersole Hospital had done handsomely with the generosity of the colonial government in Hong Kong. The member church in Hong Kong had already received a building worth about 10 million pounds sterling, which it had sold. It used the proceeds to put up a new building in the heart of Kowloon, Hong Kong. Other assets belonging to the London Missionary Society had also been transferred to the church. The Nethersole Hospital was never part of the work of the church. If this had been the case, it too would have been transferred along with other assets belonging to the London Missionary Society. I then said that the land properly belongs to the whole community of the Council for World Mission and that it should be sold and the proceeds made available for its work. Silence ensued. Then one of the members, Richard Morgan, said in a quiet voice, "You know, I think the man is right." That was the beginning of the change in direction. With the advice of the Finance Advisory Group, the Council meeting in Jamaica in June 1993 decided to sell the land and bring the proceeds to London.

The whole procedure of getting the money to London was fraught. As Andrew Morton shows in his book, just the legal ramifications in claiming this property were themselves enormous. Negotiations took more than two years. Time and again I had to reflect on the way I had handled this matter. It was another firsthand experience of having to handle dishonest mammon.

Because during the time of the negotiations the value of the land was beginning to decline, it was agreed with the Nethersole Hospital Committee that the land would be sold and proceeds placed in escrow under the names of both CWM and Nethersole until the dispute was settled. The negotiating team did well to iron out the major differences with the Nethersole Hospital Committee. It was agreed that 22.5 percent of the proceeds would be placed in a CWM-Nethersole Trust Fund for the benefit of the Chinese in Hong Kong and the mainland of China, 12.5 percent would be given to the Nethersole Hospital

Committee for chaplaincy work in their hospital, and the balance of 65 percent would be brought to London for the work of the Council for World Mission.

When it was certain that the Council for World Mission would receive a substantial amount of money from the sale of land in Hong Kong, many of us began to worry about what this windfall could do to the identity and function of the Council for World Mission as a whole. Consequently, well before negotiations were concluded and the money came, the Executive Committee asked me to organize a theological and consultative process on how this money was to be received and used. The Executive Committee knew that we could have problems unless churches in the Council for World Mission were helped to deal with this resource in an informed way. Given the magnitude of the sum, it was quite a spiritual and theological challenge.

In August 1994, even before the sale of land in Hong Kong was accomplished, a small group of persons from churches in all the six regions together with an ecumenical participant met to discuss the implications of receiving this resource.

One person who was invited but could not attend was Bernard Thorogood, who had been a missionary of the London Missionary Society in the Pacific. He was later appointed general secretary of the old LMS/CWM and had then become the first general secretary of the newly constituted Council for World Mission in 1977. He was invited to give the Bible studies at the Pacific regional meeting of the Council for World Mission, which was also to meet at the same time in American Samoa. He was not sure which meeting I felt he should attend. I urged him to go to the meeting of the Pacific region because the region had specifically asked to have him. He then wrote to me saying that he was sorry to miss the meeting in London because he doubted that any other person in the group had the historical knowledge of the policies of the London Missionary Society, which the Council for World Mission had later adopted.

After hearing of the decisions made at the meeting, he wrote a personal letter to me saying that he was of the opinion that I was trying to create a policy out of an exception just to deal with this one case. He was clear that, following existing policy, the proceeds from the sale of the land should stay in Hong Kong. He contested my position that because the CWM church in Hong Kong was well endowed, the money should come for the common use of the community. He argued that if a church is to be disadvantaged because it is already rich, then the Council for World Mission as a community must also take over the debts of churches that were poor. He conceded, though, that sufficient thought had not gone into securing adequate financial resources for the work of the Council for World Mission. This was the first time that I became aware of the fact that there had been an actual policy decision on how all properties belonging to the London Missionary Society outside Britain had to be dealt with.

I may have acted shrewdly. But had I acted in a manner that was truthful in the way I had led the Council to make the decision in July 1993 without clearly advising the Council that such a decision would contravene the decision made in 1977? The question for me was whether a decision made in 1977 should be followed when the situation in 1993 was different. Not all churches had gained equally from the transfer of resources that the London Missionary Society had previously held outside Britain, because it depended on what the society actually held in a particular country. In fact, some had not gained at all. Maitland Evans, who was present at the Singapore consultation in 1975 and later at the meeting of the new Council in 1977, was a member of the group that met to decide on how the proceeds from the sale of land were to be used. He disagreed with Bernard Thorogood. He was of the opinion that past policies, however well intentioned at the time, should not be blindly followed but tested in every new situation. However, both of us were clear that the point Bernard Thorogood made about the situation of poorer churches had to be taken up.

The group that met in August 1994 made two basic points.

The first was theological. This amount is so large and so unexpected that it can only be called "a gift of grace":

> It must be understood and received as grace—grace in the theological sense as an undeserved gift from God. Having said that, we must also recognize the fact that where grace abounds temptation is also near. The temptation for misuse or selfish use occurs because the gift (grace) has to be used in a world system which is not compatible with the grace of God. It is a world system in which sin operates as domination—the exclusion and sacrifice of the excluded to maintain the status quo. Our responsibility is to use the grace received in a system of "dis-grace."[10]

The theological argument at this consultation was shaped by our ecumenical guest, Professor Julio de Santa Ana. By "system of dis-grace" he meant the global economic arrangement in which all facets of life are being integrated through the world market, and the consequent adverse impact this integration is having especially on the poor, both on poor countries and on poor people in all countries. Given this fact, such value on a piece of land was possible only in a global economic situation that is disgraceful. In other words, the windfall was clearly mammon—dishonest wealth. To label the windfall "a gift of grace" was not a theological legerdemain. It was a theological attempt to recognize the deceitful nature of money and to recover it for management in ways that make for truth in situations of "dis-grace."

Julio de Santa Ana stated the challenge for CWM in these words: "Why has CWM been called to receive this gift of grace? Is it because you have been faithful over a little that God is calling you to be faithful over much?"

Following this relabeling of windfall (unexpected bonanza) to gift of grace (an undeserved gift from God), the group then went on to say:

> The grace/gift given to CWM is not just an accident, but has a purpose. To receive this gift is to commit ourselves to the principles of partnership and stewardship...
>
> (i) This grace/gift challenges CWM to be clear about its identity and to be firm in its commitments—who we are and what is our mission.
>
> (ii) It calls us to greater responsibility and solidarity with those who have been wronged by the world system. We have to work at levelling the injustices through health services, education, etc.
>
> (iii) It demands more careful stewardship with clear information, analysis/discernment of the information, and priorities for action.
>
> (iv) It calls for a clear understanding of and responsibility for the power in our hands.[11]

In this sense, the grace was not so much a gift to CWM as a responsibility calling for stewardship. It was also agreed that, in taking responsibility for this money, the identity of CWM as a community of churches in mission and the basic principles of partnership, which were part of its ethos, should not be distorted. The challenge was, and still is, to manage dishonest wealth in a way that is concomitant with the way we manage the things that make for truth.

The second basic point, an ergo from this theological position, was that the bulk of the money had to be used for work outside CWM. CWM must manifest its character as a missionary organization and "be for others." The group recommended that only a small part of the resource be kept for the continuing work of CWM and the bulk of the resource be managed by three trusts independent of CWM but in which CWM persons should participate, so that CWM's mission concerns are not lost. The group recommended one trust for projects on economic empowerment; the second for ecumenical initiatives in common witness; and the third for work on frontiers of mission, especially in health and education.

The Executive Committee meeting in December 1994 received the report. Roderick Hewitt, who was then secretary for education in mission, persuaded those at the meeting that there was a problem in the report. The theological part and the part that recommends setting up three trusts outside CWM do not hang together. If the resource is not to be just for CWM's use and is a gift of grace to be used in situations of "dis-grace," then CWM could not shirk its missionary responsibility and pass the responsibility on to three trusts. It had to express its ecumenical character and commitments for going "beyond ourselves," which was the theme of the Council meeting in 1993. Reflecting later on what Roderick Hewitt said, I realized that handing the bulk of the money to three independent trusts would be one way, and an unsatisfactory way, of dealing with the seductive power of mammon. CWM had to grasp the nettle and manage the money shrewdly.

The Executive Committee accepted Hewitt's argument and included it as one of the recommendations to the six regional meetings of CWM churches, which were asked to discuss the report. I was asked to collate the regional responses for discussion at the Council meeting in July 1995.

In working through the reports, I found a remarkable convergence of ideas and concerns in the regional meetings that preceded the meetings of Council in 1995 and 1996. There were also significant differences.

1. All the regions accepted the theological section of the report of the group that met in August 1994. They affirmed that the new resource should be seen as grace—that is, an undeserved gift that CWM has the responsibility to steward and share.

2. Only the European and Caribbean regions agreed with the proposals of the group that met in August 1994 that the bulk of the resource, even the capital, should be placed in trusts outside CWM and be used "beyond ourselves," though they suggested other ways in which the various trusts could relate to one another and to CWM. East Asia made no comment on this matter.

Africa, the Pacific, and South Asia disagreed and pointed to the great needs of the CWM churches. They argued that "the needs of the children should be met first." South Asia and the Pacific even had proposals on how some part of the money should be divided out among the CWM churches.

3. There was general agreement that the management of the funds should be in the hands of CWM, and that churches, regions, and trusts,

if any, should be accountable to one another and to the Executive Committee/Council of CWM. The trust to be set up in Hong Kong was to be the only exception.

4. All the regions agreed that part of the resource should be used to support the existing work of CWM and any future expansion of its work (new initiatives), especially moves toward "regional empowerment."

5. The reports also asked that part of the resource be used to strengthen the evangelistic (mission) work of member churches. This would also include health (especially AIDS) programs.

6. The reports indicated that part of the income was to be used for self-reliance projects so that churches may move from dependence to independence and then to the interdependence of mature partnership in mission relationships. Human resource development and leadership training were also stressed.

7. A majority of the reports stressed the need for widening and strengthening ecumenical relationships locally, regionally, and globally.

In one way or another, the theological position and the attendant responsibilities advocated by the ad hoc group were picked up in regional discussions. There was also the tacit agreement that to move the major responsibility for managing the gift of grace to outside trusts would be an abdication of responsibility.

The problematic area of concern, advanced by three regions, was "that the needs of the children must be met first." It was another way of saying "charity begins at home." Could this lead to a theological distortion? Would this be an opening for the perils of dealing with mammon—dishonest wealth—to creep in? I phoned a church leader from South Asia who argued that each church should receive a million pounds. "Are you sure a million would do?" His response was contrite: "I only wanted to make a point, Preman!" The point was taken and eventually expressed in a way that was rather different.

There was a general discussion of how CWM was to deal with this gift of grace at the Council meeting in 1995. But with so much to be accomplished in a shortened meeting of Council, following the bicentenary celebrations of the founding of the London Missionary Society, it was decided to call an extraordinary meeting of Council in July 1996 to deal with this matter.

Decisions were made at the extraordinary meeting in the context of prayer and worship. My colleague, Francis Brienen, thoughtfully planned the worship around the theme of community. She involved members of Council in leading the worship and developing the theme both at morning and evening worship. The theme was also developed in the bible studies led by Professor Julio de Santa Ana.

Recommendations on the use of the money were discussed in small groups and in plenary. There was also time to study the document on CWM's understanding of mission, "Perceiving Frontiers, Crossing Boundaries," which was produced in 1995. Decisions took time. Every effort was made to reach a consensus on every decision. The moderator at that time, Mrs. Andrea Adams, ensured that no decision was rushed and no person or point of view was overlooked.

The first decision was a financial one, namely, to determine in pounds sterling what was CWM's share at the point of sale and what actually came to CWM after some two years. It was agreed that the actual amount from the proceeds of the sale was 87 million pounds and that the investment in Hong Kong after the sale had provided an additional 10 million pounds. So it was the amount realized in the investment of the proceeds from the sale that had to be used or divided out.

The second decision was that 5 percent of this amount should be set aside for ecumenical work. At least in a symbolic way, the needs of the children were not met first.

The next decision was, on the surface, a controversial one. It was decided that 2.5 million pounds should be divided equally between all CWM churches irrespective of the size or economic situation of the church. It was to be used by each church as it wished in its mission. Each church did receive an equal share, which was around 86,000 pounds, a little less than the amount suggested by my colleague from the South Asia region.

The most amount of time was spent on discussing what came to be called the Self-Support Fund. Initially, it was meant to help the poorer churches. In the course of the debate, Tony Burnham, the general secretary of the United Reformed Church in the United Kingdom, said that this fund must only be for churches in economically poor countries. Maitland Evans, general secretary of the United Church in Jamaica and the Cayman Islands, one of the poor churches, responded that if some churches excluded themselves they would break the solidarity and partnership in CWM. Consequently, the discussion moved to find a method to allocate the fund proportionately. Later on, three factors were used as financial indicators—the economic situation of the country, the size of the church, and how many national churches constituted a church—that is, the transnational churches. The decision that all churches should benefit from the Self-Support Fund was not only a recognition of solidarity and partnership, it was also a recognition of the fact that in the very midst of wealth there is poverty.

The decision to divide a certain sum of money equally among the members was a way of asserting that all the churches in CWM are in a partnership and should be treated equally. The next decision took into account economic advantage and disadvantage for a more equitable distribution of economic support. Together, the two decisions represented a way of asserting partnership in the context of economic globalization.

In the private conversations leaders of well-to-do churches had with me, it was interesting that some of them had real difficulties coming to terms with aspects of these two decisions. Not only did the decisions regarding the Self-Support Fund and the equal division of 2.5 million pounds among all the churches stand on its head usual distinctions between rich and poor—the rich give, the poor receive—it also pressed upon rich churches the need to come to terms with receiving from the poor, for the poor had to give up a share for the rich to receive.

The points made in the regional reports were addressed not only at the 1996 Council meeting but also in subsequent meetings of Council and Executive Committee in 1997 and 1998. More resources were provided for the existing work of CWM, especially for regional empowerment, and for new programs such as the International Network of Theological Enquiry (NOTE). The 1997 Council meeting set up the Program on Mission Development and Education and the Mission Programme Support Fund to be used by churches for their mission work. Nine million pounds was allocated using the same formula as the Self-Support Fund to support mission programs of churches over a three- to five-year period. The amount placed in the Self-Support Fund was increased from 7 million to 10.5 million pounds. These increases were made while maintaining the "real value" of the investment of 87 million pounds.

Perhaps it was right that the mission of the churches in the Council for World Mission and strengthening their financial base for work should have received primary attention. Once this was done, it was possible to launch into the area of ecumenical relationships through which CWM as Council and as churches could express the ecumenical character and commitment of CWM, which found expression in the 1993 Council theme, "Beyond Ourselves." It was at that Council that the decision was made to sell the land in Hong Kong and realize the money for CWM. It was this theme that was taken as an unspoken framework for the theological discussions at the meeting in August 1994. Besides setting aside 5 percent from the 10 million pounds for ecumenical projects, very little else was done.

I was for the most part a listener, no doubt an interested listener, to the arguments and the decisions that were made at the meetings from 1996 onward that are given above. Those decisions having been made, the Executive Committee asked me to provide clearer leadership in helping CWM to express its ecumenical character and commitments. To do this, I provided two papers on the theme "Beyond Ourselves," which led to decisions from the 1996 Council onwards.[12] I give these in summary form accenting the area of relationship. In all of these there was an investment of money and time.

Ecumenical Relationships of CWM Churches. This area of work was set up following reminders from several Council and Executive Committee meetings that special attention should be paid to CWM churches forming ecumenical relationships locally, regionally, and globally. Money is set aside every year for projects and programs in which CWM churches work together with other churches, with other religious and secular organizations, to put into practice a multifaceted or holistic understanding of mission, which the Council for World Mission declared as its basis.

Already there are some interesting developments. The African CWM churches are coming together to work jointly with other churches in the region to combat HIV/AIDS in that continent. The Christian Medical Commission of the World Council of Churches has promised to help the churches plan their campaign of education and counseling on HIV/AIDS. The African churches have also agreed to support the Africa Reconstruction Programme launched at the Assembly of the World Council of Churches at Harare, Zimbabwe (December 1998). This may be the beginning of a new style of mission work in the Council for World Mission.

The Presbyterian Church of Taiwan has persuaded the CWM churches in the East Asia region to work together on peace and security in Northeast Asia. This is to be done with other churches in the region with the support of the World Council of Churches and the Christian Conference of Asia.

There are two principles in this style of ecumenical work. First, to begin a project by first forming a comprehensive ecumenical coalition to plan and execute a mission program seldom succeeds. A particular church or group of churches must take the initiative, get moving, and then invite others to join in. CWM churches are encouraged to be the initiators. Second, CWM, both as Council and as churches, does not have to duplicate what is being done well by global and regional ecumenical organizations. CWM churches can support the work being done by these, draw from their expertise, and work jointly with them.

Economic Justice for the Poor. This is an area of work that was recommended by the group that met in August 1994 to advise on the use of the financial resources realized from the sale of land in Hong Kong. The major initiative in this area has been to form a partnership with Oikocredit, formerly the Ecumenical Development Co-operative

Society. Oikocredit, founded by the churches in the World Council of Churches, is a lending instrument of the churches and is run by professionals. Through low-cost loans to small projects and by facilitating credit unions, it has translated issues of economic justice into action. At a time when the world market and forces behind economic globalization, including the International Monetary Fund with its structural adjustment policies, are excluding and sacrificing many, it offers an alternative credit arrangement. It has a loan repayment record of 90 percent because it allows the borrower to set the terms of repayment and is willing to reschedule debts when necessary. In more ways than one, it has also been an instrument for hope in situations of economic crisis. Many small economic projects all over the world owe much to the economic support and financial expertise that Oikocredit has provided.

The Council meeting in 1999 decided to invest 5 million pounds in Oikocredit. After extensive discussions with Oikocredit, it has been decided that part of this money should be invested as shares in the names of CWM churches. Another part will be used by Oikocredit to set up local currency risk funds in countries where it has become almost impossible to repay loans in hard currency. The balance will be used by Oikocredit to support other projects on economic justice for the poor.

CWM is now relating also to the Ecumenical Loan Fund (ECLOF), a parallel ecumenical instrument, which also provides loans, not grants, and advice for local development projects that support the struggle of the poor for economic justice.

Ecumenical Partnerships. As a symbol of CWM's admission that it is but a small part of the world church and is indebted to the ecumenical movement for providing concepts on mission that it has tried to put into practice, it supports the work of the World Council of Churches and the World Alliance of Christian Communication with annual block grants. In addition, grants are made annually to churches outside the Council for World Mission and other ecumenical bodies to support their mission programs. Preference is given to projects on justice, peace, and the integrity of creation, including health and education, new ventures in mission thought and action, and experiments in ecumenical cooperation that may include other faiths. This is an opportunity for CWM not only to spread its ethos and mission principles more widely but also to cultivate several ecumenical relationships on which CWM, as both Council and churches, can build as needed.

Partnerships with Churches and Mission Organizations. At present there are partnership relationships with the China Christian Council, the Uniting Church in Australia, the Presbyterian Church in the

Republic of Korea, and the United Church of Canada. There is an intention also to relate to the Methodist Conference in Argentina. CWM also relates to the Caribbean North American Council on Mission (CANACOM), Cevaa, and UEM. The purpose of these relationships is for enrichment and mutual challenge. In relating both to individual churches and to mission organizations, CWM seeks partners who will both contribute to and receive from CWM's thinking and practice of partnership in mission. So the specific reason and basis for each relationship is worked out on a case-by-case basis. What contribution—in mission practice and thinking—does the church or organization bring? How can CWM contribute to and cooperate with this church or organization in its mission? After a time, the relationship is evaluated.

Without a doubt, all these areas of mission have been possible because of the influx of new financial resources. CWM has trod a difficult and at times dangerous path avoiding the pitfalls that the lure of mammon always poses. It has attempted to address, as best as it could, the consequences of a prevailing economic system and its values enshrined in the processes of economic globalization. It is no more than a test case of what is and is not possible in the sharing of money in mission. In that way, it presents a specific instance and experience of dealing with the problematic nature of money and the difficulties inherent in the sharing of financial resources in mission.

The broad vision for partnership in mission made possible through the sharing of financial resources will be tested over time. When resources shrink, as they will in times of economic crisis, will CWM revert to being a community of self-interest? Will the lure of mammon be too strong to resist? Will CWM succumb and betray "the things that make for truth"? Only history can judge whether CWM has indeed met the challenge Julio de Santa Ana posed: "Why has CWM been called to receive this gift of grace? Is it because you have been faithful over a little that God is calling you to be faithful over much?" These questions will continue to challenge, perhaps even taunt, CWM. At the end of the day, was it windfall or grace?

6

Christian Mission Today: Reexamining Some Assumptions

In the previous chapters we concentrated on the ingredients necessary for the formation of a missionary community that could be the bearer of Christian mission today. A key ingredient in the formation of such a community is the way in which power is shared, not as a concession from those who previously held power in all its forms but as a result of the challenge of the powerless. To keep the discussion on the ground, we interacted with the mission thinking and practice in the Council for World Mission. The intention was not to present the Council for World Mission as the most adequate model for Christian mission today. It may be, but that is not the point. The intention was to use the Council for World Mission as a laboratory in which many of the ideas arising out of the challenges posed for Christian mission today have been tested and are still being tested both in theory and in practice.

In so doing, we have also explored several perspectives on mission, some of which press against, if not actually transgress, the borders of a model of mission the era of modern Western missions has bequeathed to us. The prevailing concern in that missionary model is to view the task for Christian mission as proclaiming the gospel to the people of other faiths (*ethne*) who need to hear the good news of Jesus Christ and convert to faith in him as Lord and Savior. That model does not preclude works of charity for the underprivileged and suffering people, but it does not reflect in its later manifestations—when it became a partner willingly or unwillingly in the colonial enterprise and with political power—the solidarity expressed through compassion that was a characteristic of the earlier period of modern Western missionary service. Looking at Jesus' ministry with the *ochlos*, it was possible not only to discern the nature of his solidarity expressed through compassion, which was characteristic of the earlier period of modern missions, but also to see something of the way in which that solidarity in a reverse flow helped to shape the Messiahship of Jesus, not as king but as the Suffering Servant of God. This is the model of sending and receiving in missionary service that needs to be recovered today if Christian mission is to move from an attitude of crusade and conquest to one of service in solidarity with the poor or the disadvantaged. The ethos of such missionary service is shaped in the service itself as we interact with the *ochlos* and meet the Suffering Servant of God who goes before us to Galilee (Mk. 16:7), the home of those who are on the margins of society. This ethos ought to inform not only the sharing of people in mission but also the sharing of money in mission. We will look at the implications of this understanding of missionary service in chapter 8, as we test a different model and understanding for Christian mission today.

Before doing that, however, more needs to be said and done in relating the *laos* to the *ethne* that goes beyond the simplistic assumption that the *ethne* are "unenlightened" or "unsaved." This is a matter that has not been dealt with at any depth in either the mission thinking and practice of the Council for World Mission or its missionary forebears. If we are to come up with a model for Christian mission today that is satisfying, that issue also needs to be faced anew at a time when religious pluralism is a fact and the vision of "the evangelization of the world in our generation" has not been realized and is likely never to be realized. Before proposing and testing a model or paradigm for Christian mission in our time, we will examine some of the assumptions that underlie the use of the terms *mission* and *evangelism* and critique attitudes that prevail in relating to people of other faiths (*ethne*), all of which prevent us from entering a new and exciting period for Christian mission in our time.

Mission Reexamined

In his book *Transforming Mission: Paradigm Shifts in Theology of Mission*, David Bosch states, "The Christian faith I submit is intrinsically missionary." He then goes on to say that other religions, notably Islam and Buddhism, and also a variety of ideologies, such as Marxism, exhibit this characteristic. Quoting Max Stackhouse, he describes these religions and presumably also ideologies as those that hold to some great "unveiling" of ultimate truth believed to be of universal import. For Christians, God's salvific plan expressed in God's reign/realm is for all humanity and is intended for the ends of the earth. Bosch then goes on to assert, "Christianity is missionary, by its very nature, or it denies its very *raison d'etre*."[1]

In his book, *A History of Christian Missions,* Stephen Neil makes the same point but is clearer in saying why some religions are missionary and others are not, or better, why some religions are more missionary than others. His observation is that most religions are local, even tribal. Neil holds that the statement in Micah 4:5, "For all the peoples walk, each in the name of its god, but we will walk in the name of the LORD our God forever and ever," is true of all religions. Each city has its temple and its god. "God" is territorial (2 Kings 5:15–19).

If a religion is territorial, then when does it become missionary? Neil's answer is that this happens when there is a founding personality who believes that he or she has received a revelation or has been enlightened, and that this revelation or enlightenment is of universal significance. The disciples of the founder are then commissioned to go out and proclaim the message. In the process of doing this, Buddhism has remained by and large an Eastern religion; Islam is largely Middle Eastern and North African and has moved from Morocco to China and into Indonesia. Neil then goes on to say, "Christianity alone has succeeded in making itself a universal religion. Something that has never happened before in the history of the world." According to Neil, it is this phenomenon that Archbishop William Temple described in 1942 as "the great new fact of our time."[2]

In different yet related ways, reflecting understandings of mission that have been with us for some time, both Bosch and Neil argue for the preeminence of the Christian faith. A critical reflection on what they say could provide us with a good entry into rethinking Christian mission for today.

Today, not just Christianity, Islam, and Buddhism but all religions are missionary to a lesser or greater degree. So Bosch's statement, "Christianity is missionary, by its very nature, or it denies its very *raison d'etre,*" is not saying very much. That may be said in varying degrees about all religions. All religions could become missionary when a religious personage, or founder, gives it a missionary push. A good example from outside Christianity is the Ramakrishna mission founded by Swami Vivekananda in the forest of religions called Hinduism. The Ramakrishna mission has spread to many parts of the world.

Neil's assertion that only Christianity has become a world religion and therefore has a certain claim to preeminence also does not hold water. The rapid spread of Islam as a world religion not only in Africa and Asia but also in Europe is a case in point. Just to get things in perspective, there are more Muslims in Britain than Methodists! The Congregationalists and Reformed lost out quite some time ago. To be sure, this increase in Europe is not just through migrations of Muslims from other parts of the world. Quite a number of the indigenous people in Europe are turning to Islam. It is estimated that in the year 2000, 32.3 percent of the world's population were Christians of all varieties and 19.2 percent of the population were Muslim. Although as a world religion Christianity is shrinking in numbers, especially in the West, with some modest gains in certain East Asian and African countries, Islam is growing rapidly all over the world.

Religions become missionary not only when a religious figure gives that religion a missionary push but also when it has to deal with an aggressively missionizing religion. The renaissance of Buddhism in Ceylon in the nineteenth century was in large measure due to the aggressive missions of Christian missionaries from Britain and a colonial government that refused to protect Buddhism as the religion of the state. Anagarika Dharmapala, a Sinhala Buddhist, and Colonel Olcott, an American Buddhist who came to Ceylon, led a movement of Buddhist resistance. In this process, Buddhism in Ceylon also became missionary, contesting the religious truth claims of Christianity and sending out missionaries to other countries. In some ways this may be seen as a political response of a religion to the manifestation of religious power by a foreign religion. The same thing could happen under the threat, real or imagined, of religions that are branded as foreign. This is the opinion the Hindutva movement in India has of Islam and Christianity. The Hindutva movement, which undergirds the present government in India, is also missionary and attempts to reclaim in India those who have left the Hindu fold to become Muslims or Christians.

Neil's progression of religion from tribal to missionary also needs to be qualified. Besides being missionary, at the same time, to a lesser or greater degree, all religions exhibit tribal or quasi-tribal characteristics. At one end of the spectrum is Zoroastrianism. To be a true Parsi, one also has to be a Zoroastrian. So in this instance it is not geography, as Neil mentions, but ethnicity that defines the tribal character of Zoroastrianism. At the other end of the spectrum is Christianity. One cannot just be a Christian. One has to have a Christian brand name. So in this instance it is neither geography nor race, but a particular creedal or denominational factor, that is determinative.

Religious self-definition, arising especially in the context of mission, in one way or another asserts why a religion is unique and therefore exclusive. This self-understanding then leads to various forms of intolerance. The two monotheistic universal religions, Christianity and Islam, are not only intolerant of religions without but also of sects within. There are constant clashes, for instance, between *Sunni* and *Shi'ite* Muslims in Pakistan. The unresolved conflict between Iran (predominantly *Shi'ite*) and Iraq (predominantly *Sunni*) is another case in point. In Christianity, besides denominational rivalries, creeds of various forms are used to define the parameters of the faith. Incantations against so-called heretics are also rife. Every time there is a new expression or a reinterpretation of the Christian faith, especially in the Third World, there are cries that it is "syncretism." Fundamentalism is another expression of intolerance of variety. Christianity's attitude to adherents of other religions is usually "convert or be damned." To be sure, not just a few but all of us so-called Christians exude an exclusivist stench.

All religions, whether they tend toward the missionary pole or the tribal pole, seek to have a growing number of adherents or they will die out.

For tribal religions, procreation is the basic answer. If the tribe dies, the religion also dies, so it is important to ensure the survival of the tribe. This aspiration is exhibited in various ways. Brahmanism attempts to maintain the purity of the caste, especially in marriage. In Malaysia, the term *Bhumiputra*, which literally means "child of the soil," is reserved for Malay Muslims; their well-being is ensured in various ways. The Russian Orthodox Church attempts to preserve itself by trying to keep out other Christian missionaries, especially those from Korea. The Russian Orthodox Church makes the tacit assumption, now often expressed, that Russian Orthodoxy is the only proper religion for Russians. Judaism, particularly in Israel, exhibits its tribal character by taking care of the Jews and their right to exist and expresses this tribal character through the ideology of Zionism. In these cases there is no real intention to propagate "the faith" to maintain or increase numbers. Procreation takes care of the problem. Maintaining the purity of the faith or religion, however defined, is the main intention. The violent and demonic expression of this tendency is "ethnic cleansing."

For the so-called universal religions or missionary religions—that is, those that advocate a particular way and understanding of salvation as normative for all—mission is the way for ensuring that a religion does not die out. In other words, mission is the means by which these religions exhibit their basic biological desire to procreate or propagate, without which a religion will die out.[3] The use of any means possible to accomplish this task is symptomatic of this anxiety. Mission in this sense is the desire to convert, to draw others into the religion.

I find that I am not the only person making these observations about religions and mission. After coming to these conclusions about mission, I came across a statement of M. R. Spindler, who refers to a remark of Otto Haendler that "the missionary drive" is inherent in the nature of the church: The church is a living organism involved in a process of shrinkage and growth, in which reproduction is inherently necessary because it is by definition an integral part of every vital process, both literally and figuratively."[4]

We have started with a phenomenological approach to mission, rather than a theological approach, just to be sure that we understand basic motives. Without such an understanding we can easily theologize approaches to mission that have their basis in basic human desires and insecurities. These are the emotional and ideological baggage we all tend to carry into the understanding and practice of Christian mission.

When we begin in this way, with the religious *angst* of religions, we note problems that we must seek to avoid. One is the challenge for Christian mission to maintain its universal character without being triumphalistic or militaristic. The other is the challenge to express universal truth as we have come to know it through Jesus Christ and the traditions of the Christian faith without being tribalistic and intolerant of other understandings of salvation, as found both in expressions of the Christian faith other than our own and in other faiths.

Evangelism Reexamined

It is against this background and analysis of mission that we approach the troublesome term *evangelism,* which in many ways expresses the biological urge of mission. Many Christians would hold that without a commitment to evangelism, one could not even be a Christian.

In a lecture delivered to the assembly of the East Asia Christian Conference in Bangkok, Thailand (1968), the Orthodox theologian Paul Verghese, later Metropolitan Paulose Mar Gregorius of the Malankara Syrian Orthodox Church in India, drew attention both to the questionable theology that underlies the term *evangelism* and to its problematic location in biblical witness.

One of the problems with the term is that it is more and more being solidly identified with the kind of instinctive or natural mission that all missionary religions exhibit. It reflects precisely those characteristics of religion that Christianity in its denominational form (is there any other form?) also has, namely, a pathological desire for human procreation in religious guise. In this case the gospel is used for propaganda, as an instrument to accomplish a human goal. Mission as evangelism is judged by human standards. How many persons have we added to a particular brand of Christianity? That is the normal test. The whole purpose of evangelism thus understood is to create more people like us, whatever that "us" is.

Following Paul Verghese on this matter, the second problem is that the term is not biblical. This may come as something of a shock to many Christians. The Greek word *euangelizma*, from which we would get "evangelism," is not found in the Bible. To look at a parallel, the Greek word *baptizma*, from which we get "baptism," is found in the Bible. The verb *euangelizomai*, "to proclaim good news," is biblical and is the term dictionaries of the Bible point to as the basis for *evangelism.* However, there are difficulties inherent in deriving the noun from this verb because, unless great care is exercised, the process tends to conflate the activity of proclamation, the content of the proclamation, and even the expected results of the proclamation.[5]

This tendency and the resulting chaos in understanding what *evangelism* means is evident, for instance, in the table of meanings Bosch gives in which the terms *mission* and *evangelism* are either distinguished or related.

He shows that after a rather checkered early history, the verb *evangelize* and its derivatives *evangelism* and *evangelization* have become very prominent "since 1970 in Protestant (ecumenical and evangelical) as well as in Roman Catholic circles." Despite the wide use of these terms, Bosch points to the uncertainty of meaning, saying that David B. Barrett lists seventy-nine definitions of *evangelize* and its derivatives to which many more could be added. The confusion or controversy prevails both in "differences (if any) between 'evangelism' and 'mission' and the scope or range of evangelism."[6]

Let us select a few of the examples Bosch gives to illustrate this confusion and note the questionable assumptions that underlie them.

1. One of the distinctions made between mission and evangelism is that mission is addressed to the so-called non-Christians overseas, whereas evangelism has to do with reclaiming lapsed Christians in Western countries.

But this distinction breaks down when the assumption that the West was originally Christian and has now lapsed is found not to be strictly true. Christianity was the state religion in many European countries, so it was usually the rich who went to church. The evangelical revival in Europe was aimed at the common people—an affirmation of their worth in God's eyes. This process never totally succeeded. It was confronted with the process of secularization and secular ideologies, which were working with the Enlightenment motto "dare to think." These began to free many realms of life from religious or ecclesiastical control. People in the West were challenged to throw away the shackles of the church as an oppressive instrument in the hands of a few privileged people. So there are as many "unreached" people in Europe as there are elsewhere.

2. Another way of understanding evangelism is to define it narrowly as the real, if not the only, missionary task of the church. This was the response of evangelicals to the use of the term *mission,*

especially in Ecumenical and Roman Catholic thinking, to refer to an ever widening number of Christian responsibilities in relating to the world. Here are two of the several evangelical reactions Bosch quotes: "Historically the mission of the church is evangelism alone" (Arthur P. Johnston). "Theologically mission was evangelism by every means possible" (Donald A. McGavran). Evangelicals continue to use *evangelism* in preference to *mission* to combat what they believe to be the dilution of mission to denote many Christian activities. Their argument would be, If everything is mission, then nothing is mission.

To recognize this position as valid is to define *evangelism* ever so narrowly, and it would signify no more than the missionary drive endemic to all religions.

3. According to Bosch, over the last four decades or so, *mission* and *evangelism* have been used synonymously. He quotes the former general secretary of the World Council of Churches, Philip Potter, as saying that mission, evangelism, and witness are as a rule interchangeable concepts. A Roman Catholic memorandum says, "Mission, evangelization and witness are nowadays often used by Catholics as synonymous."

This is needless conflation, and perhaps even confusion.

4. Finally, the terms *evangelism* and *evangelization* started replacing *mission* because the term *mission* is so closely identified with the colonial period and the crusade type of mission that certainly in the Americas wreaked havoc among native populations.[7]

The problem in replacing mission, however badly practiced, with evangelism is that whereas mission has biblical roots, the biblical roots of evangelism have not been as clear as many would hold. It is also to be noted that evangelism is a latecomer. Thomas Thangaraj quotes Kenneth Cracknell, who has this to say:

> The terms "evangelism" and "evangelization" are comparative late-comers in Christian vocabulary. Rare indeed are the sightings of either term before the mid-nineteenth century. An evangelist was one of the writers of the four Gospels or a title of an office in the early church, and that virtually was it![8]

David Bosch goes on to list some eighteen constructive ways in which the term *evangelism* may be understood. But the problem with the term remains, largely because of the way it is understood and used. Because it has no precise biblical connotation, it is so easy to make it mean things that are possibly even against the Bible. A good example is the linking of evangelism with church growth, which is how it is mostly understood today. This is a modern heresy that uses language such as "reaching the unreached" and "church planting" to control the meaning of evangelism.[9]

To get a better understanding of the word *evangelism,* we need to deal in a more discriminating way with the biblical evidence. As we noted earlier, the noun form *euangelizma* (cf. *baptizma*), from which we could get the word *evangelism,* is not used in the Bible. As Bosch points out, English translations of the Bible also do not use words such as *evangelize* or *evangelism.* The noun *euangelion* is translated either as "gospel" or "the good news," and the verb *euangelizesthai/euangelizein* as "to proclaim the gospel or the good news."

Not having a clear Greek or Hebrew equivalent to a theological term is not in itself a problem. We use quite a number of theological terms that are not in the Bible. For instance, the word *mission* is not there, but the concept of a sending or missionary God who sends the Son, who in turn sends his disciples as apostles, is there (cf. Jn. 20:21). So it is possible to root the term *mission* in its biblical moorings and then explain it in modern settings in which mission takes place. So too, the word *trinity* is not there in the Bible, but the concept of the triune God with subtle distinctions between the three persons of the Trinity is there. We need to engage in a similar exercise with the word *evangelism,* for which the basis is the verb usually translated "to take or to proclaim the good news."

To clear out the needless encrustations and theological misunderstandings this term creates, let us look at the arguments of John R. W. Stott, himself an evangelical who is committed to evangelism as the primary function of mission.

In his address to the International Congress on World Evangelization at Lausanne (July 1974),[10] he roots evangelism in the biblical usage of the verb. He identifies two secular or common uses of this verb in the Bible. Gabriel announces to Zechariah the good news that his wife Elizabeth is to have a son (Lk. 1:19). Timothy brings to Paul the good news about the Thessalonians' faith and love (1 Thess. 3:6). But the common use of the verb "relates to the Christian good news." Even when the verb is used absolutely, as in "and there they evangelized" (Acts 14:7, Stott's translation of the Greek text), Stott points out, "there is no mention whether the word that was 'evangelized' was believed, or whether the inhabitants of the towns and villages 'evangelized' were converted." He then goes on to say, "To evangelize in biblical usage does not mean to win converts (as it usually does when we use the word) but simply to announce the Good News irrespective of results." Stott quotes with approval J. I. Packer's criticism of the opening statement of the Archbishops' Committee of Enquiry into the Evangelistic Work of the Church (1919), which says, "To evangelize is so to present Christ Jesus in the power of the Holy Spirit that men shall come to put their trust in God through him." Packer's quarrel is with the words "so to present Christ," which is to define evangelism in terms of results.

Stott goes on to say, "But to evangelize is not to preach so that something happens. Of course, the objective is that something will happen, namely, that people will respond and believe. Nevertheless, biblically speaking, to evangelize is to proclaim the Gospel, whether anything happens or not."

To add to what Stott says, results are God's business. As Paul states, "I planted, Apollos watered, but God gave the growth. So neither the one who plants nor the one who waters is anything, but only God who gives the growth" (1 Cor. 3:6–7). Even the most evangelical of all New Testament books, the Acts of the Apostles, which is concerned with the growth and expansion of the church, is quite clear in saying, "And day by day the Lord added to their number those who were being saved" (Acts 2:47).

Hans-Ruedi Weber, a former missionary in Indonesia and later director for biblical reflection at the WCC, in an article titled "God's Arithmetic," stands the usual understanding of evangelism on its head. He remarks that if evangelism were indeed true, it would lay before people not only the offer of salvation but also the costliness of discipleship. This would result not in human arithmetic but God's arithmetic for measuring success. There may be a shrinking rather than an increase in numbers. Weber says,

> God's purpose is the salvation of all, of the total cosmos, yet, in order to achieve this, God elects, calls and converts a few. This began with Abraham. God judges all (Genesis 12:3a); moreover he wants all to be blessed (Genesis 12:3b). To this end he called and sent on a mission one man.[11]

Weber's point is that God is not interested in vast numbers but rather in the quality of the few who are chosen to be instruments of God's mission. As Kenneth Cracknell once said, "God is concerned with a few who will be the salt of the earth and not with our concern to build pillars of salt!"

Using the biblical evidence to argue that evangelism has to do with proclamation regardless of results may also be insufficient. As William J. Abraham points out in his article "A Theology of Evangelism," the evangelistic picture in the early church includes the presence and activity of evangelists:

> They represent those persons who did work similar to that of the apostles. That is, proclaimed the gospel and established converts in the faith in Christian communities, but they were naturally distinguished from the apostles in that they did not have that unique relationship to the risen Lord that was central to the work of the twelve and Paul.

Abraham argues that Christian nurture was as integral to evangelism as proclamation, "even though that history is far from uniform." He states:

> It is clear that in the patristic period evangelism included the formation of Christians; it was not confined merely to proclamation. This is borne out by the actual work of evangelists when they travelled into new territory. (See Eusebius, *Ecclesiastical History* 5.10.2). It is also confirmed by the extensive use of individual and corporate spiritual direction focused on the incorporation of converts into the church and into the life of faith. Especially interesting, with respect to corporate spiritual direction, is the development of the catechumenate. Considerable care was taken to ensure that seekers really knew the gospel for themselves and to see that they were well grounded in the basic content and practices of the faith.[12]

As Abraham points out, this more complete understanding of the role of evangelism dropped out when Christianity became the official religion of the Roman Empire and the church could not cope with the inrush of people into the church. However, a case has to be made for recovering this understanding of evangelism for two main reasons.

First, conversion to faith in Jesus Christ is not a once-for-all event that can prompt a glib answer to the question, "Are you saved?" Rather, conversion has to do with growth in one's faith. It takes time. People come to God much more gradually, and it takes nurture groups and other forms of support to help people attain maturity in their faith.

The second reason, related to the first, is that conversion as a change of direction in one's life is to be open to the reign/realm of God. Jesus as the Messiah, the crucified and risen One, is the content of the gospel. As Mark puts it, "Jesus came to Galilee, proclaiming the good news of God, and saying, 'The time is fulfilled, and the kingdom of God has come near; repent, and believe in the good news'" (Mk. 1:14–15). To paraphrase what Mark is saying, in Jesus the good news of the reign/realm of God is a reality. It is touchable. So turn around (repent) and receive it.

Implied in this paraphrase are two important points. First, as George R. Hunsberger notes in his article "Is There a Biblical Warrant for Evangelism?"

> In the Gospels, the most repeated and emphatic verbs directing our response to the reign of God are "to receive" and "to enter." They come at times intertwined: "Truly I say to you, whoever does not receive the Kingdom of God like a

child shall not enter it" (Luke 18:17). These two verbs represent two image clusters that, taken together, provide a portrait of the identity of a Christian community and the nature of its mission.[13]

In other words, as Hunsberger points out, expressions such as "building the kingdom" or "extending the kingdom," which in various ways betray an imperial or even a triumphalistic approach to evangelism, should be bracketed out.

The second point is that once mission/evangelism takes the reign/realm of God as its central concern, an important and required change in mission thinking ensues. To understand the implications of this orientation in a brief way, we turn to the writing of J. C. Hoekendijk, a Dutch missiologist, whose central concern was to recover the task of evangelism from the hands of those who equated the purpose of evangelism with church growth.

Hoekendijk is clear that the preoccupation with numbers is a kind of creeping Christian crypto-colonialism that is desirous of trying to reestablish Christendom. He argues that church-centered mission is opposed to kingdom-centered mission, which is to announce the breaking in of God's reign through the resurrection of the crucified Messiah.[14] Basing his argument on the witness of the Old Testament, Hoekendijk takes away the human agency from evangelism and asserts that it is

> the Messiah who is the evangelist. Only to His power and His authority will men (sic!) surrender...The great commission in Matthew XXVIII is a reference to Daniel VII [verse 13: "There was given him dominion and glory and a kingdom that all people should serve him."] Now, after the Resurrection, *now* only, Jesus says—all power is given unto Me in Heaven and in earth. Go therefore and make the heathen my disciples. Now the last days have dawned on you, you have entered the Messianic era, now you walk in the midst of the signs of the coming glory...And one of the decisive signs of the time...is that the Gospel of the Kingdom shall be preached in all the world for a witness to all heathen, and then shall the end come (cf. Matthew XXIV:14).

For Hoekendijk, the Messiah is not only the evangelist but also "the subject of evangelism." It is to announce the fact that the victory has already been won and that

> He will establish the shalom. And shalom is much more than personal salvation. It is at once peace, integrity, community, harmony and justice...The Messiah is the prince of shalom...

Evangelism can be nothing but the realization of hope, a function of expectancy. Throughout the history of the Church, wherever this hope became once more the dominant note of Christian life an outburst of evangelistic zeal followed...

Hoekendijk is clear that evangelism is not propaganda. Underlying evangelism is this metaphor: "Unless a grain of wheat fall into the ground and die, it brings forth no fruit." He then has a telling comment on the nature of the Christian community (*koinonia*) as the place where the shalom is already lived:

The Christian community, therefore, is (or should be) an open community, open to everyone who has become a partaker of the same shalom. In practice this is not the case. In an unconscious way the national churches have become closed, because they related Christian community and nationalism too exclusively, and in the West the churches have become class-churches, because they identified themselves too uncritically with one special group of society. It is nonsense to call the churches to evangelism, if we do not call them simultaneously to a radical revision of their life and a revolutionary change of their structure.[15]

Lesslie Newbigin, an English missionary who was a bishop in the Church of South India and was actively involved in evangelism, helps us to develop what Hoekendijk has to say. After his return to England from missionary service, he was invited to give a series of Bible studies on "Mission in Christ's Way" at a synod of the Church of South India. After first rejecting the equation between evangelism and successful sales tactics, he observes, with Acts 1:8 as a basis, "Please note that it is a promise not a command. It is not: 'You must go and be witnesses'; it is 'The Holy Spirit will come, and you will be witnesses.' There is a vast difference between these two."[16] To clinch his argument, Newbigin observes, with regard to Paul:

It is, is it not, a striking fact that in all his letters to the churches Paul never urges on them the duty of evangelism. He can rebuke, remind, exhort his readers about faithfulness to Christ in many matters. But he is never found exhorting them to be active in evangelism...There is an inner constraint: the love of Christ constrains him. But he does not lay this constraint upon the consciences of his readers. Mission, in other words, is gospel and not law; it is the overflow of a great gift, not the carrying of a great burden. It is the fulfilment of a promise: "You shall be my witnesses, when the Holy Spirit comes upon you."[17]

Evangelism is not about increasing numbers, but the proclamation of the good news of what God has done in Jesus Christ regardless of results (Stott). If it is true to the gospel, evangelism will lay before people the costliness of discipleship and may even result in a reduction of numbers. God's purpose is for the redemption of the whole world for which purpose God chooses and calls a few (Weber). Evangelism is not a hit-and-run matter. "Evangelism needs to be construed as a polymorphous ministry aimed at initiating people into the kingdom of God. To accomplish this will require not only proclamation of the gospel but also instruction in the faith" (Abraham).[18] Evangelism is not propaganda. At its best, evangelism is the announcement that the victory has already been won in Christ and thus projects hope (Hoekendijk). Evangelism is not a test of faithfulness. Neither is it a command. It is the receiving and sharing in joy of a great gift (Newbigin). In different ways, these missionaries and missiologists question the use of the term *evangelism* to express the activity that arises from the anxiety of Christian groups to gather adherents to their particular religious groups.

What seems clear from this examination of the term *evangelism* is that the purpose of mission has to move away from a preoccupation with results and a growth in numbers if Christian mission is to have as its central concern God's mission in the world. That concern requires a broader framework for mission that is centered on the reign/realm of God rather than on the growth of the church. Evangelistic activity should be placed and practiced within God's mission.

It is inevitable either that the terms *mission* and *evangelism* will continue to be used interchangeably or that *evangelism* will be reserved for the verbal presentation of the good news and perhaps given a certain preeminence. Our argument is that evangelism, as reinterpreted above, should inform all mission activity, which in every way possible attempts to communicate with hope and joy the good news of what God has done in Jesus Christ and continues to do through the Holy Spirit.

This position runs counter to the assumption that the primary and perhaps only goal of Christian mission is the conversion of the nations to the Christian religion. Buttressing this assumption is a particular reading of church history, which we will now reexamine and offer another interpretation that will open us to a different model or paradigm for Christian mission today.

Mission History Reexamined

Our intention in reexamining mission history is not to give another recital of it, but to evaluate the adequacy of a particular perspective from which much of our mission histories are told. There is a tacit assumption, perhaps often not so tacit, that the offer of salvation and even enlightenment goes from Christ through the Christians to the nations. In one way or another, this is the view that underlies many recitals of *Heilsgeschichte*, or salvation history derived from the Christian scriptures (Old and New Testaments), and is then carried over to the recitals of mission histories.

An approach that is typical of this point of view is that of Oscar Cullmann. In his book *Christ and Time*, Cullmann derives from primitive Christianity an understanding of linear time that has the Christ event as "the mid-point,"[19] from which redemption history has to be understood as a backward and forward movement. There is a narrowing from humankind through Abraham to the people of Israel to the remnant of Israel to the One, Christ. From that point there is a progressive advance from the One to the many:

> Thus the entire redemptive history unfolds in two movements: the one proceeds from the many to the One: this is the Old Covenant. The other proceeds from the One to the many; this is the New Covenant...The Church on earth, in which the Body of Christ is represented, plays in the New Testament conception a central role for the redemption of all mankind and thereby for the entire creation.[20]

Cullmann asserts that the narrowing and broadening of salvation history take place to deal with the realities of "divine revelation and human sin as the act of revolt against this revelation," which "makes necessary a redemptive history in the narrower sense, for the curse that now rests upon man, and upon the entire creation connected with him, is not the last word of the God who is love." He then goes on to state, "The principle of this gracious process is that of the *election of a minority for the redemption of the whole.* Otherwise expressed, it is the principle of *representation.*"[21]

To summarize Cullmann's position: The history of salvation that began in a broad-based way at creation with Adam and Eve narrows to Abraham and Sarah and to Israel their offspring, and narrows further to the "remnant of Israel" and the Suffering Servant of Deutero-Isaiah and the figure of the Son of man in Daniel. The incarnate Son of God fulfills the mission of these two figures and is the One to whom salvation history narrows. From this point the salvation history broadens out through the church, the community of those who believe in the sacrificial death and resurrection of Jesus Christ, to embrace the whole world.[22] The task for Christian mission is to make this broadening process take place.[23]

What is worrying about this position is not that a few are selected on the basis of their obedience for the redemption of the many, which is the argument of Hans-Ruedi Weber. Rather, what is worrying is the sort of ontological value that is given to those within whose history the revelation of God is locked in. Others are outside this process because of their sin. Redemption for these others is only possible through an entry into the group of elect through conversion to the Christian faith. For Cullmann, "natural revelation," at least in the time of the early church, had only a negative value:

> The intention is to show that even those who, in the time since Abraham, have no role in the redemptive process, nevertheless have preserved their relation to this process, inasmuch as even their attitude to the revelation which has been given to them can have as its result only human guilt and divine "wrath" (Romans 1:18ff.). On the other hand, however, even though they do not pass through the stage that the law occupies in redemptive history (Romans 2:14ff.), their attitude can become the presupposition of faith in the single way of salvation.[24]

The problem inherent in this understanding of salvation history becomes apparent when one asks what happened to Hagar and Ishmael, through whom Muslims in general and Arabic Muslims in particular claim Abraham as their ancestor. When salvation history narrows to the One and then broadens out in a different way, one may equally want to know what happened to the descendents of Abraham and Sarah. Even Paul, who is so concerned to interpret the obedience of Abraham in a way that would be applicable to those who are to be grafted into that history, worries about the children of Abraham and Sarah (cf. Rom. 11:17–32). Is it just my nasty, suspicious Asian mind, or is it a fact that racism is endemic to this approach, which is played out in Western mission histories and in the attempts to validate that model in present understandings of Christian mission? This racist attitude works in two ways. One is through the devaluing of cultures and histories outside Christian salvation history. The other is through the devaluing within the household of faith of the spiritualities and theologies outside white European and American theological expressions.

Coming from Asia, I would like to approach the issue of the relationship between the *laos* and the *ethne* in a different way. I would first state it as a problem. Taking the whole population of Asia from the so-called Middle East to East Asia, which has a good two thirds of the world population, centuries if not millennia[25] of mission work has yielded around 2.5 percent of Christians. Either one has to hold to the view that the goal of Christian mission, like the second coming, is still an unfulfilled dream, or one must begin to look at the purpose of Christian mission in a different way.

T. K. Thomas, an Indian Christian writer with a keen sense of humor, posed this problem in an oral response to a lecture on mission as evangelism:

> When someone offers something that is unquestionably good to another, and that person refuses the offer, there can be one of three reasons. The person does not understand what is on offer. Then the offer may be repeated, making up in volume for what is lacking in coherence! The other reason may be that the person knows what is on offer but refuses it. This is rejection. The third possibility is that the person already has what is being offered and therefore satiety prompts the person to decline the offer. It is this third reason that is theologically too horrendous to contemplate.

The argument is not that we look for another perspective from which to view mission history and the relationship between the *laos* and the *ethne*, because mission as the propagation of the Christian faith to gather more adherents has come to an end. It has not, and still continues, especially with the spread of the Pentecostal movement in Latin America, Africa, and parts of Asia and the Pacific. Rather, the unfulfilled dream of mission seen from a *Heilsgeschichte* perspective presses upon us the task to look for another, better perspective for reading mission history and for relating the *laos* to the *ethne*. To pose it as a question: Is it possible that the period of modern Western missions completed the task assigned to it, and we need to seek another perspective or model for a more satisfactory response to the challenges for Christian mission today?

Reserving for the next chapter the search for a new perspective for reading mission history, we will look again at the biblical evidence, which presents a more varied picture than do usual presentations of salvation history for relating the *laos* to the *ethne*.[26]

The biblical witness to the encounter between the *laos* and the *ethne* is usually presented in a reductionist way that holds up as absolute a particular view, namely, that because the *laos* is elected, the *ethne* are rejected. One biblical view of the *ethne*, perhaps the most prominent one, does give room for such an interpretation. This viewpoint is expressed quite clearly at the point at which Israel is to move to Canaan to possess the land. Not only are the nations—the Amorites, the Canaanites, and so on—to be driven off so that Israel may have vacant possession of the land, but Israel is also required not to have any contact with the *ethne* in the future, lest Israel be seduced into sin (Ex. 34:11–16).

First Samuel 15 provides an example of the dire consequence that could follow should Israel disregard this admonition. In this episode,

King Saul goes out to do battle with the Amalekites. In defeating the Amalekites, he disobeys the command of Yahweh given through Samuel that he should devote the whole of Amalek—king, people, animals, and possessions—to the *ban*; that is, they should be totally destroyed. This admonition, particularly in the context of holy war, works on the premise, aptly summarized by a famous Old Testament scholar, H. Wheeler Robinson, that "One man's *qodesh* is another man's *cherem*" (What is holy for one is forbidden to the other). Instead of following that injunction, Saul is more practical. He destroys what he thinks is worthless and brings back the rest, including Agag the Amalekite king as a prisoner. In great anger, Samuel beheads Agag and announces Yahweh's repudiation of Saul as king because of his disobedience. Similar anti–other nations sentiments are also found elsewhere in the Bible and particularly in the prophetic oracles against the nations. The New Testament view of the nations is not quite so bloodthirsty, yet it is clear, particularly in the Acts of the Apostles and in the Pauline corpus, that the histories of the nations would be subsumed in the history of the church as the New Israel. To put it simply, they would have to become Christians, part of the *laos*, or be damned.

As a counterbalance to this position, there is the clear statement that those who are elected can also be rejected. For instance, in Amos 3:1, the familiar election formula, "the whole family that I brought up out of the land of Egypt" (cf. Deut. 5:6), is used to state the exact opposite: "Therefore I will punish you for all your iniquities" (Am. 3:2). More pointedly, in Hosea 1:6–9, Israel is called both "not my people" and "not pitied," that is those who are not the recipients of God's compassion/grace. The prophet Hosea is clear that reacceptance (Hos. 2:1) is based on repentance—a change of direction and a return to Yahweh—and on obedience. To take another instance, for those who want to stake everything on the claim that they are descendants of Abraham, John the Baptist says scathingly, "I tell you, God is able from these stones to raise up children to Abraham" (Mt. 3:9). In essence, the view expressed in these passages is that election does not confer special privileges or a status on Israel and, by implication, on the church. Consequently, there is no place for the view that just because some are chosen, others are rejected. What is more important to remember is that those who are elected could also be rejected because of disobedience. Election is for a task. As Hans-Ruedi Weber puts it, "God's purpose is the salvation of *all*, of the total *cosmos*, yet, in order to achieve this, God elects, calls and converts a *few*."[27]

Side by side with the view that pits Israel against the nations, there are other views that present a more complex and rich set of relationships both between the *ethne* and God and between the *ethne* and the *laos*. These need to be given greater prominence.

1. The God who cares for Israel also cares for the nations:

> Are you not like the Ethiopians to me, O people of Israel, says
> the LORD. Did I not bring Israel up from the land of Egypt, and
> the Philistines from Caphtor and the Arameans from Kir?
> (Am. 9:7)

Isaiah 19:19–22 is even more startling in its admission that there
will come a time when the worship in Egypt will be acceptable to
Yahweh; and just as he heard the cry of Israel in Egypt, he will also
hear the cry of Egypt because of its oppressors, and deliver Egypt:

> On that day there will be an altar to the LORD in the center of
> the land of Egypt, and a pillar to the LORD at its border. It will
> be a sign and a witness to the LORD of hosts in the land of
> Egypt; when they cry to the LORD because of oppressors, he
> will send them a savior, and will defend and deliver them.
> (Isa. 19:19–20)

In this connection, it is also foreseen that Egypt and Assyria, like
Israel, will be a blessing in the midst of the earth: "Blessed be Egypt
my people, and Assyria the work of my hands, and Israel my heritage"
(Isa. 19:24f.). Malachi 1:11 also attests to the acceptable worship of the
nations:

> From the rising of the sun to its setting my name is great
> among the nations, and in every place incense is offered to my
> name, and a pure offering; for my name is great among the
> nations, says the LORD of hosts.

2. Besides the direct relationship that the *ethne* have with Yahweh,
they also have a role to play in Yahweh's relationship with Israel. On
the one hand, he uses them to punish Israel, as when he calls Assyria
the rod of his anger (Isa. 10:5). For a similar purpose, authority to rule
the world, including Israel, is given to Nebuchadnezzar, king of
Babylon, whom Yahweh calls "my servant"—a title usually reserved
for the Davidic king (Jer. 27:6; cf. Ps. 89:3). Also, while in Babylon,
Israel is requested to pray for that nation, because the welfare (*shalom*)
of Israel would depend on the welfare of Babylon (Jer. 29:7). On the
other hand, a nation such as Persia could be Yahweh's instrument for
liberating Israel. Cyrus, king of Persia, who plays this role, is
addressed by the royal titles of Yahweh's shepherd and anointed (Isa.
44:28; 45:1; cf. Ps. 89:38).

3. Along with these, we should also take note of the biblical
witness to the faithfulness of the nations. For instance, Ruth, as a
representative of the nations, shows remarkable faith in abandoning
her people and entrusting herself to Naomi and her people: "Where

you go, I will go; Where you lodge, I will lodge; your people shall be my people, and your God my God (Ruth 1:16). Because of her faith Ruth is awarded the distinction of being part of the ancestry of King David. It is noteworthy that in the book of Jonah, Nineveh, capital of Assyria—a city hated for all the evil that it did to Israel (cf. Nahum)—should be selected as symbolically representing the turning of the nations to Yahweh. In other words, even the nations that are inveighed against in the prophetic oracles of judgment are potentially capable of turning to Yahweh. Thus, when Jonah reluctantly proclaims Yahweh's judgment on Nineveh because of its great evil, the king and the people, in great remorse, repent and, much to Jonah's chagrin, are forgiven.

4. Of the passages that speak of Zion as the place of worship not only of Israel but also of the nations, Micah 4:1–5 is worth noting. In this passage, the nations make their pilgrimage to Zion both to learn the law (*torah*) and to accept Yahweh's justice, so that the weapons of war may be turned into tools for producing food, so that peace may reign. Yet in this context, it is admitted:

> For all the peoples walk,
> each in the name of its god,
> *And* we will walk in the name of the LORD our God
> forever and ever. (v. 5, author translation)

There is no compelling reason why the Hebrew word *waw*, which is normally understood as a conjunctive but in some instances could also be an adversative, should in this instance be translated as "but." When it is translated as a conjunctive, it becomes evident that although Zion provides an eschatological focus for the unity of the nations, so that peace may prevail, that unity does not abrogate the religious plurality that the nations represent.

Although each nation worships God by whatever name each nation knows God, God known as Yahweh in Israel is also the God of the nations. There is an attempt to transcend tribalism with the admission that Yahweh's relationship with the nations is not always adversarial. Yahweh who punishes them for not practicing justice and turning to false "gods" also punishes Israel for the same reasons (cf. Am. 1:3—2:8). Yahweh who loves Israel and has delivered and led them also loves the nations and is concerned to deliver and lead them.

Even in passages that do not speak explicitly about Yahweh's loving relationship with the nations, there is the clear view that their welfare (*shalom*) and destiny are in the hands of Yahweh. Side by side with the dominant view that Yahweh has chosen Israel as his special people from among all the nations, there are other voices that qualify this view and indeed add other dimensions to it.

Not only in this case but also in other cases, one cannot simply reduce biblical positions to any one position. The Old Testament scholar from Hong Kong Archie C. C. Lee points out the various voices in Hebrew scriptures and how and why certain voices dominate the canon of scripture as we have it. He argues that these many voices also need to be heard, especially as we address the situation of religious plurality. He goes on to say,

> As we acknowledge the polyphonic character of the biblical text and confirm the fact that many voices do co-exist side by side either in debate, in dialogue or even as suppressed silenced voices, we are reminded to be sensitive to our responsibility as readers. Who are we? Where do we stand socially and politically? What theological position have we taken and should be taking? What is the consequence of our taking sides? How much room is left for us to exercise judgment?[28]

In her book *Discovering the Bible in the Non-Christian World*, Kwok Pui-lan, another theologian from Hong Kong, echoes what Archie Lee says and takes his argument further. Using the work of the French philosopher Michel Foucault, Kwok asserts that "biblical interpretation is never simply a religious matter, for the processes of formation, canonization and transmission of the Bible have always been imbued with the issues of authority and power."[29] To surface the polyphonic character of scripture and hear again the minor and even silenced voices, she employs the method of "biblical interpretation as dialogical imagination," which many Asian theologians have employed:

> The term dialogical imagination describes the process of creative hermeneutics in Asia. It attempts to convey the complexities, the multidimensional linkages, and the different levels of meaning that underlie our present task of relating the Bible to Asia. This task is dialogical, for it involves ongoing conversation among different religious and cultural traditions. It is highly imaginative, for it looks at both the Bible and our Asian reality anew, challenging the historical-critical method, presumed by many to be objective and neutral. The German word for imagination, *Einbildungskraft*, means the power of shaping into one. Dialogical imagination attempts to bridge the gaps of time and space, to create new horizons and to connect the disparate elements of our lives into a meaningful whole.[30]

Although agreeing with Archie Lee and Kwok Pui-lan, I doubt that we will ever so create "a meaningful whole" in a permanent way.

Such creations will be time conditioned and provisional to address particular situations and specific sets of questions. Contradictions will remain in the many voices, so that scripture remains open for imagination, and will defy our attempts either to reduce gospel into law or to impose one theological position on the whole. Contradiction is of the very essence of Christian scripture. A remarkable passage in this regard is Proverbs 26:4–5. At first it says, "Do not answer fools according to their folly, or you will be a fool yourself." Then the next verse turns around to say, "Answer fools according to their folly, or they will be wise in their own eyes." Both positions are true not by themselves but in conjunction with each other.[31]

The rich set of relationships that are found in the Old Testament are also found in the New Testament, but perhaps not so fully. The reason for this reticence in the gospel accounts is that they are primarily concerned with depicting in various ways Jesus' concern with the "lost sheep of the house of Israel" and the proclamation of the good news of the reign/realm of God to them. Therefore, within the parameters of this concern, the few references that are there to the *ethne* are worthy of note. To take an example, Matthew 8, from which the title of this book is taken, speaks not only of those coming from east and west to sit with the ancestors of Israel at the messianic banquet, but also of the faith of one from the *ethne* on the basis of which Jesus speaks of this larger gathering. Jesus commends the faith of the Roman centurion and says in amazement, "Truly I tell you, in no one in Israel have I found such faith" (v. 10).

Although there are quite a few such instances in the gospel accounts, two are of particular significance. One is the so-called Nazareth manifesto (Lk. 4:18–19), in which Jesus lays out the plan and purpose of his ministry, quoting Isaiah 61:1–2. Jesus presents himself as the one who has been anointed (the Messiah) to bring good news to the poor, to proclaim release to the captives, recovery of sight to the blind, and freedom to the captives. In this way he proclaims "the year of the Lord's favor" for Israel but leaves out the second line of that couplet found in Isaiah 61:2, "and the day of vengeance of our God." As David Bosch points out, it was a commonly held expectation that the restoration of Israel would go hand in hand with the destruction of the nations that had inflicted so much suffering and humiliation on Israel. To shut the scroll precisely at the point when those who were listening to him would expect him to finish the couplet was very likely the principal cause of their amazement. That amazement later turned to anger when Jesus went on to extol the ministry and faith of gentiles. There were many widows in Israel who would have gladly ministered to the needs of the prophet Elijah during a time of famine. But God sent Elijah to the widow of Zarephath. During the time of Elisha there were many lepers in Israel, but it was Naaman, the Syrian military officer, who was cleansed.[32]

The second instance is the meeting of the woman from Syrophoenicia with Jesus, as reported in Mark 7:24–30. At first Jesus brusquely refuses her entreaty to heal her daughter with the words, "It is not fair to take the children's food and throw it to the dogs." This is one of the clearest statements in the gospel accounts that Jesus viewed his ministry as primarily to the lost sheep of the house of Israel. The statement also reflects the general contempt of Jews for these "untouchables." The woman counters Jesus with the words, "Even the dogs…eat the children's crumbs." I am indebted to José Míguez-Bonino for the insight, which he gave at a Bible study at the meeting of the Council of World Mission in Jamaica (1993), that the response of the woman exhibits more than persistence. Míguez-Bonino sees it as a challenge. In effect she is saying to Jesus that if his compassion for the children is to be truly the compassion of the Messiah, then it must also respond to the needs of all God's children. That this is indeed the case becomes evident when Jesus says to her, "Because of *this word* (GK. *touton ton logon*) go, for the demon has left your daughter" (author's translation). (The account in Matthew 15:28 has "faith.") In other words, the *logos* of the woman challenges the divine *Logos* to manifest the universality of God's compassion. She helps Jesus see beyond the limitations that his own humanity had imposed on him.

References to the nations in the Acts of the Apostles and in the epistles are set largely within the second stage of the gospel story. The gospel accounts describe the first stage, in which the ministry of Jesus was to "the lost sheep of the house of Israel." The second stage of the gospel story depicts the work of the disciples of the Risen One who are sent out to the whole world as witnesses to Jesus the Messiah.

In this scheme or progression of the missionary journey, as stated programmatically in the Acts of the Apostles, the main concern is with the spread of the good news of Jesus Christ and the gathering of those who turned to Jesus Christ, who embodies the promise of the reign/realm of God, into the various house churches. These are welcomed as part of the New Israel. Typical of this position are letters addressed to new converts. Ephesians 2:12, addressing Gentile Christian, says, "Remember that you were at that time without Christ, being aliens from the commonwealth of Israel, and strangers to the covenants of promise, having no hope and without God in the world." First Peter 2:10, after extolling the converts to Jesus Christ as a chosen race and a royal priesthood, reflects Hosea 2:23 to address them thus: "Once you were not a people, but now you are God's people; once you had not received mercy, but now you have received mercy."

To summarize: Although God's dealings with Israel are narrated in the Old Testament and the gospel accounts, in what may be called the main redemption history, the nations do not simply hover in the background either to be ignored or to symbolize God's rejection and punishment. They have an important role to play. To use the language of music, the nations provide a counterpoint to the main story. Clearly from the Acts of the Apostles onwards, they become God's special concern through the death and resurrection of Jesus Christ, and are invited through faith in Jesus Christ to become what may be called "the New Israel," which is to be an instrument in God's hands for the salvation of the whole world. But again, one cannot simply push aside the *ethne* in favor of the New Israel as God's chosen ones, as if they are the only ones through whom salvation is possible. The counterpoint continues. In the next chapter we will see how this counterpoint fits into a different sketch of mission history.

Our main concern in this chapter has been to reexamine the concepts of mission and evangelism and the prevalent perspective from which mission history is usually narrated in order to expose the problems and limitations they impose for understanding the task for Christian mission today. If we are to break through to a larger perspective for understanding the task for Christian mission today, we have to get beyond an understanding of Christian mission as simply a way of gathering more adherents so that a religion does not die out. As we have seen, a questionable understanding of evangelism is often used simply to address this anxiety. Undergirding both is a particular perspective from which mission history itself is usually narrated. Such recitals of mission history exclude the *ethne* from God's redemptive purpose. We have engaged in a clearing out process, so that we may recover these terms in a new setting with theologically more satisfying understandings for conceiving the task for Christian mission today.

7

Christian Mission Today: Exploring an Alternative Paradigm

The alternative paradigm we will explore for understanding the task for Christian mission today is "the people of God in the midst of all God's peoples." Before doing that, it would be helpful to explain the use of the term *paradigm* and the phrase "paradigm shifts."

One of the areas of meaning dictionaries give for the word *paradigm* is "pattern, a prototype, or a typical representative." The philosopher of science Thomas Kuhn uses the term *paradigm* in an extended sense to mean not simply an example that permits replication; rather, "like an accepted judicial decision in common law, it is an object for further articulation and specification under new or more stringent conditions."[1] The phrase "paradigm shift" or "paradigm change" explains the way in which scientific knowledge progresses. He argues that progress in areas of scientific knowledge—and he limits it to the natural sciences or what he calls mature sciences—takes place not just through an accumulation of scientific data, but rather by "revolutions." When a number of scientists begin to perceive that a particular paradigm, within which scientific data made sense and prompted avenues for further scientific discoveries, begins to throw up a number of anomalies that it is unable to explain or sustain, then another paradigm or framework of references begins to displace the previous paradigm. However, such displacement does not take place without a struggle, with both paradigms continuing side by side for a time until the old one is admitted to be clearly inadequate.[2]

Although Kuhn limited the use of the concept of paradigm shifts to the area of the natural sciences, the concept has caught on in other disciplines. Samuel Huntington, in *The Clash of Civilizations and the*

Remaking of World Order, uses Kuhn's work to explain the emergence and displacement of paradigms in the discipline of political science.[3] In his book *Transforming Mission: Paradigm Shifts in Theology of Mission,* David Bosch uses this concept to indicate the changes in mission thinking that have taken place in the Christian era.[4] Konrad Raiser argues in *Ecumenism in Transition: A Paradigm Shift in the Ecumenical Movement?* that perhaps the time has come to replace an older paradigm for understanding ecumenism with a new one.[5] John Hick in *God and the Universe of Faiths,* without actually using the term, argues for a Copernican revolution in theology that would replace the old Ptolemaic model that assumed that all religions revolved around a center postulated by the Christian religion.[6]

Theologians have borrowed the term *paradigm shifts* from the philosophy of science and applied it to their own fields of enquiry for epistemological reasons. There are similarities and differences between Kuhn and theologians. In several fields of theological endeavor, older paradigms for providing meaning and engendering new research are not exactly collapsing, but are seen to be inadequate in that they do not accommodate newer perspectives. So new models called paradigms are being tested. To speak of these changes as paradigm shifts is to argue that an old framework or paradigm still persists while a new one is seeking and struggling to replace it. Most would agree with Kuhn: "To be accepted as a paradigm, a theory must seem better than its competitors, but it need not, and in fact never does, explain all the facts with which it can be confronted."[7] This fact alone should make it clear that no paradigm is forever. A paradigm carries within it the possibility of throwing up anomalies that it can no longer accommodate and that could prompt the emergence of further paradigms. Epistemologically, a particular paradigm may be the most adequate for the time being. As Kuhn argues, "Paradigms gain their status because they are more successful than their competitors in solving a few problems that the group of practitioners has come to recognize as acute."[8] Our argument for a new paradigm, "the people of God in the midst of all God's peoples," for understanding the task of Christian mission today also falls into this general quest.

In the previous chapter we saw how certain themes and emphases that have emerged in the area of missiology question the adequacy of, for want of a better term, "the missionary paradigm" that worked with the premise that the main purpose of mission is to convert the "Gentiles" to the Christian faith. For one thing, as we have noted, this aspiration has not been fulfilled and is likely never to be fulfilled. In what follows in this chapter, we will need to place that historical period within a different framework for reading the history of Christian missions. We have also seen that the moving in of certain concepts—such as *Missio Dei* (the mission of God) and the emphasis on the centrality of God's reign/realm rather than Christendom—into the mainstream of thinking on mission makes it difficult to work with simply the old paradigm for mission. Equally important, the reality of religious pluralism urges us to seek a more satisfactory theological framework for conceiving the task of Christian mission today.

With these concerns in mind we will first track a specific ecumenical debate that accompanied "the conciliar process of mutual commitment (covenant) to justice, peace and the integrity of creation" to show the limitations of the paradigm for mission that sees the nations at best as objects of Christian mission. The larger ecumenical context of this debate will show how Asian theological viewpoints, in particular, that attempted to broaden this mission perspective were constantly denied a hearing. Second, we will sketch the Asian theological views that finally gained an entry into the debate. These in various ways suggest that the theme of creation rather than redemption history narrowly understood provides a better framework for understanding the task for Christian mission today. Third, we will look at a more satisfactory theological framework for mission, which emerged through several ecumenical debates and were consonant with the Asian theological positions given in the second section of this chapter. Fourth, we will sketch a course for mission history that poses the task for Christian mission more in terms of "being a blessing to the nations" than as "attempting to convert the nations." Here we will explore the appropriateness of the paradigm "the people of God in the midst of all God's peoples."

Testing an Old Paradigm

The so-called Vancouver call (1983) of the World Council of Churches, which the Programme Guidelines Committee of the Assembly formulated, was in the first instance issued to WCC programs: "To engage member churches in a conciliar process of mutual commitment (covenant) to justice, peace and the integrity of all creation shall be a priority for all World Council programmes."[9] It was an attempt to bring together the movements for Faith and Order and Life and Work to help member churches commit themselves in a solemn assembly to support and be engaged in the struggles for justice, peace, and the preservation of the environment. "To combat the threats to life in our time" was the phrase that was often used to motivate the churches. Soon after the Vancouver Assembly, it was deemed worthwhile not only to invite the member churches of the World Council of Churches but also to broaden the process to include other churches, especially through the various Christian World Communions such as the Lutheran World Federation and the World

Alliance of Reformed Churches, and to ask for Roman Catholic participation through the Vatican. What began as a WCC process became in intent, if not necessarily in result, a comprehensive global process.

Such inclusiveness was inherent in the thinking at the Vancouver Assembly itself, as is evident in its "Statement on Peace and Justice": "The biblical vision of peace with justice for all, of wholeness, of unity for all God's people is not one of several options for the followers of Christ. It is an imperative in our time."[10]

This is the setting in which the debate on whether this process should or should not include people of other faiths was placed. As the director of this ecumenical process, I had firsthand experience of how the paradigm for Christian mission drawn from the modern missionary era and neo-orthodoxy operated in this situation.

Taking into consideration the thrust for inclusiveness and recognizing the need to go further in this broadening out process, a consultation held at Glion, Switzerland (November 7–15, 1986), said in its report to the WCC Central Committee:

> In order to carry forward the JPIC process and world convocation, the WCC would have to work with other bodies that understand their witness to be in relation to justice, peace and the integrity of creation, and to remain in contact with them. Principal among these are:
>
> - the Roman Catholic and other non-member churches;
> - the Christian World Communions;
> - other international ecumenical organizations;
> - the regional and national ecumenical organizations;
> - the Christian movements which perceive themselves to be concerned with the struggle for justice, peace and integrity of creation;
> - the institutions and movements of other faiths and ideologies that are engaged in the struggle for justice, peace and the integrity of creation.
>
> It is hoped that these would also participate in the world convocation on justice, peace and the integrity of creation.[11]

Although the Central Committee of the World Council of Churches to which this report was presented accepted the first five on this list in the conciliar process, it had great theological difficulties in accepting "the institutions and movements of other faiths." At first it agreed with the Glion consultation that the churches in responding to the conciliar process "need to draw upon the resources of other faith traditions and ideologies that have important perspectives on JPIC and to collaborate with these organisations and movements for the realisation of justice, peace and the integrity of creation."[12] It went on to say:

> It is now recommended that these bodies be invited and urged to participate in the JPIC process. This recommendation includes the non-Christian bodies mentioned. The concerns comprehended in JPIC are by no means limited to the constituency of the World Council of Churches or even the Christian world, so that the process will be greatly strengthened by the participation of others.[13]

Then it turned right around to declare,

> The institutions and movements of other faiths would not be part of the conciliar process or the world convocation, except perhaps as observers. However attempts should be made to engage them in dialogue so their concerns and perspectives may be reflected in the JPIC process and the world convocation.[14]

How do we include persons of other faiths and secular movements in a Christian process, named a conciliar process, when they do not share our faith even if they do share our commitment to justice, peace, and the integrity of creation?

In the way the question is posed, it comes up against the perennial, unresolved ecumenical problem of understanding the relationship between Christianity and other faiths within a neo-orthodox framework. In his book *Hindus and Christians: A Century of Protestant Ecumenical Thought*, Wesley Ariarajah shows the difficulties inherent in using this paradigm in relating to people of other faiths, as well as in relating the Christian faith to other faiths. Taking an example from the very assembly that set in motion the JPIC process, the first draft of the report on "Witnessing in a Divided World" presented to the Vancouver Assembly read: "While affirming the uniqueness of the birth, life, death and resurrection of Jesus to which we bear witness, we recognize God's creative work in the religious experience of people of other faiths."

Speaker after speaker raised serious objections to the last part of this formulation, and it was referred back to the drafting committee. After reviewing nearly seventy written recommendations for change for this part alone, the Central Committee that followed the Assembly accepted the formulation "We recognize God's creative work in the seeking for religious truth among people of other faiths."[15] God's creative work is deemed to be in the seeking and not in the religious experience itself of other faiths. The assumption is that in the seeking they will stumble across the "real truth" revealed by God through Jesus Christ and enshrined in the Christian church. This position would be in line with what Kraemer himself had to say in terms of "unexpected fulfillment" of God's encounter and wrestling with human beings in their search for God.[16]

It is almost certain that it is such an understanding as this that made the 1987 Geneva Central Committee decide to keep out "institutions and movements of other faiths" from the conciliar process, even though it did recognize that it would be the height of idiocy to make out that justice, peace, and the integrity of creation are solely Christian concerns.

The clash evident at the Vancouver Assembly was evident at least from the time of the New Delhi Assembly (1961) of the World Council of Churches, with the Asian viewpoint, especially through the contribution of Paul D. Devanandan, losing out. According to M. M. Thomas, an earlier draft acknowledged the working of God's spirit in the lives of people of other faiths preparing them for the coming of the gospel. The draft then went on to say, "In the churches we have but little understanding of the wisdom, love and power God has given to men of other faiths and of no faith or of the change wrought in other faiths by their long encounter with Christianity. We must take up the conversation with them, knowing that Christ meets us in them." This was changed, says Thomas, so that while acknowledging "that God has not left himself without witness even among men who do not know Christ," there is uncertainty about how "to define the relation and response of such men to the activity of God among them." Hence, "we must take up the conversation with them, knowing that Christ addresses them through us and us through them." Thomas refers to the interventions of neo-orthodox theologians, such as Edmund Schlink, who argued that "the presence of Christ and the Spirit accompanied the church's historical act of preaching of repentance and forgiveness and did not precede it."[17]

The Nairobi Assembly (1975) of the World Council of Churches was no different. Wesley Ariarajah, who was present at that Assembly, notes that when the Dialogue program that was started in 1971 was officially presented to the Assembly, there was stiff resistance despite the assurances of Asian Christians Russell Chandran and Lynn de Silva that they were not against Christian mission but wanted to see a different way of relating to people of other faiths. The resistance, Ariarajah says, was the fear of compromise on "the three classical fears of the missionary movement: syncretism, compromising the uniqueness of Christ, and loss of the urgency of mission." That all these positions would not be compromised had to be stated clearly and firmly in a preamble to the Dialogue program.[18]

Ariarajah makes two comments that lead us to the next section. The first is a reference to an observation David Jenkins made. David Jenkins had been working with the WCC on the Humanum study and was later bishop of Durham. Some years after the Nairobi Assembly, Jenkins referred to the outcry about syncretism and betrayal of the gospel and said about the preamble to the Dialogue program that attempted to shackle it: "The response of the drafting committee to this outcry left many Asians and others feeling that their insights and convictions were trampled on or betrayed."[19] This was a constant response, I would add, despite the clarifying work that had been done in many consultations between assemblies. The official position, if we may call it that, was a firm *no*. The second point Ariarajah makes is a complaint:

> The doctrine of creation…is rarely spelled out in the churches' theologies in terms of plurality, certainly not of religious plurality. In much of Protestant theology creation just sets the stage or becomes no more than a prelude to the "fall" and the consequent unfolding of the drama of salvation. An undeveloped theology of creation lies at the heart of the Protestant inability to deal with plurality. *Today there is a new interest in creation, but it is more in relation to the natural environment than about the peoples who fill the earth.*[20]

The Asian contribution, which addresses this complaint, had long argued that the motif of creation, rather than redemption history narrowly understood, is a better framework for locating the task for Christian mission. As we shall see next, this perspective did come into later official ecumenical positions, but it would be good to hear this contribution in its own terms.

Creation Rather Than Redemption History

Asian theologians began to identify the motif of creation rather than redemption history as the needed theological framework for mission, largely because redemption history would assume a center, whether it be Jerusalem, Rome, Paris, London, or New York, which will inevitably attempt to control the missionary journey emanating from that center and the consequences of that mission. There will always be a location from which "redemption" is expected to flow to other locations. Consequently, "other locations" would be incorporated into a given redemption history or missionary history. In the face of this problem, Asian theologians began to realize that if there is to be true partnership in mission, then the proper theological framework for mission has to be the broader theological framework of the creation, within which the redemption of all people could be understood, rather than any construct of redemption history.

In arguing for the framework of creation for locating Christian mission, the concern was not to articulate a theology of creation, which appeared later prompted by the ecological crisis. In that instance, the move from "salvation history" to a theology of creation was an attempt to get away from a purely "God who acts in history" theology that argued for history rather than nature as the arena of God's revelation. This shift from history to creation was important to argue for a theology that focuses on all of life, for a theology of life, rather than a theology that has humanity as its primary concern, with its concomitant emphasis on "Man's dominion over nature."[21] The concern in Asian theological discussions was to see the creation as a framework within which God's dealings with all God's peoples could be located and understood.

The Taiwanese theologian Choan Seng Song is probably the one who did the most to wrench the task of mission from a purely redemption history framework and place it in the framework of creation. In his article "From Israel to Asia—A Theological Leap," he argues,

> History in the Bible derives its meaning from God's redemptive acts. Events and experiences taken into the orbit of redemption interrupt the normal course of history. They become the bearers of a meaning, which anticipates fulfilment in the future. Redemption is the power, which enables us to leap into the future and frees us from slavery to the sinful past and from an absurd fate.[22]

Having categorized God's redemption as a kind of revolution, he goes on to state: "The Christian Church which has inherited God's salvation in Christ, has not altogether succeeded in avoiding the mistake of attempting to institutionalize God's revolution."[23] Consequently, "without taking into account the realities represented by histories and cultures outside the western milieu," theologians especially from the West

> obstinately persist in reflecting on Asian or African cultures and histories from the vantage point of that messianic hope which is believed to be lodged in the history of the Christian Church, so that the relations of these cultures and histories to God's redemption become intermediate, and redemption loses its intrinsic meaning for cultures and histories outside the history of Christianity. *The universal nature of God's dealing with his creation forfeits its particular and direct application, except within the cultures and histories affected and fostered by Christianity.*[24]

The Asian theological argument for seeing creation, rather than redemption history narrowly understood, as the framework of God's mission was, as Song puts it, to see "the universal nature of God's dealing" with all of humanity.

Song follows a theological line that probably began with P. Chenchiah of India. Chenchiah was a high court judge by profession and a theologian by avocation. He was present at the world mission conferences at Jerusalem (1928) and Tambaram (1938), and presented his ideas as a rebuttal to the neo-orthodox position of the Dutch theologian Henrik Kraemer, who had a massive impact on the world mission conference at Tambaram. In his rather idiosyncratic way, Chenchiah argued against Kraemer for a creation perspective for understanding mission. Addressing the Indian theological scene in particular, he indicated how limiting a theology of incarnation and redemption would be when it is divorced from a theology of creation. He contended that the religious cultural heritage of India had its own contribution to make for an understanding of the Christian faith and argued for a theology of creation as the starting point for an Indian Christian theology.[25] He was of the opinion that once Jesus is liberated from Jewish tribalism, he might be seen as who he truly is—the incarnation of the Cosmic Christ who is both Son of God and Son of man. Not a mere Messiah of the Jews, but the Savior of the world. As Chenchiah put it:

> Viewed as an outburst or inrush into history, Jesus is the manifestation of a new creative effort of God in which the cosmic energy or *sakti* is the Holy Spirit, the new creation is Christ, and the new life order is the Kingdom of God.[26]

Following Chenchiah, Paul Devanandan made this point more clearly:

> God's act of redemption in Christ Jesus concerns the whole of his creation. Biblical faith repeatedly affirms that the work of Christ is of cosmic significance in that redemption wrought in Him has affected the entire creative process.[27]

Devanandan does not undervalue God's redemptive action in Jesus Christ. He assumes, as rightly should be assumed, that the resurrection of the Jewish Messiah released the Messiah from a specific history. For it was the Risen One and not the Jesus of Nazareth who sent his disciples out into the world as his witnesses. That is why God's redemptive work in Christ could be viewed as of cosmic significance. The disciples did not carry "God's redemption in Christ" as such to the end of the world. Rather, they were asked to witness to what God had done in Jesus Christ, which although located and interpreted within a particular history is not locked into that specific history. In some ways this position resonates with what Paul, who had his own specific revelation of the Risen Christ, had to say about now knowing Christ not "from a human point of view" (cf. 2 Cor. 5:16). Theologians such as Devanandan and Chenchiah could not accept the chauvinism of neo-orthodox theologians and the position Western missionaries assumed, that only through the history of the church is God's redemption in Jesus Christ mediated to the rest of the world.

This approach finds an echo also in the mission theology of D. T. Niles, who spoke of the "previousness of Jesus."[28] Operating within a broadly neo-orthodox framework as did Devanandan, Niles was more concerned to deal with the relationships between religious persons rather than between religions. From his own experience as an Asian Christian encountering people of other faiths, he could assert that the discussion in mission is not about religious systems or even how the gospel could be related to other religions. Rather, "[the discussion] is about the operation of the Gospel itself among those who are Christians and among those who are not. It is when the Gospel is preached that the relation we are seeking to understand is set up."[29] Niles set the task for mission in terms of God's love for the world as it found definitive expression in Jesus Christ ("God so loved the world that he gave his only Son") and in which accomplished divine action was already operative in the world through the Risen One. Reviewing his contribution to missiology, Wesley Ariarajah concludes, "[Niles] claimed the world for God; he saw the act of God in Jesus Christ as an act within the total mission of God in the whole of human life." Consequently, for Niles "the Christian activity in the world was to be part of the mission of God, [and] an important part of it, for the Christian's task was to announce what God had done in Christ, which has made all the difference in the world." It is this position that made Niles speak of "the previousness of Jesus." Or as Ariarajah puts it, "Niles claimed the world for God not only by citing natural theology, but by arguing that Christ was already present there inviting his church to join him and witness to him."[30]

Choan Seng Song broadens the God and world framework to a God and creation framework to accommodate God's saving presence in all religions. He follows on the positions of Chenchiah and Devanandan:

> When salvation gets divorced from the creation, it is bound to lose its universal dimension and significance. This inevitably leads to the impoverishment of Christian understanding of history and culture [and, we may add, "mission"] and has proved to be detrimental to the wholesome appreciation of Asian history and culture in God's revelation.[31]

Bishop Victor Premsagar of India uses the framework of creation to criticize a narrowly Christo-centric understanding of salvation, which ignores or militates against the reception of other understandings of the work of God. In his article "The Tower of Babel: An Urban Development Project," Premsagar argues, "One language and one speech indicate the will of a few with no room for the viewpoints of others...The different languages and cultures are indications of the identity and freedom of the different peoples of the earth. These are God-given gifts to men and women to overcome oppressive monolithic structures of power." Again, in his essay "The Gods of Our Fathers— Towards a Theology of Indian Religious and Cultural Heritage," Premsagar berates the Donald McGavran school with its insistence on reaching the unreached: "In such missiological circles as this [McGavran's] paper represents, there is a total lack of appreciation of the faiths and cultures of other nations. Cultures of other nations are taken into account only for evolving evangelistic strategies and not as witness to God's revelation amongst other nations."[32]

This is but a small sample of Asian Christian thinking advocating a shift from a narrow understanding of redemption history to creation and to God's mission in the world as a framework for mission. Asia was home to such thinking largely because Asian Christian thought had to come to terms with the reality of many *living* religions in whose midst Asian Christians live, usually as a minority. Asian Christian thought had to grapple with the fact that if God as revealed in Jesus Christ is the Creator of the whole world and not just the Christian part of it, then all in their religio-cultural identities and commitment are God's peoples and manifest that reality. How do we relate this fact to the task of Christian mission, which has the specific task of proclaiming what God has done in Jesus Christ for the whole of creation?

We will first look at the ways in which theological horizons were broadened to provide a framework or paradigm within which that question could be faced and explored.

The Ecumenical Debate Continued

At the Seventh Assembly of the World Council of Churches at Canberra (1991), a different Wind (Spirit) seemed to be blowing! The report of section 1: "Giver of Life—Sustain Your Creation" says,

> Our vision is of people of different faiths beginning to learn from each other's spirituality and inspiration while developing practical examples in commitment to community and sharing...Only by acknowledging the fundamental worth of all creation can we hope to reverse the direction of destructive, human-created processes.[33]

Beginning with a theology of creation and not just the motif of creation as a framework, as did Asian theologians earlier, the Seventh

Assembly recognized the spiritualities and inspirations of all faiths as part of God's creation. This was quite a shift from the limited perspective exhibited at the Sixth Assembly just eight years earlier. Such a shift of perspective could take place because this report was urging the Assembly, under the influence of the theme "Come Holy Spirit—Renew the Whole Creation!" to move theologically from, so to speak, "a Christian universe" ("Jesus Christ—the Life of the World" was the theme of the previous Assembly) to a more inclusive understanding of the universe. In a word, creation was replacing redemption history as a framework for understanding mission. Consequently, ringing the changes on "all things" (*ta panta*; cf. Col. 1:15–20), the report says:

> The Holy Spirit to whom we pray in the prayer-theme of this assembly, manifests God's energy for life present in all things and reminds us of the total dependence of all things on God...All things have been reconciled to God in Jesus Christ and through the Spirit we begin to experience God's future.[34]

This was not a sudden change in ecumenical thinking, but the result of a process of rethinking that was evident in the JPIC process, which, through those who were involved in it, influenced the thinking at the Assembly.[35]

Equally important were the discussions at the World Mission and Evangelism Conference at San Antonio, Texas (May 1989), of the Commission on World Mission and Evangelism of the WCC[36] and a meeting of the subunit on Dialogue with People of Other Faiths and Ideologies at Baar, Switzerland (1990), which put out a report titled "Religious Plurality: Theological Perspectives and Affirmations."[37]

The actual reformulation of the issue of Christian relations with people of other faiths in the JPIC process began at the international consultation on "the integrity of creation," which met at Granvollen, Norway, in February 1988. The meeting was designed to be a symposium or dialogue between the following: Orthodox, Roman Catholics, feminist theologians, indigenous people, Hindus, Sikhs, Muslims, Buddhists, Jews, and other sundry folk. It was indeed a mixed bag!

In setting up the meeting, it was decided that a discussion on the integrity of creation must be open to the insights that come from many concerned groups. This was essential for two reasons. First, the theme of creation requires that there be an openness to all creation and therefore to all God's peoples. Second, because the Judeo-Christian tradition is alleged to be the root cause of an attitude toward creation that has spawned many of the problems we now face,[38] it was felt that

Christians need to listen to the contribution and indeed the correction that comes from other religious and cultural traditions, which many a time Christian civilizations suppressed, especially during the period of European colonial expansions.

At the consultation, the open listening to others led to a realization of the radical way in which the theme of the integrity of creation could challenge our understanding of justice, peace, and creation. The report of the indigenous people perhaps made the most felicitous contribution to understanding the theme of creation as the proper starting point for a new paradigm for mission:

> For the sake of all creation, theology must begin with creation. Just as concerned Christian people have begun to learn that true peace can only be realized through the establishment of justice and that peace flows naturally out of justice, so now we must begin to learn that justice and then peace flow naturally out of a deep respect for all of creation. Thus for Indigenous Peoples a much more theologically sound expression would be "CREATION, JUSTICE AND PEACE." Not only is this more satisfying to Indigenous theology, but such a title suddenly begins to reflect the theological content and sequence of the ancient ecumenical creeds of Christianity.

> We must now clearly understand that justice is the maintenance of the wholeness of creation. Justice involves the righting of relationships not only between human beings, but also between human beings and the earth and the things of the earth. Our concept of justice must shift away from being that which protects possessions towards that which provides healing of relationships between human beings, between cultures, and between human beings and all of creation. If we begin with the perception of ourselves as a part of the wholeness of creation, and if we understand justice as the practice of human beings in maintaining the inter-relatedness of all of creation, then peace will flow naturally.[39]

The lessons learned in the process, of which the Granvollen meeting was pivotal, were reflected in the introduction to the affirmations of faith, which the World Convocation on Justice, Peace, and the Integrity of Creation made:

> We make these affirmations as Christian people aware that many people of living faiths and ideologies share these concerns with us and are guided by their understanding of justice, peace and the integrity of creation. We therefore seek

dialogue and co-operation with them, guided by a vision of the new future which is necessary for the survival for our planet.[40]

It is this expectation that was reaffirmed at the Canberra Assembly of the WCC when it said: "Our vision is of people of different faiths beginning to learn from each other's spirituality and inspiration while developing practical examples in commitment to community and sharing."

The convocation was more explicit in describing the vision of such a community of sharing:

> The covenant community is open to all. At Pentecost walls were broken down. Through the Spirit a new community is being gathered out of the dispersion and hostility of nations, religions, classes, sexes, ages and races. Through the Spirit we have access to God. The Spirit presses us to recognize and to rejoice in God's gifts in all people and in all places.[41]

Following the convocation, the Canberra Assembly spelled out a new focus for mission that assumes such a vision. In its report on "Spirit of Unity—Reconcile Your People" (section 3), it said:

> A reconciled and renewed creation is the goal of the mission of the church. The vision of God uniting all things in Christ is the driving force of its life and sharing...The diversity of cultures is of immediate relevance to the church's ministry of reconciliation and sharing for it affects both the relationships within churches and also the relationship with people of other faiths.[42]

This larger ecumenical vision has a number of fresh insights for understanding the mission of the church in a religiously plural world. First of all, the vision of God uniting all things in Christ is what prompts the mission of the church. It is a vision, not a mandate. Second, there is the assumption that the theological significance of people of other faiths can be best understood within the framework of creation and in terms of the work of the Holy Spirit rather than, by implication, from within a narrow christological framework. There is no assertion that it is only through the Christian faith that we understand the reconciling work of God in Christ. Other faith traditions also have a contribution to make. Third, an important self-understanding for discharging this mission is the recognition of the church's own plurality, which is a mirror of the plurality of the world in which it is placed.

The report of section 4, "Holy Spirit—Transform and Sanctify Us," in the section on "The Holy Spirit in the World" has the beginnings of the paradigm, "the people of God in the midst of all God's peoples":

The Holy Spirit is at work among all peoples and faiths, and through out the universe. With the sovereign freedom which belongs to God, the Wind blows wherever it wants. Recognizing this, the church rejoices in being nourished by the ministry of the Holy Spirit through the word and sacraments, thereby participating in salvation.[43]

The position that God is at work among all peoples and faiths and the position that the church bears witness through word and sacrament to the offer of God's salvation in Jesus Christ are held side by side. The tension between these two statements is not resolved but maintained as it should be maintained. It is hinted that the way to relate the two is through the recognition of the work of the Holy Spirit, who is not to be held captive in either our ecclesiologies or our christologies.

The People of God in the Midst of All God's Peoples

Shortly after I joined the Council for World Mission (July 1, 1991), I was invited to an Assembly of the United Reformed Church in the United Kingdom. As an invitation to address the Assembly, the convener of the World Missions Committee, Mary Marsden, asked me as I went up to speak, "What do you find exciting in your work as the new general secretary of the Council for World Mission?" I responded,

When I walked into Livingstone House as the newly appointed general secretary of the Council for World Mission, I read with great interest the plaque in the entrance hall which said, "This society [the London Missionary Society] was founded to send the Glorious Gospel of the Blessed God to the Heathen." I said to myself, "Isn't this exciting! Now they have the heathen himself seated right here directing operations."

After a few tense moments of silence ("Did he really say what we heard him say?"), the Assembly dissolved into laughter. My humorous opening nonetheless had a serious intention, namely, to place before a European church the necessity of dealing with a plurality of cultures within the church of Christ, so that the church is seen as holding within it the nations in a representative way.

For understanding the task for world mission today, using the paradigm "the people of God in the midst of all God's peoples," the commission to mission in Mark 16:15, "Go into all the world and proclaim the good news to the whole creation," commends itself. It broadens our ecumenical horizon to include the whole of humanity and indeed the whole of creation as the arena of God's activity.

There is another advantage in using Mark 16:15 as the basis for our missionary calling. It is well known that Mark abruptly ended his narrative at 16:8 with the women returning from the empty tomb in astonishment and fear, with the news that Jesus is risen and has gone before his disciples to Galilee where they are to join him. In stopping at this point, Mark points beyond the resurrection to the continuing ministry of the risen Christ. Jesus goes before his disciples to Galilee, as he later is to precede them to every other part of the world, and they are called to be part of the continuing mission of the risen Christ. In 16:9–20 the church appends to the gospel according to Mark its own account of the continuing story of the gospel, especially with the programmatic statement that they are bidden to "go into all the world and proclaim the good news to the whole creation." By the same token, we too are called today to be involved in the continuing mission of the risen Christ in the power of the Holy Spirit and to add our own witness to the continuing ministry of the risen Christ in our lands and in our time.

Acts 10:1—11:15 is a pivotal episode in the movement of the good news from Jerusalem to the whole world, which the Acts of the Apostles relates in a programmatic way. This passage provides a helpful entry into understanding the continuing gospel story.

In Acts 1:8 the risen Lord tells his disciples, "You will receive power when the Holy Spirit has come upon you; and you will be my witnesses in Jerusalem, in all Judea and Samaria, and to the ends of the earth." The first stage is reached with Acts 9:31 providing the notice that the church throughout Judea, Galilee, and Samaria had peace and was built up. Acts 10 gives the beginning of the movement to the rest of the world. It is pivotal for an understanding of Christian mission in that it shows the two-way traffic that comes into place as mission moves from a Jewish milieu to a Gentile milieu.

There are three characters in this story. One is Peter, the representative of the Jewish Christian church; the second is Cornelius, the representative of the Gentile people; and the third is that most troublesome member of the Trinity, the Holy Spirit.

Peter is hungry. As the meal is being prepared, Peter goes up to the roof to pray and falls into a trance. He sees a vision in which he is presented with all manner of living things. He is commanded to kill and eat. He demurs with the excuse that as a good Jew he has not allowed anything unclean to pass his lips. To which there is the rejoinder, "What God has made clean, you must not call profane" (Acts 10:15). This happens three times. Peter does not understand the full import of this vision until much later, when he meets Cornelius. Then he realizes that his religious convictions, however correct in his Jewish context, could become prejudices that could prevent him from understanding the total scope of God's redemptive work in other contexts. In this encounter, Peter is required not just to acknowledge this fact with his mind but to actually eat it, to take it into his very guts: "Get up, Peter; kill and eat" (Acts 10:13). That knowledge had to be practiced through his table fellowship with those whom he considered unclean. In this episode it is Peter, not Cornelius, who has to go through a conversion experience.

The next day the emissaries from Cornelius meet him and invite him to visit Cornelius and his household. We are told that Cornelius is a devout man who was acceptable to God long before Peter came on the scene. Peter hears Cornelius' story and makes his momentous confession: "I truly understand that God shows no partiality, but in every nation anyone who fears him and does what is right is acceptable to him" (Acts 10:34–35). To unpack what Peter is saying, he comes to the stunning realization that the God who has been revealed through Jesus Christ and whom he worships and serves is not a small God of a small people. This is no tribal God. Rather, this is the God of all the nations. Those who fear God and do what is right have already been accepted by God. This is Peter's confession of his own conversion to the God of the whole creation.

Peter then tells his own story but presents it without any arrogance. He assumes that Cornelius may already know: "You know the message [God] sent to the people of Israel, preaching peace by Jesus Christ—he is Lord of all" (Acts 10:36). Peter's story begins with its location in Israel. He speaks of the message, the gospel, spreading throughout Judea, beginning with Galilee through the ministry of Jesus. He then says that he is one of the witnesses to what Jesus did in Judea and Galilee. He recounts the death, resurrection, and resurrection appearances of Jesus. The risen Jesus did not appear to everyone but to those who were chosen by God as witnesses, who ate and drank with Jesus after his resurrection. Then comes the command given to these witnesses to proclaim that God has appointed Jesus as judge of the living and the dead and that everyone who believes in him receives forgiveness of sins through his name. This is the gospel story up to that point.

As Peter is speaking, the Holy Spirit comes. The Holy Spirit appears as the stories of Cornelius and Peter meet. The circumcised were astounded that the gift of the Holy Spirit was given even to the Gentiles. They were astounded not just because Gentiles could receive the Holy Spirit, as Gentiles who were circumcised and had become part of the story of Israel and were incorporated into Israel's salvation history could be baptized and receive the Holy Spirit. Rather, the astonishing truth that Peter and those circumcised persons who came with him had to face was that Gentiles who were not circumcised and had not been incorporated into the salvation history of Israel could receive the Holy Spirit. This is the miracle of Gentile Christianity. It signaled a decisive break with Jewish salvation history. It is this truth that Paul relentlessly kept hammering home both to Jewish and Gentile churches: Gentile Christians are not subject to the Jewish law and need not be made to bear the marks of such submission.

From our perspective, following other precedents, the gift of the Holy Spirit accompanies baptism (cf. Acts 2:38; 8:14–18). Here, as in Acts 2, the Holy Spirit appears at a crucial meeting between the *laos* and the *ethne* and turns that meeting into a crucial evangelistic event that breaks with the past. Peter, in a state of shock, impetuous as ever, asks whether anyone would oppose him if he were to baptize Cornelius and his household. Everyone is too stunned to say anything. Peter then baptizes them and thus gives the approval of the church.

When he gets to Jerusalem, he runs into trouble. The church disapproves of what he has done. It is interesting that the brunt of the criticism is not that Peter had baptized the uncircumcised but that he had had table fellowship with them. He broke a rule that defined the distinction between Jew and Gentile. In sharing the meal in the household of Cornelius, a Gentile, Peter went over to the other side and accepted them also as God's people and had a non-kosher meal with them. Peter is no theologian. He simply tells his story that now includes the story of Cornelius. In the retelling, the story of Cornelius becomes part of the continuing gospel story but introduces a decisive break with the Jewish Christian story. Peter ends with the statement, "If then God gave them the same gift that he gave us when we believed in the Lord Jesus Christ, who was I that I could hinder God?" (Acts 11:17). It is remarkable that Peter does not call for circumcision before baptism. Such a move would not have caused a problem. The problem was that Peter had given the approval of the church and granted church membership to Cornelius and his household without requiring them first to become part of the Jewish story.

As we know, the struggle continued in the Council of Jerusalem (Acts 15) and even after that as Paul, the anomalous thirteenth apostle, staked his claim to being appointed by the risen Lord to be an apostle to the Gentiles just as Peter had been appointed an apostle to the Jews (cf. Gal. 2).

This is an extremely rich passage of scripture, and we do not have the time to mine it more fully. I would like to end this exposition with a question. Could we also be attempting to stop the continuing gospel story by using baptism in the same way as the early Jewish church tried to use circumcision? Possibly quoting Jesus (cf. Jn. 4:22), the early church seems to have said, "Do you not know that salvation is of the Jews?"[44] Hence, the way to be saved is to abandon your story and be incorporated into the

Jewish story through circumcision. It is this position that the Holy Spirit contradicts and subverts in the Cornelius episode. Yet now we seem to be saying, "Do you not know that salvation is of the Christians? Therefore, the way forward is to abandon your story and be incorporated into the existing Christian story." This has been the basic thrust of neo-orthodoxy, manifested in missionary practice. A reassertion of the truth of what happened in the Cornelius episode would recognize the fact that it is the Jewish Christian story that came to be incorporated into other stories, with all their religious and cultural variety, as the gospel story continued.

To put it another way, in the process of proclaiming goods news to the whole creation, the church from time to time has to be converted to a larger understanding of the God of all creation. This is the position taken by an Asian ecumenical statement made in 1965 titled "The Confessing Church in Asia and Its Theological Task":

> We have inherited the "great tradition" of the gospel from those who brought the gospel to Asia, but we believe that Christ has more of his truth to reveal to us as we seek to understand his work among people in their several Asian cultures, their different Asian religions, and their involvement in the contemporary Asian revolution. In the past we have been too inhibited by our fear of syncretism and too tied to inherited traditional and conceptual forms of confession to make such ventures. Such formulations have been signposts and pointers to the truth, but we have often interpreted them, or had them interpreted to us, as the final word of truth so that we have encamped around them, forgetting that even as people of other times and cultures made their own confession, we too must do the same in our time and culture.[45]

It is with the challenge posed by this statement in mind that I proposed the formulation "the people of God in the midst of all God's peoples" as the overriding paradigm for mission at a joint Christian Conference of Asia and Council for World Mission roundtable on mission held in Hong Kong in November 1999. I put forward this formulation because I was convinced that no amount of argumentation, qualification, or clarification would make the neo-orthodox formulation for the task of Christian mission provide us with a satisfactory paradigm for understanding the task for Christian mission in our time. I felt that a clear break was necessary to articulate a new paradigm that was emerging through various ecumenical discussions and positions for conceiving the task for Christian mission in our time.

The paradigm I proposed is sharper than what it has become, the people of God among all God's peoples. This formulation, although affirming that all peoples are created by God in the image of God, could quite easily, with the reduction of "in the midst of" to "among," be interpreted to mean that we among all God's peoples have been privileged.

The formulation "in the midst of" emphasizes a spatial paradigm that I would hold is very biblical. To understand this paradigm in terms of its biblical roots would require us to hold in view the canon of scripture, rather than just its parts.

Usually Genesis 1—11, which begins our canon of scripture and tells the general human story, is dismissed as a mere preamble to the real Israelite or biblical story that begins with the call of Abraham in chapter 12. A better view would be to understand Genesis 1—11 as a theological setting for what follows. Thus understood, Genesis 1:26ff. presents an account of the creation of humanity (*adam*) with a differentiation into male and female to carry forward the blessing given at creation: "Be fruitful and multiply, and fill the earth" (Gen. 1:28). After several vicissitudes in the general human story we come to Genesis 11, the story of the tower of Babel, which speaks of a further differentiation of humanity into several *ethne* or nations.

In large measure, the interpretation of the tower of Babel episode has been conditioned by the way in which Genesis 1—11 as a whole is usually understood. The fall of humanity, reported in Genesis 3, colors the interpretation of the rest of the general human story, so that it is seen as an unmitigated account of human perversion and sin that culminates in the tower of Babel episode in Genesis 11. Genesis 12 is then viewed as a fresh start with the call of Abraham as the centerpiece in a new human drama. From this perspective, the nations, who are part of the general human story narrated in Genesis 1—11, are expected to find their redemption through Abraham (cf. Gen. 12:3), because their collective histories have already been repudiated.

An important element in this understanding of Genesis 1—11 is how the story of the tower of Babel is itself interpreted. In his article "Unity and Diversity in God's Creation: A Study of the Babel Story," Bernhard W. Anderson surveys various interpretations of Genesis 11. He notes two main positions with their advocates. One position, made particularly during the medieval period, is that several languages and races are the result of God's punishment for the hubris exhibited at Babel, with the key text being "let us make a name for ourselves" (Gen. 11: 4), which is taken as the effort to build a tower reaching to the skies presumably to reach God. Because the story has as a background a picture of the Babylonian ziggurat, stairs leading up in Babylonian temples to *babillim* (gate of the gods), this interpretation of the story is acceptable. The other position, which is as old as the interpretation of the Jewish historian Josephus, is as one Jewish rabbi put it, God's response to the human "resistance to the divine will that the children of men be dispersed over the whole world." From this viewpoint, the purpose of the story is not to narrate a tragic loss of unity, with diversity as the consequence of sin, but rather, as John Calvin understood Genesis 11, diversity "flowed from the benediction and grace of God."

As Anderson argues, although both positions could be derived from Genesis 11 taken by itself, the more important question is "How does it function in the total context of Genesis 1—11?" Why did the Priestly Writer, who brought the whole of the Pentateuch together, place this well-crafted story, which has no antecedents in the earlier part of Genesis, at this particular point? For Anderson the key motif is the blessing given to humanity at creation: "Be fruitful and multiply, and fill the earth" (Gen. 1:28). After the flood, which almost reduced the whole of God's creation to its primeval watery chaos, God reissues the same blessing in the covenant with Noah and his descendents, with creation being restored (Gen. 9:1–17). Verses 18–19 form a bridge to Genesis 10 and 11: "The sons of Noah who went out of the ark were Shem, Ham, and Japheth…These three were the sons of Noah; and from these the whole earth was peopled."

After a brief interlude narrating the sin of Ham, Genesis 10 presents a table of nations as descendents of the sons of Noah. In its context in the text, Genesis 11 functions to explain theologically Genesis 10. It presents the diversity of the human race as a consequence of God's, ensuring that the blessing given to humanity at creation and renewed with Noah did not stagnate in one place with a false unity, which a single language imposed.[46]

Independently, Choan Seng Song comes to the same conclusion. "Very few exegetes," argues Song, "have understood dispersion in the world not as God's punishment for human pride but as fulfilment of God's command." He then quotes with approval the insight of a British Semitist, S. R. Driver, who makes the discerning remark that the story of the tower of Babel "shows how the distribution of mankind into nations, and diversity of languages, are elements in [God's] providential plan for the development and progress of humanity."[47]

Although it is true that Genesis 1—11 is relentless in its depiction of all forms of human sin and depravity and the condign punishment that follows, it is equally clear in portraying the divine concern, or grace, that overrides both human failing and the ensuing punishment, so that God's creation may be both preserved and sustained. From this revised perspective, Genesis 10 may be seen as providing a table of nations, as known to the biblical writer, exemplifying the fact that several nations are a consequence of the blessing given to humanity in creation and renewed in the covenant with Noah. Genesis 11 follows with an explanation of how this happened.

The episode begins with the explanatory statement that until then the whole earth had one language and a limited vocabulary. While migrating from the east—that is, from Eden (Gen. 2:8)—in response to the blessing to fill the earth, the people came to a plain and attempted to settle down. Instead of moving sideways over the face of the earth, they planned to move upward and make a name for themselves through the construction of a tower reaching to the sky. Then God thwarted the human attempt to move upward and scattered them over the face of the earth by turning a monolingual situation into a multilingual one.

God does not break down the tower being built, which would be a response to human arrogance and pride that attempts to reach God. In fact, the text only speaks of a very high tower reaching to the skies that would be a memorial. The important divine response is the scattering of the people, for which God comes down.

The Argentinean biblical scholar Néstor O. Míguez also agrees that the Babel story is not about punishment. After noting that the words *language* and *land* (in Hebrew one word *'eretz* means both "land" and earth") are in the opening and closing sentences (vv. 1 and 7ff.) of this story, he then goes on to say:

> So, God descends and decides to put an end to that project (v. 7). Now, in the biblical tradition, when God descends from heaven it is a liberative act. We never read that God comes down in order to punish. God does not need to move from heaven to punish. But God comes down to join the people to overcome oppression. So, for example, we read in Exodus 3:8, that God comes down to deliver Israel from the Egyptians and take them again to their assigned land.[48]

The problem of noncommunication and suspicion that appears in Genesis 11 is symbolically resolved in Acts 2:5–12 when a representative group from the nations is caught up in the Pentecostal experience, and all groups receive the message in their own language. The miracle of Pentecost is not that the representatives of the nations were enabled to hear and understand Aramaic, which would have been the language in which Peter spoke, but rather that they heard the message each in his or her own language. They then spoke among themselves, marveling at what was happening. They understood one another and the purpose of what God had done in Jesus Christ. Thus, Acts 2 does not abrogate plurality as a divisive human condition, but rather affirms it as an enriching of one another in a receptive plurality.

Going back to the account in Genesis, chapter 12 follows chapter 11 to pick up one story among the many, the story of Abraham, and immediately links it with the other stories by saying that Abraham is called to be a blessing to the nations (12:3). Toward the end of the canon of scripture we have Revelation 21, with its heavenly vision of the "New Jerusalem," which appears as a gracious gift of God, when the old heaven and the old earth and the sea have passed away (21:1ff.) It is the new creation of God, without even an earthly temple, so that the sacred and secular are collapsed into one in which God's reign and realm are realized. Its gates are never shut during the day and there is no night, so the city is open to the traffic of life. The kings as the representatives of the nations bring their treasures (21:22–27). These do not find their way into the Holy City either *through* the history of the old Israel or *through* the history of the New Israel (the *laos*). In some ways it is redolent of Matthew 8:11, where Jesus says in response to the faith of one outside Israel that many will come from east and west and sit with the patriarchs at the messianic banquet. As Lakshman Wickremesinghe of Sri Lanka put it:

> The nations have distinctive histories in the providence of God, so that in the final kingdom of Christ their sicknesses are healed and their riches become an acceptable offering to enrich life in heaven. National histories have a significance and autonomy which the church must both appreciate and assimilate as it engages in mission...And so, we must enfold in one overall vision what the Lord is doing both in the church and in our nations, when we engage in mission at the present time.[49]

Within this total perspective, the call of Abraham, to which we too are heirs in Jesus Christ, is to be a blessing to the nations: "I will bless those who bless you, and the one who curses you I will curse; and in you all the families of the earth shall be blessed [or will bless themselves]" (Gen. 12:3; see also Isa. 19:23–25).

Lest this vocation of the church being a blessing and inversely being a cause for cursing be misunderstood, let me illustrate with the example of the Catholic and Protestant churches in India. The majority of those in these churches are from the caste group called untouchable, or better, the term they themselves use, *Dalits*, meaning "the broken ones." Much of the missionary evangelistic work in India was done among these largely because the usual missionary strategy of beginning with the "top," with the Brahmins and other high caste people, did not work too well. The assumption in this strategy is that once those at the top of the social ladder are converted, others will follow. In India, as in several other parts of the world, the Brahmins and other high caste groups were by and large impervious to the Christian message. The Dalits, on the contrary, found the church to be a liberating community that treated them as human beings and not as untouchables. Having experienced this liberation and acceptance, Christian Dalits have done much to draw the attention of Indian society and the world at large to the plight of the Dalits. Dalit theology has been instrumental in working for the liberation of the Dalits and in articulating a theology that is critical of Brahminic attitudes in society, as well as in Indian churches and Indian Christian theology.[50] The Hindutva movement, which brands Christianity as a foreign religion that interferes in the religious life of the Indians, is led by Brahmins. This, in my opinion, is the real reason for the Hindutva antipathy to both Christianity and Islam. Both these religions have accepted the Dalits and thus have upset the stratification of Indian society along caste lines.

The history of the church in India, as in other parts of the world, is replete with instances of the church being perceived both as a blessing and as a curse. Sometimes it is for the same reason. When it has opposed untouchability and opened its doors to the poor and the marginalized, it has been seen as a blessing. When it has opposed *sati*[51] and other forms of oppression of women in the church and in society, it has been seen as a blessing. Those whose power and vested interests it has thus challenged and undermined see it as a curse. It has been perceived as a blessing when it has put itself and its services at the disposal of the whole community and as a curse when it has attempted to exercise its power to protect institutional interests. A self-critical examination of its own history would provide the church with the criteria it needs not only for its ongoing mission to be a blessing in the midst of the nations but also for the theological exploration that is needed to undergird this emerging missiological emphasis.

To return to our earlier discussion, the Acts of the Apostles, with chapter 2 as its centerpiece, depicts the church or Christian community being scattered over the face of the earth and locates Christian communities or churches in the midst of the nations. The Christian community, taken as a whole, holds within it the plurality of cultures and languages given by God in a receptive plurality offered through the gift of God's Spirit. To be scattered in the midst of the nations is our geographical location in terms of which the missionary task has to be grasped.

The matter of geographical location can be explained also in another way. The Christian faith does not call for a specific "Christian" geographical location to give our faith existential validity. We do not have to perform an earthly pilgrimage. Geographical references in the Bible have been spiritualized. When we sing John Newton's hymn based on Psalm 46, "Glorious things of thee are spoken, Zion city of our God," like Newton we have no great urge to go to Jerusalem, the earthly Zion. Zion has been spiritualized. If anything, it refers to the new Jerusalem descending from the clouds, whose builder and maker is God (cf. Rev. 21 and Heb. 11). Likewise Jordan and quite a few of the other geographical locations in the Bible have been spiritualized. Few Christians have been moved to visit the so-called Holy Land—which of late has become quite an unholy place—as an essential element in the practice of their faith.

This is another way of expressing the conviction that we have no earthly city or land that is specially ours except the lands in which we are located. On earth we have been placed in the midst of the nations as were the people of Israel during the exile. The exhortation of Jeremiah to the people of Israel scattered in the midst of the nations is apposite for us. Jeremiah says to them, "Settle down, get married, bring up your children, and, more importantly, pray for the *shalom* (peace, well-being) of those people, for on their *shalom* depends your *shalom*" (cf. Jer. 29). In other words, our salvation, *shalom*, or well-being is mixed up with the salvation of the nations. We have a dual identity: the identity of our faith and the identity of the nation in the midst of which we live. To relate these two identities is an inevitable part of understanding the task of Christian mission in our time. In so doing, Christian mission also has to deal with the problem of religion itself. Not everything in every religion, including Christianity, is good. Nor is everything bad. The continued retelling of the gospel story as it moves forward among the nations is expected to gather in and affirm what is good and eliminate what is bad.

From this perspective, the modern era of Western missions accomplished an unfinished task. Through their work, Christian communities have been placed in almost all the countries of the world. The way forward is not to berate those missionaries, whatever their faults might have been, or to repudiate that history in its totality with the facile assumption, only partly true, that Western missions were nothing but religious clones of colonialism. Whether we like it or not, we are part of that history and gain from that history. The task, rather, is to recover that heritage within a better plotting of the course of church history that now places us in a new missionary situation, which the paradigm "the people of God in the midst of all God's peoples" attempts to capture. It is a paradigm that urges us to explore missiologically the interrelationships that ought to exist between understandings of people as *laos*, *ochlos*, and *ethne*.

In the next chapter we will test the appropriateness of this paradigm for understanding the task for Christian mission with regard to one specific circumstance, namely, that of religio-ethnic strife, in which we are called to express our missionary vocation as channels of God's peace.

8

Christian Mission Today: Testing a Paradigm

We will test the adequacy of the paradigm "the people of God in the midst of all God's peoples" as we explore a particular challenge for Christian mission today, namely, the situation of religio-ethnic strife that is characteristic of the world in which we live. First, we will derive from the Letter to the Ephesians a theological basis for seeing our vocation as channels of God's peace, which vocation translates this paradigm to face the challenge that religio-ethnic strife specifically poses. Second, we will read the signs of the time in terms of a political paradigm, "the clash of civilizations," which grapples with the fact that enmity defines relationships within and between nations understood as civilizations. This political paradigm is at variance with and is antagonistic to another political paradigm that presses upon us the reality that, whether we like it or not, whether we accept it or not, we belong to "one world." Third, we will look at an alternative political paradigm, which attempted to translate into political action the love ethic of Jesus: "Love your enemies; do good to them that hate you." Fourth, we will set out the consequences for the church as it appropriates this alternative to express its vocation to be a channel of God's peace. Here we will argue that only a church holding within itself a multiplicity of nations that are reconciled to each other can be a channel of God's peace in a world situation that is rife with hatred. Finally, we will explore how this missionary vocation could be expressed using the paradigm of God's people in the midst of all God's peoples.

A Theological Basis

The challenge for Christian mission in a situation of religio-ethnic strife was well stated at the Canberra Assembly (1991) of the World

Council of Churches, which spoke of a reconciled and renewed creation as the goal of the mission of the church.

The basis for this understanding of the task for Christian mission is derived from the epistle to the Colossians and the epistle to the Ephesians. In proposing this goal for mission, it also states that "the diversity of cultures is of immediate relevance to the church's ministry of reconciliation and sharing for it affects both the relationships within churches and also the relationship with people of other faiths." In other words, reconciling the diversity of cultures within churches seems to be a precondition for Christian engagement in the work of reconciliation with and within people of other faiths.

The ingredients for this understanding of the task for Christian mission is drawn particularly from Ephesians 2:12–22, where the author of the epistle presents a particular relationship between Israel and the world of nations that has been accomplished through Christ's death on the cross. To grasp the distinctive insight that Ephesians provides, it would be helpful to compare it with how other New Testament writers view the same relationship.

All the New Testament writers are clear that something new has happened in the relationship between Israel and the world of nations in and through Christ's death on the cross and Christ's resurrection. They perceive a new relationship between the people of God and all God's peoples.

For some, especially the writers of the gospel accounts, the church supplants Israel. However, for Paul, a rabbinic Jew, as the New Testament theologian J. Christiaan Beker says, "Israel has not only a positive function in past-salvation history, but also a positive function in future salvation history."[1] Addressing the church in Rome, Paul says,

> I want you to understand this mystery: a hardening has come upon part of Israel, until the full number of the Gentiles has come in. And so all Israel will be saved...As regards the gospel they are enemies of God for your sake; but as regards election they are beloved, for the sake of their ancestors. (Rom. 11:25–29)

Compared with these two understandings, the author of Ephesians has a different perception of the relationship between Israel and the world of nations. The author perceives two things to have happened through Christ's death on the cross. First, the death on the cross is perceived not so much in terms of an atoning sacrifice (i.e., expiation for our sins) as God making a new covenant through "the blood of the covenant" that includes the nations with Israel: "But now in Christ Jesus you who once were far off have been brought near by the blood of Christ" (Eph. 2:13). Israel and the nations have become one in Jesus Christ through the cross, or rather through Christ's death on the cross.[2] Second, through Christ's death on the cross the dividing wall of hostility between Israel and the nations has been torn down: "For he is our peace; in his flesh he has made both groups into one and has broken down the dividing wall, that is, the hostility between us. He has abolished the law with its commandments [i.e., those things that define and keep Israel separate]…that he might create in himself one new humanity in place of the two, thus making peace" (2:14–15). The author of Ephesians is not concerned with divisions and hostilities in social, economic, or even overtly political matters. Rather, the author's concern is with the hostility that divides nations.

Using the metaphor of the body (Eph. 4), the author affirms two things. First, it is the hostility and not the difference that has been abolished through the shedding of Christ's blood. Second, the practice of unity that witnesses to what God has accomplished in Christ values each member of the body. Although neither of these realities are yet true of the world of nations, they are held to be true of the church.

Drawing from this theological position to speak to our situation, the church, which holds within itself persons from many nations, is called to bear witness to the good news that, in Jesus Christ, God is proposing to put an end to the factionalism and hostilities that define a divided world.

Clearly, we cannot talk of the church in the abstract or about a "universal church" without reference to the local church. Although the epistle talks of the mission of the church, as universal church, it is addressed to a particular church, the church in Ephesus. Through its practice of unity, each church is to give evidence of the reconciliation between "nations" within itself as a sign and foretaste that in Jesus Christ the walls of hostility between nations has been broken down. In this way, each church is to give credence to its vocation to be a channel of God's peace.

Reading the Signs of the Time

The location of this vocation is in a world situation, which the political scientist Samuel Huntington characterizes as "the clash of civilisations." In a book with the same title and with the additional words "and the Remaking of World Order," published in 1996, he speaks with deadly clarity about our present situation. He writes,

One grim *Weltanschauung* [worldview or world outlook] for this new era was well expressed by the Venetian nationalist demagogue in Michael Dibdin's novel, *Dead Lagoon*: "There can be no true friends without true enemies. *Unless we hate what we are not we cannot love what we are.* These are old truths we are painfully rediscovering after a century and more of sentimental cant. Those who deny them, deny their family, their heritage, their culture, their birthright, their very selves. They will not lightly be forgiven." (italics added)

Huntington then goes on to say,

The unfortunate truth in these old truths cannot be ignored by statesmen and scholars. For peoples seeking identity and reinventing ethnicity, enemies are essential, and the potentially most dangerous enmities occur across fault lines between the world's major civilizations.[3]

In presenting the clash of civilizations as the prevailing political paradigm of our time and therefore as a framework for reading the signs of the time, Huntington enables us not only to perceive why something as horrendous as a September 11 could happen together with the tragedy of the bombing of Afghanistan, but also to see why political leaders of powerful nations feel constrained to identify an "axis of evil" and seem to be engaged in a neverending search for enemies.[4] This political paradigm also explains why the Rashtrya Swayamseveka Sang and the Vishwa Hindu Parishad, with their varied and often confused confrontational messages, have such an appeal in India. To be Indian, according to this ideology, one must be Hindu.

Such an understanding of identity presents in rather stark terms the fact that pluralism, at least in terms of religious cultures, has always been intolerant of itself. There are two classical forms of intolerance. One is the Semitic form evident especially in Christianity and Islam. (Judaism remains largely as a tribal religion.) This form of intolerance urges that differences either have to be converted or destroyed. "Choose either the Book or the sword" has many a time been manifested in history as these two religions clashed with each other or with other religions. The other is the Hindu form, which holds that all religious differences are but accidents of history and geography. "All roads lead to Vrindhavan" may be a metaphor for this form of intolerance. Hinduism would then posit an eternal religion, *sanatana dharma*, which transcends all specific religions. Soon it becomes apparent that, in some form or another, Hinduism is that eternal religion. It then seeks to absorb other religions and thus to kill them. This is what happened to ancient Buddhism in India and what almost happened to Buddhism in Ceylon. The Hindutva movement in India is a modern, virulent expression of this form of intolerance, which expects people of all religions to locate their religion within the

Hindu fold to claim their right to be considered citizens of India. Those who cannot and will not conform to this expectation are deemed to be non-Indian and are identified with foreign enemies. As a speaker in a talk-show on an Indian television channel said, "Every Muslim in India has 'Pakistan' [the arch-enemy of India] written on his heart."

In this situation it is also possible to perceive why any paradigm for mission that presents the people of God over against rather than in the midst of other peoples of God will play into the hands of the prevailing political paradigm of the clash of civilizations. In contrast, to understand our missionary vocation in terms of God's people in the midst of all God's peoples is to accept the fact that scattered among the nations, the Christian community or the church, which holds within it a plurality of cultures and languages, is called to enable the communication and receptiveness that is needed to overcome suspicion and to lead the nations, as they learn from one another, to a deeper understanding and appreciation of God's purpose for the whole creation.

Writing after the events of September 11, Peter Singer presents as an alternative to the clash of civilizations the paradigm of "one world."[5] Although the paradigm of the clash of civilizations provides a good basis for analyzing the prevailing political situation, it cannot and should not be the basis for "the remaking of world order," as Samuel Huntington himself concedes.[6] The interlinkage that "globalization" provides both for good and for ill cannot be ignored. As Singer argues, what is done in one part of the world affects other parts of the world. For instance, the overconsumption of fossil fuels in the U.S. and Europe creates global warming, leading to rising sea levels and floods that adversely affect other parts of the world. These are usually poor nation-states that are powerless to resist the excesses of the more powerful nation-states. It is therefore ethically unacceptable, says Singer, for political leaders to speak narrowly of the non-negotiable lifestyle of the citizens of a rich country,[7] for what adversely affects one part of the world sooner or later will have an impact on the nations that caused the problem. Even if altruism does not persuade, self-interest should, for as a United Nations panel, which Singer quotes, said shortly before the attacks of September 11, "In the global village, someone else's poverty soon becomes one's own problem: of lack of markets for one's products, illegal immigration, pollution, contagious disease, insecurity, fanaticism, terrorism." Singer then goes on to say,

> Terrorism has made our world an integrated community in a new and frightening way. Not merely the activities of our neighbors, but those of the inhabitants of the most remote

mountain valleys of the farthest-flung countries of our planet, have become our business. We need to extend the reach of the criminal law there and to have the means to bring terrorists to justice without declaring war on an entire country in order to do it. For this we need a sound global system of criminal justice, so justice does not become the victim of national differences of opinion. We also need, though it will be far more difficult to achieve, a sense that we really are one community, that we are people who recognize not only the force of prohibitions against killing each other but also the pull of obligations to assist one another.[8]

Although we may not and need not agree with all of Singer's arguments and the details of his analysis, he does present an alternative, which is an ethical response to the trends of globalization expressed in "One Atmosphere," "One Economy," "One Law," and "One Community" (the headings of the chapters in his book). If this global vision of "A Better World?" (the last chapter of his book) is to become a reality, even though not necessarily in terms of the specifics he suggests, then there need to be credible, concrete responses. This is the location in which Christian mission needs to be understood and practiced. Although the clash of civilizations remains the prevailing political paradigm, "called to be channels of God's peace" is a way of understanding Christian mission today in pressing for the recognition and operation of the paradigm "one world."

The Challenge for Christian Mission: "Love Your Enemies"

A major barrier in expressing the vocation to be channels of God's peace in translating the paradigm for Christian mission, God's people in the midst of all God's peoples, is the operation of the political paradigm, the clash of civilizations, also in many churches. The problem is, How do I claim my identity as a black unless I hate the whites in my midst? How do I claim my identity as a feminist unless I hate the men in my midst? How do I love myself as a Tamil unless I hate the Sinhalese in my midst? The list is endless. There may be many reasons, good reasons, why we should hate our enemies. But we have to remember that all these enmities have been nailed with Christ on the cross. Not to recognize and give expression to this truth is to deny the very essence of being the church in the world.

The choice is both simple and difficult. Either we can be defined as churches by the law of the world and therefore conform to the world under the banner "unless we hate what we are not, we cannot love what we are" or we can be defined by the law of Jesus, "love your enemies; do good to them that hate you."

In this situation, the challenge to the church that the love ethic of Jesus can indeed be demonstrated comes from the political arena itself. For some time, especially in the philosophies and actions of Mohandas Gandhi, Martin Luther King, Jr., and Nelson Mandela, this saying of Jesus found political expression to address specific situations. Each translated the love ethic of Jesus into a political philosophy leading to action that has a particular continuity from Gandhi to Mandela, though each translation is specific to its context.

Gandhi translated the love ethic of Jesus into *satyagraha*, which means "truth force." In other words, to counter evil with love is the political operation of truth. For Gandhi, hate and the expression of hate were untruthful because hate is not the quality of God. Truth builds, whereas hate destroys. Gandhi believed that to achieve the truth in sociopolitical life, one must use means that enhance the truth. He stood on its head the Machiavellian principle that the end justifies the means. For Gandhi, the end could not vindicate the means if the end was achieved through untruth. Following recognized Hindu beliefs, Gandhi believed that good motives would produce good results and bad motives would produce bad results. He was clear that the means would shape the end or even that the end was implicit in the means. To illustrate, when he was accused of selfish motives in setting up the Indian Congress Party so that he could be independent India's first prime minister, Gandhi responded publicly. Normally he did not bother to respond to his detractors, but this for him was a serious allegation. After stating that he had already asked Jawaharlal Nehru to be the president of the party, so Nehru would become the first prime minister, Gandhi then went on to say that it is one thing to accuse a person of bad judgment and quite another thing to accuse a person of a bad motive. To accuse a person of a bad motive is to impugn that person's integrity and declare that person untruthful. Gandhi felt he had to confront this accusation because it questioned not only his motives but also his political philosophy, which was premised on the position that only the practice of truth would produce a truthful end.

The Hindu doctrine of *ahimsa* (nonviolence) provided him with the means to resist what was patently untrue, namely, the colonial oppression and exploitation of a nation. This truth Gandhi carried even to advocating a lifestyle that would essentially be nonexploitative. It is said that when someone asked Gandhi whether he expected India to become a powerful nation like Britain, he responded, "Britain used nearly half the planet's resources to become what it became. How many planets do you think there are to use?"

In the practice of *satyagraha* expressed in *ahimsa*, Gandhi and his followers received violence without a reciprocal use of violence to counter the violence inflicted on them. He believed that this was the way to unmask the untruth of violence. Violent force was encountered and resisted with truth force.

British colonial power was able to counter the violence of insurrection with violence. However, it had no weaponry to deal with the moral resistance of those who would not resort to violence. The British prided themselves on being a moral people. Brute force from the soldiers of His Majesty's government against unarmed civilians was often punished to prove this point. The practice of *satyagraha* through *ahimsa* laid bare Britain's claim to be a moral people. Of course, the economic condition of Britain after engaging in two costly world wars also made it difficult to maintain an empire. India won its independence.

For Martin Luther King, Jr., truth was in the preaching/proclamation of the truth that all human beings have equal rights and have a right to be treated equally. This truth was taken to the streets with people of all colors in the fight against discrimination of people of color. He appealed to the constitution of the United States. The only way his position could be declared untrue was for "the enemy" to hold publicly that Negroes are of a lower racial order and therefore need not be treated as equal to the white Caucasoid people. This position had already been denied in the Civil Rights Act of 1866, which said that "such citizens, of every race and color...shall have the same right...to make and enforce contracts." This position was strengthened four years later in the Fifteenth Amendment to the Constitution, which said that the right to vote "shall not be denied...on account of race." This was also the basis on which King spoke against the war in Vietnam. The truth to be realized on U.S. soil also needed to determine U.S. behavior outside U.S. soil. Like Gandhi, King refused to resist violence with violence.

For Nelson Mandela, the truth in the fight against apartheid was not to replace white rule with black rule, but rather to debunk the concept of apartheid, expose its untruth, and dismantle its institutions. This had to be done so that a multiethnic, multireligious South Africa could prove that apartheid—the separate cultural and economic development of ethnic groups, imposed on the basis of a questionable ideology of racial differences—was patently untrue. The ideology of apartheid gave expression to the false notion of a racial gradation of humankind known as the "the great chain of being." Supported with a questionable exegesis of certain passages of Genesis, it used a form of social Darwinism to argue that humankind was divided into races, with the black Negroid people at the bottom, leading through other racial groups to the white Caucasoid people at the top. This is why in the fight against racism the World Council of Churches declared that "apartheid is a sin against God and fellow human beings" and denounced "any theological justification of apartheid as a heretical perversion of the Gospel."[9] The doctrine of the separate development of races imposed by an Afrikaaner government was not only unjust but patently untrue.

Against the brute force of untruth devoid of any semblance of morality, Mandela did not deny the use of force to resist, as did Dietrich Bonhoeffer in contesting the evil of national socialism that was manifested in the Third Reich under Adolf Hitler. However, Mandela was against the indiscriminate use of force, which the Truth and Reconciliation Commission was asked to deal with. Few realize that the Truth and Reconciliation Commission was in the first instance set up to deal with "excesses" by the members of the African National Congress.[10]

In the practice of truth, these three leaders did contest their enemies and resisted the efforts of the enemy to have dominion over them. However, they refused to get dragged into a hate war.

Nelson Mandela demonstrated this fact when he invited the wives of former presidents of South Africa to the President's house for tea. These ladies are labeled collectively in some circles in South Africa as the "womb of apartheid." From the moment they came to the moment they left, it is said that Mandela spoke to them only in Afrikaans. They left saying of Mandela, "What a gracious man!" Many think of it as a wonderful gesture from a great statesman. That may be true. But I wonder whether Mandela did it for them or for himself. To meet them face to face in table fellowship and to speak the language of the enemy would have been for Mandela a spiritual exercise that contradicted the dictum that "unless we hate what we are not, we cannot love what we are."

Besides bearing witness to the fact that "love your enemies; do good to them that hate you" could be translated into a political philosophy and the hard realities of political action, these three political leaders also present an insight into the formation of community. All three were concerned with building communities that were more than natural religio-ethnic communities. The political communities they were intent on building were to be plural communities, which would be home to several religio-ethnic communities. In fact, they were giving political expression to what the epistle to the Ephesians is saying: "For he is our peace; in his flesh he has made both groups into one and has broken down the dividing wall, that is, the hostility between us" (2:14).

To use the imagery of Archbishop Desmond Tutu, which he seems to have borrowed from the U.S. civil rights leader Jesse Jackson, all three political leaders in various ways were saying, "We are a rainbow people." Although different colors make a rainbow, together they constitute the light of truth. It would not be incidental to Desmond Tutu's use of this image that the rainbow is also a sign of hope (cf. Gen. 9:11–15).

So both norms—"unless we hate what we are not, we cannot love what we are" and "love your enemies; do good to them that hate you"—are realistic norms for political action. One reinforces natural community through an identity that excludes others with the utmost violence. The other, although affirming natural community, attempts to transcend the limitations of the natural community of race and religion to build plural communities

Today, our missionary calling to be channels of God's peace, to a ministry of reconciliation, is to choose the option of Gandhi, King, and Mandela, who have demonstrated an alternative to the political philosophies and actions built on the premise that unless we hate what we are not, we cannot love what we are. Over against this political ethos we are called to proclaim, through word and deed, that there is another reality that is operative in history, namely, that through his death on the cross, Jesus Christ has put to death the hostility that has become the defining character of our time, to create a new humanity that holds many communities in an inclusive community. To do this, we first have to be reconciled communities ourselves if the message we proclaim is to be credible.

Appropriating the Challenge: The Road to Reconciliation

The issues of racism and casteism and all forms of ethnic strife have created deep divisions within churches. Let us take just the case of racism as one of the forms of hostility that needs to be addressed.

Speaking specifically to the theological scene in the U.S., the black theologian James Cone states why reconciliation between blacks and whites in U.S. churches is difficult if not impossible. Although black theologians have addressed the legacy of slavery and have attempted to recast the identity of black people so that they may jettison the slave term *Negro* for the positive term *black,* white theologians have by and large refused to address this blight in the continuing history of the country. The title of Cone's article, "Theology's Great Sin: Silence in the Face of White Supremacy,"[11] itself identifies the problem. He begins by quoting Dietrich Bonhoeffer: "Silence in the face of evil is itself evil: God will not hold us guiltless. Not to speak is to speak. Not to act is to act." Alongside this statement of Bonhoeffer, he sets a quotation from Martin Luther King, Jr.: "We will have to repent...not merely for the vitriolic words and actions of the bad people but the appalling silence of the good people."[12] Cone then goes on to say that even thirty years after black theologians, such as he, had attacked racism in American theology, nothing significant has happened. While American theologians have been engaged in the "death of God" controversy and much more, hardly a word has been spoken on the prevalence of racism. Europeans and white North Americans inflicted unspeakable horror on many native people, either confiscating their land and destroying the people or stealing the people from their land and turning them into slaves. He then goes on to say,

> Racism is particularly alive and well in America. It is America's original sin and as it is institutionalized at all levels of society; it is its most persistent and intractable evil. Though racism inflicts massive suffering, few American theologians have even bothered to address white supremacy as a moral evil and as a radical contradiction of our humanity and religious identities.[13]

Cone argues that it is not sufficient for a person to admit that racism is wrong and refuse to countenance it in his or her own social behavior. White people must come to terms with the history of black slavery, its pain and its sin, and the fact that it has advantaged one group at the expense of the other and continues to do so. Unless the systemic operation of racism in church and society is identified and combated, reconciliation in the church is not possible. This is a theological problem. Cone identifies the major cause for the silence in American theology: "White theologians avoid racial dialogue because talk about white supremacy arouses deep feelings of guilt. Guilt is a heavy burden to bear."[14] But, as Cone points out, this divisive issue must be faced because "we are all bound together, inseparably linked to a common humanity. What we do to one another we do to ourselves."[15]

In contrast, the churches in Australia and New Zealand are tackling the blight of racism head on and are accepting and coming to terms with both the guilt and the consequences of racism. For reasons of space, we will look briefly only at the Australian scene.

Having built white settler Australia, beginning in 1770 (with the arrival of Captain James Cook), on the questionable application of the doctrine of *terra nullius*, "unoccupied land," native populations were driven from their ancestral lands and declared, in effect, a "no-people." It is therefore no surprise that in the ·eighteenth and nineteenth centuries, in cases involving white atrocities against Aboriginal people, courts of law were often required to settle the question of whether the Aboriginals could even be considered as human beings. Substituting Aboriginals for foxes in organized hunts is just another unspeakable horror inflicted on the no-people.

Lately, two court cases in particular have turned the tide of government actions and have forced non-Aboriginal people (a term that is now being used with increasing frequency) to recognize the fact that the Aboriginal people not only were the original inhabitants of the land but also have a history in the land stretching back for more than four millennia. This fact has been established through the carbon dating of Aboriginal artifacts and archaeological excavations of Aboriginal sacred sites.

Koiki Mabo, a Torres Straits Islander, challenged in 1982 the illegal occupation of islands belonging to the Meriam people. After ten years of hearings and debates among the High Court judges of Australia, Mabo's challenge was upheld,[16] though Mabo himself died before the verdict was announced. Equally significant was the Wik case (1996),[17] in which it was declared that Aboriginal native rights to lands that were leased in perpetuity to white graziers (sheep and cattle farmers) had not been extinguished. In this situation, against all the racist hype that land is being taken away from white Australians, all that the Aboriginal people are asking for is access to their ancestral religious sites, from which they had been alienated. They are not seeking to dispossess the present holders of the lease. Where land was taken away from them wrongfully, just compensation is being paid.

Repentance, reparation, and reconciliation at last seem possible, as all Australian people are being asked to work together in a treaty that would go at least some way to put right past wrongs and make reconciliation possible.[18] Through this and other such processes, non-Aboriginal and Aboriginal people are learning to live together lest they perish together. Attempts are being made to deal with the deep divisions that racism has caused and to come to terms with white guilt and Aboriginal hurt.[19]

The churches in Australia have been active participants in this struggle, and there have been theological responses also from non-Aboriginals. They have not only initiated government action to deal with the race issue but have also accompanied government decisions to put right past wrongs. Churches at all levels—congregational, regional, and national—have sought to bring about reconciliation between the people both in church and society. The Aboriginal-Islander Congress of the Uniting Church in Australia, set up in 1985, not only provides a forum for the native inhabitants of the land to debate issues that would be of particular consequence to them but also provides them with a platform to voice their position on issues concerning the whole church. Seldom, if ever, are their views and positions disregarded.

This ministry has been costly and has often been done in the face of enormous resistance. The slogan "Reconciliation: The Way to Australia's Future" seems credible as a goal to be achieved, though the road to it is still rocky and rife with pitfalls.

Let us return to Paul's letter to Philemon, which we discussed in chapter 3, for a further exegesis to locate the specific challenge for the church and seek a way to resolve the "hostility that separates us."

Paul sent Onesimus, the runaway slave, back to Philemon, the slave owner, so that Onesimus may recover and affirm his dignity as a child of Christ in the presence of Philemon, the slave master. To keep running away from that confrontation would only have reinforced his slave-consciousness. To recall another episode, Moses did not simply run away with the people of Israel from slavery in Egypt in the dead of night. The exodus from Egypt was liberative because Moses had already confronted Pharaoh with the words "Let my people go!" Nonetheless, Pharaoh with his forces pursued the slaves he was losing, because Pharaohs will always do that. Domination and exploitation is the name of the game.

However, Philemon was required to give a different response. Paul not only sent Onesimus back for the sake of Onesimus to confront Philemon, he also challenged Philemon. Philemon was asked to accept Onesimus as a brother in Christ. Only then could Philemon demonstrate the truth that he, Philemon, was a child of Christ. In other words, the return of Onesimus was necessary for Onesimus and for Philemon, for it was in that confrontation that true reconciliation could take place and each could demonstrate that they were indeed children of God.

Clearly, only love, not force, could make this happen. But having pleaded in love with Philemon, Paul adds a deft touch. Although Paul is in prison, he yet says to Philemon, "Prepare a guest room for me, for I am hoping through your prayers to be restored to you" (v. 22). In effect, he was saying, I will be checking up on you!

A reconciliation that overcomes the hostility that divides us cannot be a cheap reconciliation that papers over the cracks. It happens through Christ's death on the cross. To accept that fact as operational in the church and in society is to recognize that it is through the victims of the present system that such reconciliation can take place. To be channels of God's peace, we need one another and need to learn from one another. But if such knowledge is to liberate both oppressed and oppressor, both within the church and in the world of politics, the basic framework for such theology and its major insights must come from those who are on the periphery and at the margins of life. It must come from those whom we have placed outside the system to hang with Jesus on the cross. This has been and still is a hard pill to swallow. That is why quite often the challenges that Dalit theology, Black Theology, and Womanist theology—to name but a few—pose are not taken into account, and the theologies themselves are branded as sectarian and left on the periphery. Is it ignorance, or is it arrogance, that makes us think that these theologies are the febrile inventions of insignificant people? At their best, these theologies are about the liberation of the oppressor and the oppressed through the creation and operation of liberating relationships that affirm fullness of life for all. Not to recognize this fact is to deny that it is those on the periphery who are to be at the very center of our theology. Indeed, for Jesus of Nazareth, as it should be for us, the periphery is the center. The church, which holds within itself a plurality of nations, is required *both* to provide space for those who are "acted upon" to claim their identity *and* to embrace them for the contribution they can make to express the vocation to be channels of God's peace.

In this regard, it is not accidental that Gandhi, King, and Mandela, who exposed the untruth of racism and oppression and struggled to create inclusive and reconciled communities, came from the periphery, where their respective oppressing societies had placed them.

Having taken into account the challenge to Philemon, there is also a challenge to Onesimus. The challenge to Onesimus is that he be willing to participate in a joint task with Philemon to seek a new framework of relationships and theological dialogue within which *all voices* could be heard and valued. In other words, Onesimus alone cannot do the job. We need one another, and we need to learn from one another, *albeit in a new framework*, to come up with a theology in dialogue to appropriate our calling to be channels of God's peace.

To shift the discussion to a different forum to illustrate this point, for quite some time, as I pointed out in chapter 1, Asian theologians argued to be free from the deadening weight not only of European theology but also of Latin American liberation theology. We needed space to find and express our plural identities in situations characterized not only by the reality of Asian poverty and suffering but also by the reality of Asian religiosity. Having done that, we have been challenged to re-engage in the broader theological arena not to justify ourselves but to bring the riches of the nations into the world church.

Taking this challenge into account, let us look at a few examples of Asian understandings of peace to communicate understandings of peace that go against the grain of what the powerful understand as peace.

There is a basic human yearning for peace all over the world, and the bearers of this yearning are ordinary people—women, children, farmers, and so on—who have no political ambitions. If anything, they are the victims of political ambitions and power games. They use different metaphors for peace that depict this yearning. The two words normally used in my language, Tamil, are *amaidhi* and *samadhanam*. *Amaidhi* has its source in the Dravidian family of languages and literally means "rest" or "quiet." It is the absence of turbulence. It is the cessation of desiring after things that cause unrest. It is stillness. It is like the primordial stillness from which creation arose. *Samadhanam,* which comes from Sanskrit, has a different image. It has the same root as *samadhi,* which refers to the concentration of the mind as in meditation. From this understanding arise steadiness, composure, and the bringing together, or reconciling, of two groups. The ideogram *hei-wa* or *ping-he* in the Chinese family of languages is made up of two characters: One denotes harmony or level, and the other has a mouth and grain. When all are fed, there is peace.

The argument is not that these understandings of peace, which have their source in Asian religions and Asian peasant experience, should replace the English word *peace.* Rather, they challenge an understanding of peace that has its source in political understandings of peace based on power relations. The English word *peace* has its roots in *pax Romana,* leading to *pax Britannica,* and now to *pax Americana.* In this sense, to keep the peace is to impose the will of the Emperor or Pharaoh. It is to eliminate dissent and silence the voice of the people. It denies the participation of the many.

Then there will be a cry for justice. Political understandings and practice of peace from the powerful and the yearning for justice of the powerless are often at loggerheads. Justice questions the status quo. It calls for a more equal distribution and accounting of power. In this situation, as M. M. Thomas once reminded us, "We are called to be messengers of peace in situations of strife, and messengers of strife in situations of false peace."[20]

The metaphor for peace that the Letter to the Ephesians carries is Christ on the cross, which is foolishness to the Greeks (philosophy), sedition to the Romans (politics), and a stumbling block to those within the church who would rather follow either of these (bad theology).

What is the metaphor for peace that the church should carry? That would be a meaningful question for a church that takes seriously its vocation to be a channel of God's peace. Through the reconciliation realized between the representatives of the nations within itself and thus opening the way to learn from one another, it would incarnate its missionary calling to be God's people in the midst of all God's peoples. It would then strive to demonstrate the communication and receptiveness that is needed to overcome suspicion, and to lead the nations, as they learn from one another, to a deeper understanding and appreciation of God's purpose for the whole creation.

Without a doubt, this is a costly vocation. In his chapter on "Discipleship and the Cross," Dietrich Bonhoeffer argues that "the call to follow is closely connected with Jesus' prediction of his passion." As

Bonhoeffer points out, it is both suffering and rejection. If it were passion without rejection, then the whole world would have seen it as a terrible tragedy. However, to suffer and be rejected is "passion without honour...and every attempt to prevent it is the work of the devil."[21] He then goes on to say, "The cross is laid on every Christian. The first Christ-suffering which every man must experience is the call to abandon the attachments of this world...Thus it begins; the cross is not the terrible end to an otherwise god-fearing and happy life, but it meets us at the beginning of our communion with Christ." Then in words that were to be prophetic of his own life with Christ, Bonhoeffer says to us today, "When Christ calls a man, he bids him come and die."[22] It is a call to costly discipleship that goes against the tide of a prevailing worldview that says, "Unless we hate what we are not, we cannot love what we are."

In the face of such hostility, our vocation to be channels of God's peace needs to be turned into a prayer: "O God, make us channels of your peace." On the one hand, it is to rely on God's grace, knowing that, as Reinhold Niebuhr put it,

> Nothing that is worth doing can be achieved in our lifetime; therefore we must be saved by hope. Nothing that is true or beautiful or good makes complete sense in any immediate context of history; therefore we must be saved by faith. Nothing we do, however virtuous, can be accomplished alone; therefore we are saved by love. No virtuous act is quite as virtuous from the standpoint of our friend or foe as it is from our standpoint. Therefore we must be saved by the final form of love which is forgiveness.[23]

On the other hand, it is a prayer to live by that forgiveness, which is the final form of love. It is a prayer that calls for cleansing that echoes the sentiments of the prophet Isaiah: "Woe is me...for I am a man of unclean lips, and I live among a people of unclean lips" (Isa. 6:5). We cannot be channels of ethnic and religious prejudice and strife and also at the same time expect to be channels of God's peace. We cannot be channels of corruption—corruption in all its forms—and expect to be channels of God's peace. We cannot conform to the expectations and standards of this world and at the same time attempt to be channels of God's peace.

There is also the sin of churches as institutions from which we need to be cleansed. Church leaders are often more concerned with protecting vested institutional interests than with engaging in the mission of the church. Often, the protection of institutional interests becomes such a "holy" (read: "unholy") enterprise that we are willing to use any means necessary to punish those who put those interests at risk. In his book *The Silencing of Leonard Boff*, Harvey Cox makes a comment about the Vatican that is applicable to all churches as institutions. Thus amending what he says, "Even in a negative way the church is a witnesses to God's grace, because no mere human institution could survive so many scoundrels."[24]

"Make us channels of your peace!" is a prayer that acknowledges the fact that as human beings we cannot rise to this high calling. Only God's grace can transform us into being channels of God's peace.

Incarnating the Challenge: Called To Be Channels of God's Peace

To recall what David Bosch had to say about being a missionary church and recasting it in relation to our missionary concern—namely, to be channels of God's peace—not everyone in the church is required to be a missionary. However, a missionary church sends out missionaries into the world with a message, which the church itself must embody if that message is to be credible. Only a church that is home to the nations can indeed be a missionary church that could proclaim in word and deed to the world that in Jesus Christ God is proposing to put an end to the religio-ethnic hostilities and factions that divide our world. To be God's people in the midst of all God's peoples is to elicit from all God's peoples an equal response in terms of their own religious traditions and together with them begin a process of healing that leads to reconciliation.

There are several factors that we need to take into account in expressing this vocation if we are indeed to be a blessing to the nations.

The first has to do with power analysis to understand the basis of the hostility that exists between religio-ethnic groups, because it seems to be a negative manifestation of a far more positive trend that is characteristic of the postcolonial and postmodern mindset. This mindset is a basic refusal to accept identities imposed during the colonial period and its aftermath.

Colonial powers had to deal with civilizations, which were more than races. The term *race* is a European word and is very much on a par with other words such as *pagan, heathen,* and *Gentile.* "Nation" is not only a good translation of the Greek *ethnos,* but it also refers to people collectively as civilizations. In this case, *nation* refers to a linguistic community with a shared culture and a shared history and therefore a shared destiny. It also refers to a particular geographical location in which that nation is situated.

It is this sense of nationhood that colonialism sought to destroy; it had two rather distinct ways of doing it. Whereas colonial powers were nervous about attacking a written culture, they seem to have had no qualms about denigrating an oral culture, because an oral culture is not open to scrutiny. It stays with a nation. It has to be either learned or ignored. Anthropologists learn it. Colonialists ignore it. When it is ignored, the nation and its people are assumed to be nonhuman or subhuman and are treated as such. This is what happened in Australia.

The pattern continued elsewhere as well. African peoples, who have oral cultures, were wrenched from their lands and cultural roots and brought over to work the land in the Americas and the Caribbean, while the indigenous people in these places were decimated. All were nations with an oral culture.

When it came to the nations with a written culture, the subjugation was still there, but often it was subtle. The method was cooption rather than decimation through an approach that was benign at least on the surface, but the result was almost the same. Subjugate and rule was the name of the game, though the ways in which it was done were different. As Samuel Huntington put it, "The West won the world not by the superiority of its ideas or values or religion (to which few members of others civilizations were converted) but rather by its superiority in applying organized violence. Westerners often forget this fact; non-Westerners never do."[25]

We are using the term *nation* in a way that is quite different from its use in the term *nation-states*. Our use of the term *nation* connotes a people's collective identity and is not to be confused with *nation* as in *nation-states*. Several nations need to negotiate with one another to form a viable nation-state. To try to impose one national identity on another, as is the prevailing approach of many nation-states, is what often causes conflicts within nation-states, as is happening, for example, in Sri Lanka.

Now, in the postcolonial period, almost all formerly suppressed civilizations, oral and written, in new and different ways are claiming their right to be a nation. Those in power find this trend frightening, because it is an affirmation of who we are. To call an identifiable civilization a nation is to carry the pride of a people. It resists encroachment. It refuses cooption. To give just two examples, it is one thing for a black person in America to say, "I am a Muslim." It is only when that person says, "I belong to the nation of Islam," that the authorities find it annoying. When the term *Negro* is jettisoned and *black* takes its place, there is an affirmation of nationhood out of which arises black power. The Aborigines of Australia in seeking a treaty with non-Aboriginal Australians are saying that as Aboriginal nations, they never ceded sovereignty to the British Crown. They are claiming the right to be considered as nations.

There is a further complicating factor. Quite a number from the civilizations that claim to be nations now live in the midst of other nations and have a dual identity. Using North America as an example, there are African Americans, Indian Americans, Japanese Americans, Indigenous Americans, Mexican Americans, Hispanics, and so on. On the one hand, these are in a search to express their dual identity in a responsible way. On the other, they are prevented from engaging in this search. Their identities are preempted and prescribed. They are not given the space to dissociate themselves from what is pernicious or bad in the nation with which they are identified. If they are not European American, then it is assumed that their primary loyalty is with the "enemy."

In large measure, the clash of civilizations cannot be understood, so to speak, as a phenomenon on the flat. It is almost always the result of nations resisting the imposition of power and their being labeled "enemy." The irrational resistance to such power, often with religious justifications, is what leads to their being defined as "terrorists." It needs to be recognized that these activities are the result of the imposition of power and the rejection of power in various forms. This is the source of the hostility. A reconciled and renewed church is a countersign that has already resolved this hostility.

This leads to the second factor, which is to recover the role of the church as a confessing church to express its identity as a missionary church. A confessing church is not so much concerned with preserving the gains of the past and glory in the past as with drawing on the traditions of the Christian faith to address the present. A confessing church goes against the grain. It is a church that is not afraid to take risks in being channels of God's peace. With a multiplicity of nations within it, it bears witness to the reconciling power of God in Jesus Christ. It confronts a worldview that proclaims, "Unless we hate what we are not, we cannot love what we are." A confessing church challenges the mindset that pits security against peace.

The confessing church engages in an analysis of power that looks at reality with the intention of placing its resistance to false peace in ways that are effective, with a message that says, This is not what life should be about. It also expresses hope, holding itself to scrutiny, to declare that it is God's intention through the cross of Christ and the suffering of the many to put an end to the hostilities and factionalisms that divide nation from nation and people from people.

We will look at two examples from Asia, which seem to have drawn their inspiration from the confessing church in Germany during the Third Reich, to illustrate what it meant to be a confessing church during an earlier time when Asian countries suffered under dictatorships.

The confessing church in Korea discovered that it had no protection before "Pharaoh" when it resisted the dictatorships of Park Chung-hee, Chun Du-hwan, and Ro Tae-wu in the 1960s through the 1980s. The confessing church in Korea was a gathering of students, workers, and professors, who met outside Seoul on Sunday afternoons after attending regular morning services in their own churches. Meeting outside the capital city Seoul, the seat of Pharaoh, they called themselves the Galilee Church. I attended one of the services and heard the late Professor Suh Nam-dong preach on Christ's solidarity with the *Minjung* (Korean) or *ochlos* (Greek) and how that compassion led him to witness to God's love on the cross. The service ended as usual with the singing of "We Shall Overcome" in Korean. After the second round of singing, it turned into a dance led by two eighty-year-old women, mothers of the poet Kim Chi-ha and of the theologian Timothy Moon. Both their sons were in prison. Wives of workers who had been tortured to death were also in the dance. It was a dance of hope. It was a dance of life. It was a dance that took place in the midst of the realization that many who were there would themselves be imprisoned and perhaps also killed.

Despite the realization that suffering and death were staring them in the face, it was that dance of hope taken to the streets, in concert with the struggles of Buddhist priests and other Korean resistance fighters, that finally brought down a dictatorship that had abolished the rights of workers in the interests of accelerated economic growth, which, as we know, benefits the rich and subjugates the poor.

The confessing church in Sri Lanka also discovered the high cost of resistance. My friend Fr. Michael Rodrigo, an eminent Pali and Buddhist scholar, was warned that his life was in danger and was asked to hide. The Sunday mass in a small village church, seating around twenty-five people, was to begin. Before celebrating the mass, he passed slips of paper with a question asking his small Catholic congregation of religious sisters and ordinands who served a poor Buddhist village, "Should we withdraw temporarily?" The answers scribbled on the pieces of paper were unanimous: Let us stay, for the people want us. Fr Mike responded, "We should not be afraid to die for the people if and when the time comes." The mass began. As it was ending, Fr. Mike raised his hands to pronounce the blessing. Hearing the window behind the altar being wrenched open, he turned to receive the full blast of a rifle shot from security forces. He collapsed on the altar and died. As one of the religious sisters wrote to me, "His blood filled the chalice and mingled with the blood of our Saviour."

There are many more such small confessing churches in Asia and all over the world. These churches are not situated on hilltops but in the midst of the poor—whether they are Buddhists, Hindus, Muslims, or Christians—with whom they identify and whom they serve. They all carry a simple and yet profound and dangerous message: A confessing church is called to resist "systems of injustice" (WCC) and "structures of sin" (Vatican) and to celebrate hope. It will go against the tide.

The "Conciliar Process of Mutual Commitment (Covenant) to Justice, Peace and the Integrity of All Creation" gave prominence and validity to the confessing activity of the church when it said,

> The foundation of this emphasis should be confessing Christ as the life of the world and Christian resistance to the demonic powers of death in racism, sexism, caste oppression, economic exploitation, militarism, violations of human rights, and the misuse of science and technology.[26]

Confessing Christ as the life of the world or as the reconciling power of God at work in the world and Christian resistance to the powers of death are not two separate activities, but one and the same activity. To confess Christ as the reconciling power of God at work in the world is also to say a clear and unequivocal no to the powers of death and translate that no into concrete acts of resistance and of hope. It is an expression of our baptismal vow, which responds to two questions: "Do you confess your faith in Jesus Christ as Lord and Savior?" "Do you renounce the devil and all his ways?"

The confessing church, whether local or national, with its ecumenical linkages locally, nationally, regionally, and globally, is the witnessing church. It would follow the invitation of Jesus: "If you want to follow me, then take up your cross." It would also incarnate in a credible way the task for Christian mission today.

To summarize: "Called to be channels of God's peace" is a specific, though not the only possible, application of the paradigm of God's people in the midst of all God's peoples to understand and address a particular challenge for Christian mission today. In addressing the situation of religio-ethnic strife embodied in the political paradigm of the clash of civilizations, the challenge is to incarnate the love ethic of Jesus, "Love your enemies; do good to them that hate you." Our contention has been that only a church that has managed the plurality of nations within itself and that views itself as set in the midst of and not over against all God's peoples can take up this costly missionary vocation, because it is a mission that will attempt to go against the tide.

9

The Journey Continues:
Some Concluding Remarks

I have firmly resisted the temptation to pull all the discussions in this book into a clear, tight conclusion: to try and resolve the contradictions and tie up the loose ends. I leave all these as they are, because the thoughts and arguments in this book are only a small contribution to a continuing missionary journey. If what I have said prompts corrections and further explorations, and above all opens up avenues for imagination, as the journey continues, I would be satisfied.

In essence, my conviction is that we are at a stage of the journey of Christian mission when we will have to work with the tension inherent in holding on to two truths: God's grace is evident both in the lives and in the religious systems of people of other faiths; God has been revealed in a definitive way in the life, ministry, death, and resurrection of Jesus the Messiah, the Suffering Servant of God, to which truth we are called to witness. This tension cannot be resolved and perhaps should not be resolved. I have suggested the paradigm "God's people in the midst of all God's peoples" as a way of addressing this tension in a creative way. In facing the challenges for Christian mission today, the interplay of understandings of people as *laos, ochlos,* and *ethne* is crucial, both in the formation of a missionary community and in the expression of its missionary vocation.

I end as I began, with a conversation that I had with my father, D. T. Niles, a few months before he died. He had popularized the aphorism "Evangelism is one beggar telling another beggar where to find food." I had already begun to mark out my own directions in theology and was beginning to get allergic to the term *evangelism.* Neither was I exactly pleased to be thought of as a beggar! When I

179

accosted him about this aphorism, he said, "That is not mine. That is Visser 't Hooft's." I then asked him what he meant by evangelism. His answer was something like this: "Evangelism is the power of the gospel to work in the lives of people and in the world irrespective of the messenger who proclaims it. Our task is to point to the source of that power, so that the work of the gospel is secure in the lives of people and in the creative movements in the world which God loves and for which Jesus gave his life." This was a somewhat long speech for one who had a predilection for verbal pictures and aphoristic utterances. He then ended with these words: "The problem is that we are so busy wanting to populate heaven that we forget to get on with the business of the Kingdom." With that position I could heartily agree.

The mystery of the aphorism on evangelism had to be tracked down. Having known that august and at times austere leader of the ecumenical movement, I was reasonably certain that Willem Visser 't Hooft could not have coined it, though he may have provided an idea for it. By the time I came to work at the World Council of Churches, Visser 't Hooft was no more. So I asked another ecumenical leader and theologian, José Míguez-Bonino from Argentina. After listening to the account of my conversation with my father and my doubt about Visser 't Hooft coining the aphorism, he thought for a moment and then said, "That is from Martin Luther, who said, 'Before God we are all nothing but beggars.'" The mystery was solved, and so too the theology! Before God, not only us but all God's peoples are nothing but beggars. We live by God's grace. It is this truth that makes it possible to engage in the confrontations and conversations that a continuing missionary journey evokes.

Echoing words an Indian Jesuit friend of mine, Samuel Rayan, spoke at a meeting on Indian theology, I end my essay.

> Now, my words must return to the Silence from which they arose. At the end, the struggle that mothered that Silence into uttering the Logos (the Word), from which all theo-logies (God-talks) derive, would become *amaidhi, shanti, peace,* in the palm of God's hands. And the earth shall be filled with the knowledge of God as the waters cover the sea.

Notes

Introduction

[1]Wesley Ariarajah, *Not Without My Neighbour: Issues in Interfaith Relations* (Geneva: WCC Publications, 1999), 122f.

[2]John Hick, *God and the Universe of Faiths: Essays in the Philosophy of Religion* (Basingstoke and London: Macmillan Press, 1988), 146f.

[3]Ibid., 138f.

[4]Aloysius Pieris , *An Asian Theology of Liberation* (New York: Orbis, 1988), 54f.

[5]M. Thomas Thangaraj, *The Common Task: A Theology of Christian Mission* (Nashville: Abingdon Press, 1999), 22.

[6]Ibid., chaps. 1–3.

[7]Ibid., 59f.

[8]M. M. Thomas, *Man and the Universe of Faiths* (Madras: CLS Publications, 1975), vi.

[9]C. Lakshman Wickremesinghe, "Togetherness and Uniqueness: Living Faiths in Inter-relation," *CTC Bulletin* 5, no. 1–2 (April–August 1984): 8. Aloysius Pieris, *Love Meets Wisdom: A Christian Experience of Buddhism* (New York: Orbis Books, 1988), makes a similar point: "In the very process of approving and appropriating the basic insights of *Homo religiosus*, each religion also sets itself apart from all other religions by ordering these insights according to its own cultural pattern, formulating them doctrinally within its own conceptual framework, and crystallizing them into its own hierarchical structure of symbols, so that the resultant synthesis…not only corroborates the common contents of all religions but also *judges* every other synthesis as a minor or major deviation from what it regards as Ultimately and Salvifically True. Phenomenologically, therefore, religions are so many alternative configurations of human values. And as such it is in their nature to provoke *comparison* and mutual *criticism*, *confrontation* and reciprocal *correction*, these being the intermediary stages between mere tolerance, with which dialogue begins, and positive participation, in which dialogue should culminate" (p. 17, emphasis original).

[10]Wickremesinghe, "Togetherness and Uniqueness," 6.

[11]Ariarajah, *Not Without My Neighbour*, 112. See chap. 7, "Dialogue or Mission: Can the Tension be Resolved?"

[12]Philip L. Wickeri, ed., *The People of God Among All God's Peoples: Frontiers in Christian Mission* (Hong Kong and London: Christian Conference of Asia and Council for World Mission, 2000).

[13]Lakshman Wickremesinghe, "Christianity Moving Eastwards," *CTC Bulletin* 5, no. 1–2 (April–August 1984): 58–68.

[14]See Bernhard W. Anderson, *The Living Word of the Bible* (Philadelphia: Westminster Press, 1979), chap. 1, "Word of Imagination," for a fuller articulation of his position. Anderson says that historical criticism has made us aware of the fact that a long history of transmission lies behind the text as we have it: "For we come to sense that the text is not dead: it is pulsating with historical life." The way forward is not to attempt to solve how the various layers of historical life have been laid upon each other. "The major weakness of historical criticism," says Anderson, "is not that it is 'historical' (concerned with history) or 'critical' (faith seeking understanding) but that it tends to take us away from the text in its final form and fails to deal with the Word of God as Scripture, as literature. It leads us into excursions behind the text, into hypothetical areas of the text's origin and process of transmission, into reconstructions of the situations that gave rise to the original text or its subsequent re-interpretations, and it tends to leave us in that far

country." (pp. 28, 29). Using the story of Abraham's testing (Gen. 22), he indicates the way forward. Comparing it to Homeric poetry, where no details are missed and every intention sketched in, "the story of Abraham's testing...has a dimension of depth and mystery; it is fraught with 'background.' Instead of objective clarity, we find various levels of meaning, ambiguity about time and circumstance, lack of the thoughts and feelings of actors. The story is told in such a way as to appeal to the imagination. It has a 'gappy' open-ended quality, requiring that the reader fill in the gaps as he is drawn into the movement. The reader must go with Abraham step by step, co-experiencing his love for his only son, his bafflement about the strange command he was called to obey, and finally the moment of release when, just as the knife was upraised, his son was given back to him. Scripture in this case is word of imagination." (p. 31). See also Walter Brueggemann, "Imagination as a Mode of Fidelity," in *Understanding the Word: Essays in Honor of Bernhard W. Anderson*, ed. James T. Butler, Edgar W. Conrad, and Ben C. Ollenburger (Sheffield: JSOT Press, 1985), 13–36, for a linguistic, biblical exploration of the role imagination played in the articulation of Israel's faith.

[15]Bernhard Anderson's student and my colleague in the doctoral program, Edgar W. Conrad, takes Anderson further than Anderson himself may want to go. Anderson takes the position that "The time has come for the kind of literary criticism that calls on our poetic imagination, without sacrificing the insights that historical criticism has provided" (*Living Word of the Bible*, 29f.). In his book *Reading Isaiah* (Minneapolis: Fortress Press, 1991), chap. 1, "Choosing Reading Strategies," Conrad presents a trenchant analysis of the debatable assumptions and limitations of various forms of historical criticism. He argues that historical criticism not only leads us away from the text but also imposes a form on the text from without which is but an abstraction of the scholar's social location and literary assumptions. He also shows how misleading historical criticism is in assuming that the authorial intention of an ancient text could be found and the historical circumstances of its origin (*Sitz im Leben*) could be established. Instead of searching for the authorial intention and the historical circumstances of the text, all of which are hypothetical, Conrad urges us to recognize the fact that meaning does not reside in the text itself but is generated in the reading of the text. Utilizing modern literary critical methods, he then presents a persuasive case for a reader-response approach. See also his article "How the Bible Was Colonized," in *Scripture, Community, and Mission: Essays in Honor of D. Preman Niles*, ed. Philip L. Wickeri (Hong Kong and London: Christian Conference of Asia and Council for World Mission, 2003), 94–107.

[16]For a good illustration of how this happens, see Néstor O. Míguez, "A Comparative Bible Study of Genesis 10—11:9: An Approach from the Argentine," in *Scripture, Community, and Mission*, 152–65. Míguez tracks his changing interpretation of the Babel story as he moved from the classroom to working with the Qom, the indigenous people in Argentina.

[17]Dulcie A. Niles, *The Stranger: A Book of Meditations*, 5th ed. (Melbourne: Australian Christian Youth Council, 1965), 7.

Chapter 1:　My Ecumenical Formation

[1]See D. Preman Niles, "Some Emerging Theological Trends in Asia," *CTC Bulletin* 2, no. 1–2 (March 1981): 10f.

[2]See Commission on Theological Concerns of the Christian Conference of Asia (CTC-CCA), *Minjung Theology: People as the Subjects of History* (New York: Orbis Books, 1983). See also *CTC Bulletin* 3, no. 1 (1982); and *CTC Bulletin* 5, no. 3 through *CTC Bulletin* 6, no. 1 (1984–1985).

[3]Maitland Evans, ed., *Learning for Leadership: Reflections on the ITLD as a Model for Ministerial Formation* (London: ITLD & CWM, 2003), 3.

[4]See my reports in *Hayyim* (later *CTC Bulletin*) 1, no. 1 (January 1979) and *CTC Bulletin* 2, no. 1–2 (March 1981).

[5]Robin Boyd, foreword to *An Introduction to Indian Christian Theology* (Madras, India: Christian Literature Society, 1969), vi.

[6]Henrik Kraemer, *The Christian Message in a Non-Christian World* (London: Edinburgh House Press, 1938), which was specially written for this conference. Kraemer

revised some of his positions and restated them in *Religion and the Christian Faith* (London: Lutterworth Press, 1956). Although his position and arguments were well nuanced, it is the view given here that was received as normative.

[7]*Hayyim* (later *CTC Bulletin*) 1, no. 1 (January 1979): 5.

[8]Aloysius Pieris, *An Asian Theology of Liberation* (New York: Orbis, 1988), 91.

[9]See *CTC Bulletin* 1, no. 2 (November 1979), for material on theologies from Taiwan that emerged during the theological dialogue there. Because of the clampdown of martial law and the imprisonment of church leaders during a human rights protest, a book on theology in Taiwan that was to have been published had to be stopped.

[10]D. Preman Niles, "The Report of the Secretary for Theological Concerns," *CTC Bulletin* 2, no. 1–2 (March 1981): 13. See this article also for a report on the theological dialogues that had taken place until then, and "A Continuing Ecumenical Journey— Report of the Secretary for Theological Concerns, CCA January 1983," *CTC Bulletin* 4, no. 1 (April 1983): 46–64, for reports on all the theological work done until the end of 1983.

[11]*Sharing in One World Mission: Proposals for the Council for World Mission* (London: CWM, 1975), 7 (2.7).

[12]David Gill, ed., *Gathered for Life: Official Report of the Sixth Assembly of the World Council of Churches, Vancouver, Canada, 24 July–10 August 1983* (Geneva: WCC Publications, 1984), 255.

[13]"Statements and Recommendations from the Glion Consultation on Justice, Peace and the Integrity of Creation, 7–15 November 1986," in *Central Committee Minutes of the WCC*, January 1987, Appendix 7, 141.

[14]See Lukas Vischer, "Conciliar Fellowship and Councils: Churches on Their Way to a Universal Council," *Interpretation* 41, no. 4 (October 1989): 501–14. Also see my essay, "Covenanting for Justice, Peace and the Integrity of Creation," *Interpretation* 39, no. 4 (October 1987): 470–84.

[15]Michael Kinnamon and Brian E. Cope, eds., *The Ecumenical Movement: An Anthology of Key Texts and Voices* (Geneva: WCC Publications, 1997), 463–68.

[16]See Ans van der Bent, *Commitment to God's World: A Concise Critical Survey of Ecumenical Social Thought* (Geneva: WCC Publications, 1995), chap. 5, "Three Ecumenical Concepts of Society," as well as chaps. 3 and 4, for a good, concise presentation of the range of differences and disagreements in matters relating to ecumenical social thought.

[17]*Baptism, Eucharist and Ministry*, Faith and Order Commission of the World Council of Churches (Geneva: WCC Publications, 1982).

[18]For reflections on several aspects of the conciliar process, see the essays in D. Preman Niles, ed., *Between the Flood and the Rainbow: Interpreting the Conciliar Process of Mutual Commitment (Covenant) to Justice, Peace and the Integrity of Creation* (Geneva: WCC Publications, 1992).

[19]See D. Preman Niles, "Now We Are in a Covenant: The Dynamism of an Ecumenical Process," in *Festschrift for Dr. Kim Yong-bock, Asia Pacific Journal of Theology*, no. 1 (October 1998): 97–114. See also Marc Reuver, "The People of God and the Conciliar Process," and Kim Yong-bock, "People's Participation and the JPIC Process in Asia," in Niles, *Between the Flood and the Rainbow*.

[20]*Ideas and Services: A Report of the East Asia Christian Conference 1957–1967 by the General Secretary* (New Zealand: National Council of Churches, 1968), 8.

[21]See M. M. Thomas, *My Ecumenical Journey 1947–1975* (Trivandrum, India: P. M. Oommen Of Ecumenical Publishing Centre, CLS Bookshop, 1990).

[22]David Bosch, *Transforming Mission: Paradigm Shifts in Theology of Mission* (New York: Orbis Books, 1991), 137f.

[23]See my report to CWM Council July 1997: D. Preman Niles, "Called To Be a Community of Blessing," section 2: "Trends in CWM's Work."

[24]See Psalm 89:9–11 for a similar account of creation that names the sea monster Rahab. See also Psalm 104:5–9.

[25]For a detailed discussion of the theme of creation as control over chaos, see Bernhard W. Anderson, *Creation Versus Chaos: The Reinterpretation of Mythical Symbolism in the Bible* (Philadelphia: Fortress Press, 1987).

[26]Richard Lovett, *History of the London Missionary Society 1795–1895*, vol. 1 (Oxford University Press, 1899), 49f.

Chapter 2: Exploring a Metaphor for Mission

¹Christopher Duraisingh, "CWM's First Decade and Beyond," *International Review of Mission* 76, no. 304 (October 1987): 482.

²Fred Kaan, "The Church Is Like a Table," *Rejoice and Sing: Hymnal of the United Reformed Church in the United Kingdom* (Oxford: Oxford University Press, 1991), hymn 480.

³Masao Takenaka, *God Is Rice: Asian Culture and Christian Faith* (Geneva: WCC Publications, 1986). See p. 18 for his use of Kim Chi-ha's poem "Heaven Is Rice."

⁴Although the Puritan understanding of the church as a pilgrim people is the source for the use of this metaphor here, this understanding in fact seems to go back to the Franciscans. See Harvey Cox, *The Silencing of Leonardo Boff: The Vatican and the Future of World Christianity* (Oak Park, Ill.: Meyer-Stone Books, 1988), 40: "For Thomas [Aquinas], the bridge was provided by the church, the sole custodian of revealed truth, the only trustworthy bridge between knowledge and faith. For Bonaventure, on the other hand, the church means something else. Rather than the ladder between the pinnacle of earth and the lowest gate of heaven, he sees the church more as a party of pilgrims, seeking to follow Christ, sustained by the sacraments and constantly becoming more aware of the source of the inner light that makes them human." The discussions in Cox's book, especially on Francis and Bonaventure, provide a good Catholic backdrop to the exploration of the metaphor of "being on a journey" in this chapter.

⁵Details regarding the churches that constitute the Council for World Mission are given in *Church Profiles: CWM Member Churches at a Glance* (London: Council for World Mission, 2002).

⁶For this reading of the early history of Israel, see Norman K. Gottwald, *The Tribes of Yahweh: A Sociology of the Religion of Liberated Israel, 1250–1050 BCE* (New York: Orbis Books, 1979).

⁷Kosuke Koyama, *Three Miles an Hour God* (London: SCM Press, 1979).

Chapter 3: A New Arrangement for Mission

¹The concerns of partnership in mission, autonomy in government, and unity in life that Asians raised at the World Missionary Conference in Edinburgh in 1910 continued to permeate the life and thinking of Asian churches. The East Asia Christian Conference (later Christian Conference of Asia) kept these concerns alive. Of particular importance in this connection was a consultation on partnership in mission held in Hong Kong (1954) between U.S. and Asian church leaders. It must be remembered that the World Mission Conference on Salvation Today (1973), which promoted the concept of partnership in mission, was also held in Asia. See "Record of a Consultation Held by the Council for World Mission at Singapore, 31 December — 6 January 1975," 18–22.

²Hans-Ruedi Weber, *Asia and the Ecumenical Movement 1895–1961* (London: SCM Press, 1966), 131f.

³*World Missionary Conference 1910 Edinburgh: The History and Records of the Conference*, vol. 9 (Edinburgh & London: Oliphant, Anderson & Ferrier, 1910), 110.

⁴Ibid., 306–15.

⁵Ibid., 306.

⁶Ibid., 313.

⁷Ibid.

⁸Ibid., 315.

⁹Ibid.

¹⁰Weber, *Asia and the Ecumenical Movement*, 133.

¹¹*World Missionary Conference 1910*, vol. 2, 358f.

¹²*World Missionary Conference 1910*, vol. 9, 294–305.

¹³*World Missionary Conference 1910*, vol. 8, 197.

¹⁴Ibid., 196.

¹⁵Richard Lovett, *History of the London Missionary Society 1795–1895*, vol. 1 (Oxford: Oxford University Press, 1899), 49f.

¹⁶See Weber's *Asia and the Ecumenical Movement*, pp. 118 and 132, for the important role that John R. Mott played in bringing in the Asians and encouraging them to speak.

See pp. 115–63 for a fuller discussion of the Asian contribution to the missionary movement and the ecumenical movement.

[17]Ibid., 116f.

[18]"Record of a Consultation," 12.

[19]*Sharing in One World Mission: Proposals for the Council for World Mission* (London: CWM, 1975), 3 (1.3).

[20]For the debate on moratorium and mutuality, see *Bangkok Assembly 1973: Minutes and Report of the Assembly of the Commission on World Mission and Evangelism of the World Council of Churches*, 23–25. The theme of moratorium, first raised at a meeting of Asian and U.S. church leaders, was then picked up and pressed by some church leaders in Africa, who in fact were the ones who insisted that there be a section on moratorium at the Bangkok meeting. It was, in essence, a radical proposal for putting an end to the missionary power of ideas and money so that a truly African church belonging to its context and serving Christ in its context could emerge. Canon Burgess Carr, the first general secretary of the All Africa Council of Churches, and Dr. John Gatu, the General Secretary of the Presbyterian Church of Kenya, were its major proponents. Although the plea for a moratorium on Western missionaries and Western funds was short-lived and African churches by and large did not heed the call, its influence lived on, and it had a major impact on restructured mission organizations such as Cevaa and CWM in their call for a sharing of power. The words of Gatu on this subject are worth remembering: "Surely election of this option may cause many existing structures of our churches to crumble. If they do, thanks to God, they should not have been established in the first place and again it would be profound theology, for to be truly redeemed, one must die and be reborn…Should the moratorium cause missionary sending agencies to crumble, the African Church would have performed a service in redeeming God's people in the northern hemisphere from a distorted view of the mission of the Church in the world." In Michael Kinnamon and Brian E. Cope, eds., *The Ecumenical Movement: An Anthology of Key Texts and Voices* (Geneva and Grand Rapids, Mich.: WCC Publications and Eerdmans, 1997), 364.

[21]*Sharing in One World Mission*, 7 (2.7).

[22]Ibid., 5 (2.1).

[23]Ibid., 5 (2.2). Italics added.

[24]Ibid., 5f (2.3).

[25]"Holistic," from the Greek *holos*, means "whole, entire, complete in all its parts." In CWM circles, the Church of North India, used the phrase "toward a holistic understanding of mission" to denote its mission thinking and practice. Bishop Pritam Santram gave this exposition: "God's mission is God's mission. It is our understanding of God's mission that needs to change. We need to have a holistic understanding of God's mission." The phrase "holistic understanding of mission" was then used in the thinking of the Council for World Mission as a way of bringing together and inter-relating all aspects of the ministry of Jesus and the areas of engagement of the church in the world into a comprehensive understanding of mission. See in particular the mission statements of the Council for World Mission: *Perceiving Frontiers, Crossing Boundaries* (London: CWM, 1995), and D. Preman Niles, ed., *World Mission Today* (London: CWM, 1999). The major documents on mission produced by the Council for World Mission are available on the internet at www.cwmission.org.uk.

[26]*Mission and Evangelism: An Ecumenical Affirmation* (Geneva: World Council of Churches, 1982), and also in Kinnamon and Cope, *Ecumenical Movement*, 372–383.

[27]*Handbook of the Council for World Mission* (London: CWM, 1984), 5 (3.2).

[28]"CWM's First Decade and Beyond," *International Review of Mission*, 76, no. 34 (Ocotber 1987): 477–81.

[29]Jan van Butselaar, "Structural Changes in Mission: New Shoes or Stocking Feet?" (English translation) Dutch original: "Structuurveranderingen in de Zending" Wereld en Zending (1994:1), 3–15.

[30]*Sharing in One World Mission*, 6 (2.6).

[31]Letter from Sam H. Smellie and Maitland Evans to Aubrey Curry (Secretary for Finance, CWM), April 17, 1987, quoted in Roderick Hewitt, *A Missiological Analysis of the Thinking, Practice and Structures That Have Emerged in the United Church of Jamaica and Grand Cayman* (Master's thesis, Department of Theology of the University of London, 1995), 156f.

[32]*International Review of Mission* 76, no. 304 (October 1987): 458–72.

[33]See appendix H1 of CWM Executive Committee papers, November 1992. See also the report of Aubrey J. Curry, "Sharing of Material Resources," Executive Committee, November 1992.

[34]This problem, especially as it impacts on United Churches in CWM, was flagged early in the life of CWM by its first chairperson, Daisy Gopalratnam, "Partnership in Practice: The Council for World Mission after Four Years," *International Review of Mission* 76, no. 304 (October 1987): 491.

Chapter 4: Sharing People in Mission

[1]Choan Seng Song, *Christian Mission in Reconstruction: An Asian Analysis* (Madras: CLS, New York: Orbis Books, 1975), 2.

[2]Bernard Thorogood, "A CWM View of Missionary Service," introduction to part 2 of 1979 Council meeting, 3.2.

[3]T.V. Philip, *Reflections on Christian Mission in Asia: William Carey Lectures and Other Essays* (Delhi: ISPCK, 2000), 31.

[4]Richard Lovett, *History of the London Missionary Society, 1795–1895*, vol. 1 (London: Oxford University Press, 1899), 8.

[5]Alec H. Vidler, *The Church in an Age of Revolution* (Baltimore: Penguin Books, 1965), 248.

[6]See Michael Banton, *Racial Theories*, 2d ed. (Cambridge: Cambridge University Press, 1998), especially chaps. 1 ("Race as Designation") and 2 ("Race as Lineage"), for the views on race prevalent at that time.

[7]Philip, *Reflections on Christian Mission in Asia*, 28.

[8]Professor Graham Stanton of the University of Cambridge made these observations in a lecture he gave on "Mission in Matthew." See his book *The Gospels and Jesus* (Oxford: Oxford University Press, 1991), 59–80, and his essay in G. N. Stanton, ed., *The Interpretation of Matthew* (Philadelphia: Fortress Press, 1983).

[9]Philip, *Reflections on Christian Mission in Asia*, 29.

[10]Ibid., 36.

[11]Ibid., 30.

[12]Ibid., 32f.

[13]Ibid., 34.

[14]See Lovett, *History of the London Missionary Society*, vol. 2, chap. 15, "The Demerara Martyr," 336–59.

[15]Ibid., vol. 1, 543f.

[16]Ibid., 546f.

[17]See Ahn Byung-mu, "Jesus and the Minjung in the Gospel of Mark," in *Minjung Theology: People as the Subjects of History*, Commission on Theological Concerns of the Christian Conference of Asia [CTC-CCA] (New York: Orbis Books, 1983), 138–52.

[18]In this regard, see the mission statement of the Council for World Mission, *Perceiving Frontiers, Crossing Boundaries* (CWM: London, 1995).

[19]Konrad Raiser, "Laity in the Ecumenical Movement: Redefining the Profile," *The Ecumenical Review* 45, no. 4 (October 1993): 379.

Chapter 5: Sharing Resources of Money

[1]*Communities of Churches in Mission: A Joint Consultation of Cevaa, CWM and UEM, Wuppertal, Germany, February 1–5, 2000*, (Wuppertal: UEM, 2000) 64f.

[2]Ibid.

[3]David Gill, ed., *Gathered for Life, the Official Report of the Sixth Assembly of the World Council of Churches, Vancouver, Canada, 24 July–10 August 1983* (Geneva: WCC Publications, 1984), 131: "Humanity is now living in the dark shadow of an arms race more intense, and of *systems of injustice* more widespread, more dangerous and more costly than the world has ever known. Never before has the human race been as close as it is now to total self-destruction. Never before have so many lived in the grip of deprivation and oppression" (italics added). The specifics may have changed, but not the situation.

[4]John Paul II, *Sollicitudo Rei Socialis* (encyclical letter, December 30, 1987), 69 (para. 36). The encyclical describes "structures of sin" as "rooted in personal sin, and thus always linked to the *concrete acts* of individuals who introduce these structures, consolidate them and make them difficult to remove." Although the analysis differs significantly from that of the World Council of Churches, both come to a similar conclusion. As the encyclical says in the same paragraph: "Sin and structures of sin are categories which are seldom applied to the situation of the contemporary world. However, one cannot easily gain a profound understanding of the reality that confronts us unless we give a name to the root of the evils which afflict us." Both positions may describe globalization as it impinges on those whom the system has marginalized.

[5]D. Preman Niles, ed., *World Mission Today* (London: CWM, 1999).

[6]See Joseph A. Fitzmyer, "The Gospel According to Luke, X–XXIV," in *The Anchor Bible* (Garden City, N.Y.: Doubleday, 1985), 1104–11.

[7]From *Communities of Churches in Mission.*

[8]Andrew Morton, *In All Good Grace* (London: Council for World Mission, 2000).

[9]Minutes of the CWM Council, 1977, resolution 77CNL35.

[10]See appendix H, submitted at the meeting of Executive Committee of CWM, November 1994.

[11]Ibid.

[12]See my reports to meetings of Executive Committee, "Beyond Ourselves: Toward Refining CWM's Ecumenical Relationships" (December 1996) and "Beyond Ourselves II: CWM's Ecumenical Relationships" (appendix N, June 2000).

Chapter 6: Christian Mission Today: Reexamining Some Assumptions

[1]David Bosch, *Transforming Mission: Paradigm Shifts in Theology of Mission* (New York: Orbis Books, 1991), 8f.

[2]Steven Neil, *A History of Christian Missions* (London: Hodder & Stoughton, 1965), 13–15.

[3]Canon Burgess Carr, the former general secretary of the All Africa Council of Churches, reflected this fact in a cynical remark he made: "If there is one single thing I have learned about the church during these seven years that I have lived and worked in Europe and Africa, it is this. You here in the North Atlantic world need us in Africa. This has been a revelation to me, since all along I have been led to believe that the situation was just the reverse." From a lecture he delivered at a meeting of church leaders in the U.S. in April 1971, quoted by Choan Seng Song, *Christian Mission in Reconstruction: An Asian Analysis* (Madras: CLS; New York: Orbis Books, 1975), 14.

[4]M. R. Spindler, "The Biblical Grounding and Orientation of Mission," in *Missiology: An Ecumenical Introduction*, ed. F.J. Verstraelen, et al. (Grand Rapids, Mich.: Eerdmans, 1995), 123f.

[5]Professor James A. Bergquist, a New Testament scholar who kindly read this chapter in manuscript form, made two important comments. (1) He agreed that *evangelism* is not a biblical term. (2) He pointed out that key words such as "to proclaim the good news," "to witness" (*martureo*), and "to proclaim" (*kyrusso*) occur almost always as verbs. For example, there are sixty instances of *kyrusso* in the New Testament, as opposed to eight instances of the noun form *kyrugma*. As Bergquist puts it, "Key terms in the New Testament are verbs not 'isms.'"

[6]Bosch, *Transforming Mission*, 409–20.

[7]See George (Tink) Tinker, *Missionary Conquest: The Gospel and Native American Cultural Genocide* (Minneapolis: Augsburg Fortress Press, 1993).

[8]Kenneth Cracknell, *Protestant Evangelism or Catholic Evangelization?* (England: Methodist Sacramental Fellowship, 1992), 3, quoted in M. Thomas Thangaraj, *The Common Task: A Theology of Christian Mission* (Nashville: Abingdon Press, 1999), 79.

[9]See, for instance, A. F. Glasser and D. A. McGavran, *Contemporary Theologies of Mission* (Grand Rapids, Mich.: William B. Eerdmans, 1983).

¹⁰John R. W. Stott, "The Biblical Basis of Evangelism," in *Evangelization*, Mission Trends, no. 2, ed. Gerald H. Anderson and Thomas F. Stransky (New York: Paulist Press, 1975), 4–23.

¹¹Hans-Ruedi Weber, "God's Arithmetic," in *Evangelization*, 64–69.

¹²William J. Abraham, "A Theology of Evangelism," *Interpretation* 48, no. 2 (April 1994): 119.

¹³George R. Hunsberger, "Is There a Biblical Warrant for Evangelism?" *Interpretation* 48, no. 2 (April 1994): 138.

¹⁴J. C. Hoekendijk, "The Church in Missionary Thinking," *International Review of Mission* 41 (1952): 324–36.

¹⁵J. C. Hoekendijk, "The Call to Evangelism," *International Review of Mission* 39 (1950): 167–75, reprinted in *The Ecumenical Movement: An Anthology of Key Texts and Voices*, ed. Michael Kinnamon and Brian E. Cope (Geneva: WCC Publications, 1997), 332–42.

¹⁶Lesslie Newbigin, *Mission in Christ's Way* (Geneva: WCC Publications, 1987), 16.

¹⁷Ibid., 21.

¹⁸Abraham, "A Theology of Evangelism," 117.

¹⁹Oscar Cullmann, *Christ and Time*, trans. Floyd V. Filson (Philadelphia: Westminster Press, 1949), 93.

²⁰Ibid., 117f.

²¹Ibid., 115. Emphasis original.

²²Ibid., 116f.

²³A good example of how this position is reflected in narrations of mission history is Stephen Neil, *A History of Christian Missions*. He begins asking the question: "How is it that a religion of the Middle East, radically changed its character by becoming the dominant religion of Europe, and now is changing its character again through becoming a universal religion, increasingly free from the bounds of geography and of Western civilisation? This is the theme of this book" (p. 15). He begins his conclusion with these words, "But in the twentieth century one phenomenon has come into view which is incontestably new—for the first time there is in the world a universal religion, and that the Christian religion." After pointing to the decline of Buddhist and Islamic missions, which we would now contest, he argues that despite several failings, "Christianity alone has acclimatized itself in every continent and almost every country." He then goes on to sketch how the religion may grow in several political situations.

²⁴Cullmann, *Christ and Time*, 180f.

²⁵See Ian Gillman and Hans-Joachim Klimkeit, *Christians in Asia Before 1500 AD* (Ann Arbor: University of Michigan Press, 1999).

²⁶For a more complete picture of relationships than the one presented here, see S. Wesley Ariarajah, *The Bible and People of Other Faiths* (Geneva: WCC Publications, 1985), 1–18.

²⁷Weber, "God's Arithmetic," 65.

²⁸Archie C. C. Lee, "Refiguring Religious Pluralism in the Bible," in *Plurality, Power and Mission: Intercontextual Theological Explorations on the Role of Religion in the New Millennium*, ed. Philip Wickeri, Janice Wickeri, and Damayanthi Niles (London: Council for World Mission, 2000), 230.

²⁹Kwok Pui-lan, *Discovering the Bible in the Non-Biblical World* (New York: Orbis Books, 1995), 9.

³⁰Ibid., 13.

³¹For Asians, typical of this approach would be the "yin-yang" way of thinking, in which yes and no, the positive and the negative, are held in balance. See Lee Jung Young, "The Yin-Yang Way of Thinking," in *Asian Christian Theology: Emerging Themes*, ed. Douglas J. Elwood (Philadelphia: Westminster Press, 1980), 81–88. A good pictorial representation of yin-yang is the emblem on the flag of the Republic of Korea. Hindu thinking about God also attempts this kind of balance. One may use attributes for God—such as God is Love, God is Righteous, God is Wrathful—through which God is manifested, if at the same time one says "but that is not so!" For God is "nirguna"—who as Absolute is "One without attributes" or "One who negates attributes."

³²Bosch, *Transforming Mission*, 110.

Chapter 7: Christian Mission Today:
Exploring an Alternative Paradigm

¹Thomas Kuhn, *Structure of Scientific Revolutions*, 2d ed. (Chicago: University of Chicago Press, 1970), 23.

²Ibid. See in particular his chapters on "The Priority of Paradigms," "Anomaly and the Emergence of Scientific Discoveries," and "Crisis and the Emergence of Scientific Theories."

³Samuel Huntington, *The Clash of Civilizations and the Remaking of World Order* (New York: Simon & Schuster, 1996), 29–39.

⁴David Bosch, *Transforming Mission: Paradigm Shifts in Theology of Mission* (New York: Orbis Books, 1991), 183–87.

⁵Konrad Raiser, *Ecumenism in Transition: A Paradigm Shift in the Ecumenical Movement?* (Geneva: WCC Publications, 1991), 31–53.

⁶John Hick, *God and the Universe of Faiths: Essays in the Philosophy of Religion*, chap. 9, "The Copernican Revolution in Theology," 120–32, and chap. 10, "The New Map of the Universe of Faiths," 133–47. See also Kuhn, *Structure of Scientific Revolutions*, 68ff., for the way in which the Copernican paradigm replaced the Ptolemaic paradigm, which had served for some four centuries.

⁷Kuhn, *Structure of Scientific Revolutions*, 17f.

⁸Ibid., 23.

⁹David Gill, ed., *Gathered for Life: Official Report of the Sixth Assembly of the World Council of Churches, Vancouver, Canada, 24 July–10 August 1983* (Geneva: WCC Publications, 1984), 255.

¹⁰Ibid., 132.

¹¹"Statements and Recommendations from the Glion Consultation to the Central Committee of the WCC," appendix 7, in *Central Committee Minutes*, Geneva, Switzerland (January 16–24, 1987), 143.

¹²*Minutes*, 51.

¹³Ibid., 53.

¹⁴This particular decision is not recorded in the official minutes but is in the fuller minutes the JPIC staff recorded. The official minutes present a more edited and coherent account of the debate than what actually took place. The Glion consultation presented the Central Committee with far too many concepts than it could adequately handle. An involved and at times desultory debate, with all manner of recommendations, went on for several sessions. It was abruptly brought to a close, as the official minutes show, when a resolution supported by the WCC administration was presented to invite the Roman Catholic Church to co-sponsor the World Convocation on JPIC.

Even the official minutes reflect the problems inherent in inviting institutions and movement of other faiths in a conciliar process of the churches. Not only does the main argument in the minutes on the process record the primary and even sole concern of involving the churches and Christian institutions, but there was also a resolution put forward to limit the participation to official partners of the WCC. This attempt did not find favor. The decision given above, not noted in the official minutes, seemed to be the best compromise. In the event, despite efforts to include people of other faiths, the JPIC Convocation was limited to Christians, and was a Christian process of covenanting. As mentioned later in the chapter, participants at the convocation expressed the hope that while we as Christians make these commitments, others would also do the same.

The JPIC staff produced a "Working Paper on Justice, Peace and the Integrity of Creation" (1987) that brought together the Glion (1986) and Central Committee (1987) discussions. See also D. Preman Niles, "Now We Are in a Covenant: The Dynamism of an Ecumenical Process" (*Asia Pacific Journal of Theology, Festschrift for Dr. Kim Yong-bock* no. 1 (October 1998): 97–114), for an account of the stresses and strains in the Central Committee debate and decisions on JPIC.

¹⁵Wesley Ariarajah, *Hindus and Christians: A Century of Protestant Ecumenical Thought* (Grand Rapids, Mich.: Eerdmans, 1991), 170.

¹⁶Henrik Kraemer, *The Christian Message in a Non-Christian World* (London: Edinburgh House Press, 1938), 123–24: "To be sure, in many men and in the religions of

mankind there stir deep aspirations, longings and intuitions which find their fulfillment in Christ, for man 'is groping for God' as Paul said on the Areopagus. Because of that many a convert to Christianity has had this experience of liberating fulfillment. Nevertheless, as the revelation of God in Christ transcends and contradicts all human wisdom by its divine folly, and all human aspiration and expectation by its entirely unexpected way of fulfilling them, it is wrong to use the term fulfillment. Conversion and regeneration would be truer to reality."

[17]M.M. Thomas, *Risking Christ for Christ's Sake*: *Towards an Ecumenical Theology of Pluralism* (Geneva: WCC Publications, 1987), 111.

[18]Wesley Ariarajah, *Not Without My Neighbour: Issues in Interfaith Relations* (Geneva: WCC Publications, 1999), 102f.

[19]Ibid., 105.

[20]Ibid., 114f. Emphasis added.

[21]There is burgeoning literature on this subject. For a brief presentation of the concerns in "a theology of life," see Martin Robra, "Theology of Life—Justice, Peace, Creation," *The Ecumenical Review* 48, no. 1 (January 1996): 28–37. See also Lukas Vischer, "Climate Change, Sustainability and Christian Witness," *The Ecumenical Review* 49, no. 2 (April 1997): 142–61. See also D. Preman Niles, "Caring for the Earth: Healing the Broken Communities," *CTC Bulletin* 9, no. 1 (April 1990): 5–12, which attempts to address both the many religious cultures aspect and the ecological aspect in a theology of creation.

[22]Choan Seng Song, "From Israel to Asia—A Theological Leap," in *Third World Theologies*, Mission Trends, no. 3, ed. Gerald H. Anderson and Thomas F. Stransky (New York: Paulist Press; Grand Rapids, Mich.: Eerdmans, 1976), 211–22, esp. 213f.

[23]Ibid., 214.

[24]Ibid., 215. Emphasis added.

[25]M. A. Thangasamy, *The Theology of Chenchiah with Selections from His Writings* (Madras: Christian Literature Society [CLS]; Christian Institute for the Study of Religion and Society, 1967), especially "Introduction: The Theology of Chenchiah—Basic Theological Convictions," 1–47.

[26]Chenchiah, "Rethinking Christianity," in *The Theology of Chenchiah*, 172. See also Thangasamy's "Introduction: The Theology of Chenchiah," 16f.

[27]Paul D. Devanandan, *Our Task Today: Revision of Evangelistic Concern* (Bangalore: CISRS, 1958), 5.

[28]D. T. Niles, *Upon the Earth*: *The Mission of God and the Missionary Enterprise of the Churches* (London: Luthernorth Press, 1962), 46.

[29]Ibid., 233.

[30]Ariarajah, *Hindus and Christians*, 111.

[31]Choan Seng Song, *Mission in Reconstruction: An Asian Attempt* (Madras: CLS, 1975), ixf.

[32]Victor Premsagar presented these arguments in two articles in *The South India Churchman,* September 1985 and December 1985.

[33]Michael Kinnamon, ed., *Signs of the Spirit: Official Report of the Seventh Assembly of the World Council of Churches, Canberra, Australia, February 1991* (Geneva: WCC Publications, 1991), 59.

[34]Ibid., 54f.

[35]In an unusual move, under pressure from the JPIC staff, a special category of advisor on JPIC concerns was created for the WCC Assembly. Dr. Roger Williamson from England was invited to be this special advisor. JPIC staff assigned to him as his main responsibility the role of coordinating an "unofficial gathering" of persons concerned with JPIC issues at the Canberra Assembly. It met almost every evening to assess progress and to see how the broad spectrum of concerns expressed in the JPIC process could be reflected in the reports of the Assembly. Many of the drafters of section reports also attended this meeting. The JPIC staff, as did most other WCC staff, assiduously avoided these gatherings.

[36]Frederick R. Wilson, ed., *Your Will Be Done: Mission in Christ's Way*, The San Antonio Report (Geneva: WCC Publications, 1990), 32: "In re-affirming the 'evangelistic mandate' of the ecumenical movement, we would like to emphasize that we may never claim to have full understanding of God's truth: we are only the recipients of God's grace. Our witness among people of other faiths presupposes our *presence* with them,

sensitivity to their deepest faith commitments and experiences, *willingness* to be their servants for Christ's sake, *affirmation* of what God has done and is doing among them, and *love* for them."

[37]Michael Kinnamon and Brian E. Cope, eds., *The Ecumenical Movement: An Anthology of Key Texts and Voices* (Geneva: WCC Publications, 1997), 417–20.

[38]See especially the seminal essay of Lynn White, Jr., "The Historical Roots of Our Ecological Crisis," *Science* 155 (1967): 1203–7, reprinted in *The Environmental Handbook,* ed. Garrett de Bell (New York: Ballantine Books, 1970), 12–26.

[39]"Integrity of Creation: An Ecumenical Discussion," in *Justice, Peace and the Integrity of Creation: Documents from an Ecumenical Process of Commitment,* ed. D. Preman Niles (Geneva: WCC Publications), 151f., paras 31 and 32.

[40]"Entering into Covenant Solidarity for Justice, Peace and the Integrity of Creation" (final document), in *Between the Flood and the Rainbow: Interpreting the Conciliar Process of Mutual Commitment (Covenant) to Justice, Peace and the Integrity of Creation,* ed. D. Preman Niles (Geneva: WCC Publications, 1992), 168.

[41]Ibid., 166.

[42]Michael Kinnamon, ed., *Signs of the Spirit,* Official Report of the Seventh WCC Assembly, Canberra, Australia, 7–20 February, 1991 (Geneva: WCC Publications, 1991), 100.

[43]Ibid., 116f. para 38.

[44]It should be remembered that because Judaism was more concerned with orthopraxis than orthodoxy, Jewish Christians could continue or masquerade as a Jewish sect until the synod of Jamnia (C.E. 85), when the Rabbinic Judaic community pronounced the so-called Twelfth Benediction: "Let the Nazarenes and the heretics be destroyed in a moment...Let their names be expunged from the Book of Life and not be entered with those of the just."

[45]"The Confessing Church in Asia and Its Theological Task," an EACC Statement in *Asian Christian Theology: Emerging Themes,* ed. Douglas J. Elwood (Philadelphia: Westminster Press, 1980), 145.

[46]"Unity and Diversity in God's Creation: A Study of the Babel Story," *Currents in Theology and Mission* 5 (1978): 69–81.

[47]Choan Seng Song, *The Compassionate God* (New York: Orbis Books, 1982), 22f.

[48]Néstor O. Míguez, A Comparative Bible Study of Genesis 10—11:9: An Approach from the Argentine," in *Scripture, Community, and Mission: Essays in Honor of D. Preman Niles,* ed. Philip L. Wickeri (Hong Kong and London: CCA and CWM, 2003) 154–55.

[49]Lakshman Wickremesinghe, "Mission, Politics and Evangelism," *CTC Bulletin* 5, no. 1–2 (April–August 1984): 48.

[50]See the essays in V. Devasagayam, ed., *Frontiers of Dalit Theology* (Delhi: ISPCK; and Madras: Gurukul, 1997); and James Massey, ed., *Indigenous People: Dalits, Dalit Issues in Today's Theological Debate* (Delhi: ISPCK, 1994). It needs to be noted that not all the writers in these two volumes are Dalits. Non-Dalit Christians have also taken the approach and viewpoints of "subalterns." See also James Massey, *Dalits in India: Religion as a Source of Bondage or Liberation with Special Reference to Christians* (Delhi: Manohar Publishers, 1995).

[51]*Sati* is the Hindu practice of the forced immolation of widows on the funeral pyres of their dead husbands. This practice is now legally banned.

Chapter 8: Christian Mission Today: Testing a Paradigm

[1]J. Christiaan Beker, *Paul the Apostle: The Triumph of God in Life and Thought* (Philadelphia: Fortress Press, 1980), 330.

[2]See Francis W. Beare, "The Epistle to the Ephesians," in *The Interpreter' Bible,* vol. 10 (New York: Abingdon Press, 1953), 606, col. 2.

[3]Samuel Huntington, *The Clash of Civilizations and the Remaking of World Order* (New York & London: Touchstone Books, 1996), 20.

[4]For an analysis of how the paradigm Huntington puts forward is played out through leaders of powerful nations, especially as it affects Asia, see Ninan Koshy, *The War on Terror: Reordering the World* (Delhi:LeftWord Books, 2002). "The war on terror,"

says Koshy, "was declared by George W. Bush, the President of the United States of America in response to the horrific events of September 11, 2001. The war goes on unabated, with shifting aims, new targets, expanding scope and refurbished strategies." Koshy then quotes the ominous words of Bush to the whole world: "Every nation in every region now has a decision to make. Either you are with us or you are with the terrorists." Koshy continues, "It is a command, which just had to be obeyed and no debate was allowed. The President of the mightiest nation on earth was laying down the law for the whole world" (pp. 1 and 2).

[5]Peter Singer, *One World: The Ethics of Globalization* (New Haven, Conn. & London: Yale University Press, 2002).

[6]Huntington, *Clash of Civilizations*; see especially chap. 12, "The West, Civilizations, and Civilization." Huntington has often been criticized for advocating a self-fulfilling prophecy. In actual fact, he presents a paradigm that serves to understand the world situation and that needs to be taken realistically into account in the political reordering of the world. The last sentence of his book makes this telling remark: "In the emerging era clashes of civilizations are the greatest threat to world peace, and an international order based on civilizations is the surest safeguard against world war" (p. 321). As will become evident later on in this chapter, in a modified form, I too subscribe to this position.

[7]Singer, *One World*, 1f.

[8]Ibid., 7.

[9]"The Statement on Southern Africa," in *Gathered for Life, the Official Report of the Sixth Assembly of the World Council of Churches, Vancouver, Canada 24 July–August 1983*, ed. David Gill (Geneva: WCC Publications, 1984), 151f.

[10]See Albie Sachs, *Post-Apartheid South Africa: Truth Reconciliation and Justice*, D. T. Lakdawala Memorial Lecture (Delhi: Institute of Social Studies, 1998), 20f. Albert L. Sachs, of Jewish descent, is presently a Justice of the Constitutional Court of South Africa. He was twice detained without trial during the time of the apartheid regime and almost lost his life in an assassination attempt in which he lost the use of his right hand and eye. He is a member of the African National Congress.

[11]James Cone, "Theology's Great Sin: Silence in the Face of White Supremacy," *Union Seminary Quarterly Review* 55, no. 3–4 (2001): 1–14.

[12]Ibid., 1.

[13]Ibid., 3f.

[14]Ibid., 7.

[15]Ibid., 3.

[16]See Henry Reynolds, *Aboriginal Sovereignty: Three nations, One Australia?* (St. Leonards: Allen & Unwin, 1996), for a discussion of the issues dealt with and the decisions reached in the Mabo case.

[17]See Henry Reynolds, *This Whispering in Our Hearts* (St. Leonards: Allen & Unwin, 1998), for a discussion of the Wik case.

[18]The Aboriginal and Torres Strait Islander Commission have put out a series of booklets on the treaty proposals: *Treaty Yeh, Treaty Now; Treaty: Let's Get It Right! (Frequently Asked Questions); Treaty: Let's Get It Right: Issues*. Their publications are available on www.treatynow.org.

[19]See Delphine Delphin-Stanford and John Brown, *Committed to Change: Covenanting in the Uniting Church in Australia* (Melbourne: Uniting Church Press, 1994). John Harris, *One Blood: 200 Years of Aboriginal Encounter with Christianity: A Story of Hope*, rev. ed. (Sunderland: Albatross Books, 1994); David J. Tracey, *Edge of the Sacred: Transformation in Australia* (North Blackburn, Vic., Australia: HarperCollins, 1995). See also Reynolds, *This Whispering in Our Hearts*.

[20]M. M. Thomas, "Report of the Chairman of the Central Committee," *Minutes and Reports of the Twenty-Fifth Meeting of the Central Committee of the World Council of Churches, August 13–23, 1972* (Geneva: WCC, 1972), 128.

[21]Dietrich Bonhoeffer, *The Cost of Discipleship* (New York: Macmillan, 1961), 76.

[22]Ibid., 79.

[23]Reinhold Niebuhr, *The Irony of American History* (New York: Charles Scribner's Sons, 1952), 63.

[24]Harvey Cox, *The Silencing of Leonardo Boff: The Vatican and the Future of World Christianity* (Oak Park, Ill.: Meyer Stone Books, 1988), 46. Cox refers to the notes Leonardo Boff made for his meeting with Cardinal Joseph Ratzinger, Prefect of the Sacred Congregation for the Doctrine of the Faith. The notes listed the seamy side of Vatican politics over several centuries. Commenting on this, Cox says, "Perhaps here also, Boff's edgy Franciscan spirituality may help explain what to some might sound merely gratuitous. Many Catholics believe that, in an odd way, the endurance of the papal office despite the villains, rakes, and debauchers who have occupied it provides a kind of inverse proof of God's providence. No merely human institution, it is argued, could have survived so many rascals."

[25]Huntington, *Clash of Civilizations*, 51.

[26]"Conciliar Process of Mutual Committment (Covenant) to Justice, Peace and the Integrity of All Creation," in *Gathered for Life*, ed. David Gill, 255.

Index of Names

(Page numbers in italics indicate that the reference is in the notes)

Index of Biblical Passages

(Page numbers in italics indicate that the reference is in the notes)